Integral To Islamic Finance
A Semiotic Approach

Insights in Semiotic Economics

Series Editors: Tony Bradley and Ronnie Lessem

Commendations

This book demonstrates a perfect blend between the theoretical foundations of ethical finance, practical Islamic finance, and the future of finance, where financial laboratories are moulded for human happiness. On the other hand, it advocates Shariah-compliance, profitability and a societal impact that is measurable. In these respects, it makes for a fascinating read.

ADENIYI AKINLUSI
CEO TrustBond Mortgage Bank Plc and President,
Mortgage Banking Association of Nigeria (MBAN)

For decades I have been fascinated with the four directions as an archetype for the world we inhabit. Because of my grandfather's famous discovery of Machu Picchu, I have spent many hours contemplating the four directions. All this is to say that I believe these economists are onto something that is meaning making. As an impact investor for most of my adult life, even when there was no language for it, I welcome this exploration that integrates the four directions, the great religions and the practical experience of centuries. Thank goodness for this initiative to transform the way money works in the world. Money is an expression of intention, and how we transact, lend, borrow, invest or gift—it is a measure of who we are. As an investor, I look forward to putting the principles to work, that this book and series uncover.

BENJAMIN BINGHAM
Founder and CEO, 3 Sisters Sustainable Management
and Scarab Funds for Impact Capital and Positive Growth

A much-needed and timely work on a semiotic approach to Islamic finance. A must-read for anyone looking for an in-depth and insightful reading in this area.

DR. ASAD GHALIB, PhD
Senior Lecturer in Management Sciences,
Liverpool Hope University Business School, UK

The issues created by neoliberal capitalist economic models have prompted the need to emerge a vital quest for alternatives. Semiotic Economics holds huge potential as an alternative discipline. The application of Semiotic Economics to Islamic economics and finance is a new phenomenon, to make it more exciting and applicable to the modern world. This inspiring book is pioneering an innovative approach in this field. It contains effective solutions on how Semiotic Economics can be applied in Islamic economics and finance respectively. I strongly commend it as a first text to open up this area, for both academics and practitioners.

DR. NECMETTIN KIZILKAYA, PhD
Associate Professor of Islamic Law,
Istanbul University

In the current era of creative destruction in development and economic models, it is imperative and insightful to rethink the conventional models to overcome the global state of tipping points in society, economy and ecology. This book is a fresh look in the journey of re-thinking and exploration of meaning, for the current models of development and finance.

PROFESSOR ODEH AL-JAYYOUSI, PhD
Professor of Technology and Innovation Management,
Arabian Gulf University, Bahrain

While the world goes in search of financial freedom, and while emerging economies struggle to find their feet, this book sets forth a unique path to impact investment. Such an integral approach to finance is, then, lodged in communal emancipation, with recognition of social realities. It is this emerging measurement of societal impact that shines a new light on finance, both Islamic and more conventional.

ARIYO OLUSHEKUN
CEO Capital Assets Limited

This book recognizes the needs of struggling economies and the kind of funds that can be used to effectively emancipate weak communities from poverty and inequality. The diffusion of money into impactful investment and the measurement of such, then, becomes the most amazing proposition. I highly commend it for detailed study.

AKEEM OYEWALE
CEO Stanbic IBTC Nominees Limited

The constant boom and crash of unbridled greed, manifested through conventional capitalism, has demonstrated that the world needs a more equitable form of finance. It needs to be inclusive and to create opportunities for social mobility. This book brings Islamic principles of finance to life, showing that they represent a genuine alternative to the status quo, when they are adopted in a true spirit and form.

UMER SULEMAN
Head of Ethics Committee, Islamic Council of Europe and UKIFC Senior Associate

First published in the UK by Beacon Academic
103 Washway Rd, Sale, M33 7TY, UK.

First paperback edition published in 2020

www.beaconacademic.net

ISBN: 978-1-912356-40-9 Paperback

Cataloging-in-Publication record for this book is available from the British Library

Cover design by Joel José

Integral To Islamic Finance
A Semiotic Approach

Editors:
Tony Bradley
Ronnie Lessem
Aneeqa Malik
Basheer Oshodi

Foreword by Abu Jimoh, CFA

Insights in Semiotic Economics, Volume 1

Series Editors: Tony Bradley and Ronnie Lessem

BEACON ACADEMIC

Contents

About the Editors

Tony Bradley is Professional Tutor in Social Economy and Catherine Booth Hall Fellow, at Liverpool Hope University Business School. He has had a varied career as an Anglican Priest, social entrepreneur, academic, TV and musical theatre producer, radio presenter, adult educator and playwright. Tony has recently completed his doctorate, investigating ways in which arts-based social innovation can be developed using criteria derived from the Judaeo-Christian scriptures and other faith traditions. His other main research publications are on the subjects of 'greening markets', the relationship between UK business and political social movements, associated with environmentalism and the climate emergency, and the intersection of faith-based and social science interpretive frameworks.

He is the author of nine previous books, including (with Ronnie Lessem and Anselm Adodo) *The Idea of the Communiversity*, for Beacon Academic. Tony has instigated the new discipline of Semiotic Economics, investigating alternative economic models, as the age of the 'meaningful economy' gathers pace. His next two books, for Beacon Academic's Series in Insights in Semiotic Economics, are *Uncovering the Biblical Quaternity Archetype* and *Introducing Semiotic Economics*. Outside his university work, Tony is Chair of the Board of Wigan Arts and Community Heritage Trust and a Fellow of Trans4m. He is married to Carol and lives in the English Lake District with their two dogs, their two daughters, their partners and twin grandsons.

Ronnie Lessem, born in Zimbabwe and now based in the UK, was co-Founder of TRANS4M (France) which has since evolved, together with Dr Anselm Adodo and Aneeqa Malik, into Trans4m Communiversity Associates (TCA) in the UK, which focuses on the regeneration of particular societies. It is currently mainly active, through its emerging Communiversities—promoting Communal learning, a Regenerative Pilgrimium, Research academy and integral Laboratory—in Southern Africa (South Africa, Zimbabwe), West Africa (Nigeria), the Middle East (Egypt, Jordan), the Near East (Pakistan), and Europe (UK). Hitherto Ronnie Lessem has launched projects on European management, with IMD in Switzerland, European-ness and Innovation, with Roland Berger Foundation in Germany, African management, with Wits Graduate Business School in South Africa, and Arab as well as Islamic Management, with TEAM International in Cairo and Jordan.

He studied economics at the University of Zimbabwe, the economics of industry at the London School of Economics, Corporate Planning at Harvard Business School, and has since written some 50 books, the most recent, with Anselm Adodo and Tony Bradley, on *The Idea of the Communiversity* (Beacon Academic, 2019), and, with Munya Mawere and Daud Taranhike, *Nhakanomics: Harvesting Knowledge and Value for Regeneration Through Social Innovation* (African Talent Publishers, 2019).

Aneeqa Malik is the initiator and co-creator of iSRA. She refers to herself as a Soulidarity stewardess, as well as a facilitator of societal regeneration, having multi-functional experience in a wide variety of business settings and sectors. For the past 3 years, she has worked closely with Akhuwat Foundation, Pakistan, as their Global Research Strategist and an Associate Research Fellow for the Trans4m Centre for Integral Development, France. She is now developing Trans4m Communiversity Associates, alongside Professor Ronnie Lessem and Father Anselm Adodo.

Aneeqa has founded iSRA (Integral Soulidarity Research Academy). This aims to tune-in to the deeper impulses of a universal calling, seeking to invoke the 'spiritus' of economics and finance, giving way to a new economic discipline, which Aneeqa terms as the Soulidarity Economy. It is inspired by the Prophetic tradition of Mawakhat (spiritual brotherhood) and Akhuwat Foundation's (in Pakistan) model of Qard-e-Hasan (benevolent loan). Her book, *Integral Finance: Akhuwat – A Case Study of the Solidarity Economy* was published in 2018 by Routledge, as part of Trans4m's Transformation and Innovation Series.

Basheer Oshodi is the head of Islamic Banking at Sterling Bank and has over 20 years' work experience in finance and real estate. Basheer was Head, Non-Interest Finance and Head, Research at EFInA. He was Head, Islamic Banking Risk & Compliance at Stanbic IBTC Bank (a member of Standard Bank Group) and set up the non-interest banking window. He also initiated products compliant with Islamic finance principles at Stanbic IBTC Asset Management Ltd. He holds a BSc and MSc in Estate Management and General Management respectively from the University of Lagos. He has a PGD from the Institute of Islamic Banking & Insurance (IIBI), London and he is an Associate Fellow of the institution. He obtained a master's in research (MRes) Business & Management from London Metropolitan University; and a PhD in Management of Innovation & Technology from DaVinci Institute for Technology Management, South Africa in conjunction with Trans4m Center for Integral Development, Geneva. He has completed the Executive Programme on International Housing Finance at Wharton, University of Pennsylvania, USA and starting a Diploma in Global Business at the University of Oxford.

He is a Senior Fellow at Trans4m; Research Fellow – Centre for Housing Studies, University of Lagos; Research Fellow and Co-founder – Centre for Integral Socio-Economic Research, Lagos; and Senior Associate, Chartered Institute of Islamic Finance Professionals, Malaysia. Basheer is a member of the International Atlantic Economic Society (IAES) and American Economic Association (AEA). He is the author of An Integral Approach to Development Economics: Islamic Finance in an African Context published by Gower, UK. He has also published several academic articles and chapters.

Insights in Semiotic Economics

Semiotic Economics is a new sub-discipline. It relates to the current ferment about the teaching of economics and its connection to real-world events. Since the global financial crash (2007–09), groups such as Post-Crash Economics, Rethinking Economics, and Alternative Economics have formed, led by students and many young, radical academics. They have questioned why so little conventional textbook and taught economics explains real-world experience and phenomena, especially at a macro-level. As such, a range of models have been dusted off, fashioned and re-emphasised, many of which are centuries old, to challenge the dominance of neoliberal, market-based, capitalist economics.

At the same time, there has been a surge in the development of heterodox approaches to economics, which reflect many contemporary concerns. These include ecological, feminist, indigenous, well-being, core/non-monetary, social-solidarity, Islamic, spiritual, love and mutualist economics—to name but a few perspectives—each of which contests the idea of TINA (there is no alternative to neoliberalism). In consequence, there is an urgent need to examine the ways in which economic meaning is reflected in each of these alternative perspectives, alongside the assumptions of more conventional approaches. This is the primary purpose of Semiotic Economics.

Even so, beyond the narrow academic objective of examining the meanings of alternative economic models, there is a deeper requirement, which is to document and develop cases that reflect the distinctive cultural genius of particular societies, out of which these approaches are emerging. In this respect, our perspective on Semiotic Economics is an evolution of the work of leading theorists and commentators in integral economics over several decades, notably Professor Ronnie Lessem and his co-workers (1). One of these co-workers, Tony Bradley, has taken a pioneering role in developing this new perspective of Semiotic Economics. Together they are the editors of this series for Beacon Academic, reflective of the need for a Northern world Research Academy, as part of the global movement for communiversities (2).

Insights in Semiotic Economics will address four specific aspects of this community-based and academic movement. Firstly, the meaning-systems that are used to define alternative economics; secondly, the questions, theories and models generated within these approaches; thirdly, empirical and philosophical studies of culturally located cases, considered through the lens of semiotics, or the study of meaning-systems, signs and significance; fourthly, we will directly address the lacuna in classical semiotics which neglects the deep structures and archetypes that shape meaning, and which are so important in interpreting the significance of economic models.

But, we describe the development of Semiotic Economics as urgent for more than academic reasons. As leading economist Professor Neva Goodwin (3) has commented:

> The neoliberal experiment… contributes to poverty and inequality, while gravely damaging communities, natural resources, democratic processes and human well-being. In the new economy the reorganisation of important aspects of work and ownership will make it possible for people to be happier and more fulfilled, while extracting a lower level of resources. The transition to a new economy needs to be as inclusive and inviting as possible. There is great urgency to making the transition before we cross socio-political as well as ecological tipping points.

Yet this doesn't go far enough in focusing on what we mean by Semiotic Economics. In the summer of 2019 (when we are writing), it appears that many of these tipping-points are already being crossed. As such, the need for dissemination of alternative economics is vital. This is already beginning to happen. However, few people are systematically presenting the alternative meaning-systems (semiosis) that lie behind these alternatives. This edited book series will do just that. And in doing so, it will empower academics, students and educated lay-people alike, who are making these meanings, to pursue their activities and studies, in alternative economics more fully. Additionally, it will offer an opportunity for those researching and teaching—through the lens of Semiotic Economics—to bring the fruit of their work to a wider audience. This is the first book series on Semiotic Economics. Its appearance could hardly be more timely for the challenges we face, as the crises of the 21st century deepen, threatening cultures and the very sustainability of human life on earth, because of our conventional economic system.

1 **Lessem** R and **Schieffer** A (2010) *Integral Economics: Releasing the Economic Genius of your Society*. Abingdon. Routledge
2 **Lessem**, R, **Adodo**, A and **Bradley**, T (2019) *The Idea of the Communiversity: Releasing the natural, cultural, technological and economic GENE-ius of societies*. Manchester. Beacon Academic
3 **Goodwin**, N (2014) Rethinking Economics Conference Address, New York
Tony Bradley and Ronnie Lessem, Series Editors

Foreword

As we move deeper into the 21st century, many of the old certainties are disintegrating before our very eyes. In the West, the so-called post-War consensus has evaporated. In the decade since the great financial crash, the spectre of economic meltdown has never been far from the headlines. Just as I am writing, at the end of the Northern hemisphere summer of 2019, uncertainties surround the future of the UK economy as a result of Brexit, and the movement for increasing political integration in Europe is threatened, reflecting instability in one of the world's largest economic blocs and financial markets.

Equally, the Chinese economy is rebalancing. Germany is threatened with a recession. The US Federal Reserve has just reversed its decision to raise interest rates, prompting President Trump to castigate his Fed Chief for being 'a greater economic foe than China'. The entire global economy seems to be slowing down. Assuredly, you know what happened next, in respect of each of these news stories.

Yet, as I write, even greater calamities threaten to engulf us. The apparent seriousness of US President Donald Trump to use money and power to buy the continental island of Greenland, over the heads of its population, the societal chaos of Brexit in the UK, and political instability in Africa (cf. Zimbabwe) and Asia (cf. Hong Kong), each indicate that social democracy and ecological sustainability are under threat, as at no time since the Second World War. And in terms of the environmental catastrophe, we are in the most perilous state since humanity first emerged out of Africa. Fires in the Amazon rainforest are an appalling tragedy, of catastrophic proportion for life on earth. And on and on.

In light of these emergencies, the current book could not be more opportune. The work of our investment funds is only one small piece in a jigsaw for revitalising economic and financial markets. Yet, we believe it to be a vital one. More generally, Islamic finance—which hitherto has not always lived up to the promise of a *Shariah*-based system, for bringing genuine economic justice to millions, if not billions—is on the cusp of transformation, to fulfil its prospect. And whilst Islamic finance is significant in and of itself, it is only one part of a much wider movement for channelling societal well-being and true prosperity through new economic models, many of which are based in the faiths and humanitarian values.

As such, this excellent collection of essays, which draws together Islamic and other value-based financial models within an integral framework and the new discipline of Semiotic Economics, offers a vital perspective on how to address the current crises. For many, finance and accounting may appear dull as ditchwater. But in reality, when yoked to the human values and, in particular, for Muslims, the God-given principles of the Holy Qur'an, alternative and integral financial models are a gift of the Divine to help us out of the pit of our own making. It is in this light that I wholeheartedly commend this brilliant contribution to the work of building a new financial system that is fit for 21st century purposes. It is our hope and intention at ATG that we will not only learn from these essays but will implement their meaning to bring new economic and financial hope to millions, in Africa, across the developing world, and throughout the globe.

Abu Jimoh, CFA
Group CEO, TrustBanc Financial Group

Introducing the Semiotics of Integral to Islamic Finance

Tony Bradley and Ronnie Lessem,
Series Editors

As We Begin

In the spring of 2019, Trans4m Communiversity Associates Ronnie Lessem and Tony Bradley in the UK, and Father Anselm Adodo in Nigeria, published their book with Beacon Academic, entitled *The Idea of the Communiversity.* Such a 'communiversity' seeks to reconstitute economics and enterprise in its communal guise. In the present book they are joined by their close integral colleagues, bankers Robert Dellner in the UK and Dr. Basheer Oshodi in Nigeria, economist Mark Anielski in Canada, and Pakistani philosopher and financier, Aneeqa Malik. Together, this team, within the wider community of Trans4m, introduce features of how to understand finance from a communiversity perspective.

This is the initial volume in a new book series for Beacon Academic on *Insights in Semiotic Economics.* Semiotic Economics is a relatively new discipline. Apart from a small number of monographs and articles on the theme of the semiotics of economic language (1), mainly from continental Europe, this is a topic that has hardly been addressed within the Anglo-Saxon world. Yet, since the 'global financial crash' of 2007–09, an increasing number of voices have been questioning why there are no alternatives to the current neoliberal economic model.

Neoliberalism pertains to the (apparent) commanding heights of the Western world and influences all other worlds. The reasons for this will be addressed in various volumes of this series, either directly or tangentially. But movements—often led by students and young academic economists—such as Rethinking Economics, Post-Crash Economics, and Alternative Economics, have sprung up on campuses across the world, beginning in the UK and US.

These movements are starting to influence policy-makers and even central bankers. Why? Because the range of global challenges that societies face—in terms of anthropogenic climate change; the extreme nature of inequality, both within and between nations; the failure to provide adequate social service and medical care for vulnerable people in an age of austerity and demographic transition; the challenges of automation and the evolution of work, under conditions of AI, AR and robotics; the need to accommodate mass migrations of people; and the increasing awareness of other economic modes than those that are ruled by markets, to name only a few—are signalling that the current phase of capitalism is unstable, at the very least.

This is not to herald a glorious new day for the Soviets, the communes or international socialism—far from it. Rather, it is to point to the urgent requirement to interpret the meaning-making of alternative economic systems, in order to present societies with a richer understanding of what is possible, beyond the failures of economic models that were helpful for several decades, but seem to have reached their sell-by date. That is the core purpose of Semiotic Economics. The volumes in this series will address a wide range of perspectives, asking the foundational question: what are the meaning-systems underpinning different economic cultures and what do they point towards, in policy and practical terms?

As such, it seemed a good place to begin the series with a volume addressing alternative perspectives on money and finance. After all, money is what most ordinary people (who often make the best economists) think of when questions of economics are raised. Without wishing to invoke Margaret Thatcher's image of macro-economics as simply a scaled-up version of household budgeting, each of us is concerned with whether or not the money in our account will stretch to buy the things that we need. Frequently, we forget that the things that make life worth living are not traded on markets or, if they are, their commodification robs them of their core value.

We tend to equate value with money price. Price is the *sign*—the core concept of semiotics—that we look at to gauge whether or not something is 'worth it'. This is part of the dark genius of capitalism. But there are alternative perspectives on value, and each of these offers different meaning-making and systems for interpreting the nature of money and its significance.

When we address questions of semiotics, it is significance, signification, signs and codes that are our primary concerns, which may sound highly abstruse. In fact, the signposts that alternative understandings of money generate, point to very different ways of running economies for societal benefit. So, in addressing the semiotic economics of money and finance, we are considering what alternative models of money point to. What are they signs of? How do they demonstrate a different form of signification in society, which may indicate a radical and integral shift in the ways in which we view financial systems? And so, to help us look in a new direction, we need to ask the basic question: what is the meaning of money? This, together with each of the other questions, is raised in the subsequent chapters. But, by way of preface and opening this series on Semiotic Economics, we can address something of this question.

The Meaning of Money

What *is* the meaning and significance of money? This is a more perplexing question than may first be recognised. If we think of money as a material fact of life, we look to the dollar, pound sterling, euro or rand bills that bulge from our wallets, if we are lucky. Equally, we can hear the jingle of change in our pockets. These assert that money is, actually, a physical means of exchange that we carry with us. But as soon as we consider the money that is transferred in billions of dollars every microsecond across the world's markets, we need to be aware of the digits, algorithms and electronic data that are, really, the carriers of money.

Then we need to challenge the assumption that money is always, or even primarily, a means of exchange. For financial institutions, those who command wealth and for national and global central banks, money is less about exchange and more about holding stocks of guarantees, insurance, and a commodity to be valued in itself. Those institutions and the very small number of persons, relatively speaking, worldwide, who control electronic money transfers—or the banks of computers that create and destroy the money—recognise that the commodity is, largely, intangible. It exists as bits and bytes and rarely crystallises out as actual things that can be touched or held.

So, where does money come from and where does it go? Very few people, it seems, understand that retail or wholesale money is not a direct reflection of some physical resource. Instead, it is a *sign* of a bank's desire to loan and charge interest. Or, in a more ethical vein, money is a signifying commitment to *trust*, a fiat. Many bank notes display the words 'I promise to pay'. Money, whether physical or digital, is a promissory note, pointing towards the level of trust and integrity in an economy and society. It is a sign of a valid social contract, or in times when the value of money fails, as in periods of massive economic instability, war, famine or hyper-inflation, it becomes a sign of an invalid social system.

Money doesn't grow on trees, except in certain indigenous people cultures such as Skagway in the Klondike of Alaska, where spruce tips are traded for goods, or in places where timber or coffee is the primary means of exchange. However, it can be created out of thin air. Indeed, to some extent, that is the

3

origin of most money in digital circulation. Several decades ago, the eminent North American economist J.K. Galbraith (2) famously commented:

> The process by which banks create money is so simple that the mind is repelled. With something so important, a deeper mystery seems only decent.

Private banks (but not governments) can effectively create money out of nothing, by placing deposits in an account. So, we may ask: why isn't there more of it to go around? This is an extremely good question, the answer to which lies in what the sign points to in neoliberal-based economies: the need to maintain *scarcity* in a market-based economy that fuels inequality.

Equally, it is remarkable how many people believe that the money in circulation is somehow backed up by vast hoards of gold bullion, precious jewels or some other store of mythic value, kept in a Fort Knox or Bank of England. Whilst central banks do keep considerable reserves in things like gold bars, they are not very relevant to the circulation of money in society. You may or may not be surprised to know that only about 3% of the money in circulation is in the form of tangible cash. The other 97% exists as electronic money, script money, bank money and other forms of intangible money assets that are traded and can be created, virtually out of thin air, by private banks. Nor are European banks advised to hold more than 7% of their loan book in reserves, and some hold far less, although they are working to that target. So everyone shouldn't ask for their money all at once, unless you want to see another bank run, such as happened with the UK bank, Northern Rock, in 2008.

Of course, whether or not bank money is realisable may not appear to be much of an issue, so long as I have that tenner in my pocket—except when a financial crash, such as 2007–09, occurs. Then the assets on which bank loan books were based proved to be close to worthless: the notorious CDS's (credit default swaps), securitisation vehicles and the like. In that case, my tenner could have turned to paper value, had not the UK Treasury intervened to stabilise the international financial system.

But it *is* an issue. Governments, in an age of austerity, argue that they have insufficient money for addressing climate change, providing effective schooling and hospitals, adult social care, enough house construction, combating poverty or a myriad of other real, tangible, social needs. There just isn't enough money to go around. Or, so it is argued in the current financial system. This is largely because of the scale of national debt in debt-based economies. On October 1st 2008, time famously stood still in New York when the massive debt clock in Times Square, which had recorded the national debt for 20 years, ran out of digits after the US Federal debt surpassed $10TN (trillion)! This was a perfect semiotic *sign of the times*.

However, there are other ways of signifying money and finance and they can lead to very different ways of organising integral financial systems. If you would like to read a very good guide to the conventional neoliberal system and how it can be changed into one that works for the betterment of society, we recommend Frans Doorman's booklet *Our Money* (3). Alternatively, for a longer read on the same theme, you might wish to consult Andrew Jackson and Ben Dyson's superb work (4) on how the monetary system is broken and can be fixed.

What Does Integral Finance Point Towards?

Commenting on how to make the current system work better is not, however, the primary aim of this volume. Rather, as the initial book in our series on *Insights in Semiotic Economics*, the following chapters have a complementary purpose. As we indicated above, our opening question was a sign pointing us to our main aim. The intention of this book, then, is to address a question that emerges once we've raised the basic one of what money means. It is the question: what do money and finance *point to*? What are they, in turn, signs *towards*, in the various parts of the world—which we understand as fourfold, in our integral worlds model—and which present alternative financial approaches to the current dominant system?

Over many years and volumes, Ronnie Lessem and his co-workers have identified the fourfold nature of social research, development and innovation, GEN*E*rating an integral approach to social transformation. Each of these aspects of real-world transformation—at personal, organisational, societal and cultural levels—can be understood as having distinctive 'Southern', 'Eastern', 'Northern' and 'Western' forms. Consequently, we can identify ways in which innovation, enterprise, management and economy are **g**rounded in a Southern mode, connected to nature and community; **e**merge as new ways of awakening, through culture and spirituality; **n**avigate towards alternative transformational operations, through systems, science and technology; and **e**ffect enterprises and social innovations (Western) that build on the grounding (Southern), emergence (Eastern) and navigational aspects (Northern) of the other three worlds. This is what we refer to as the GEN*E* dynamic model of integral development, aligned to the more static understanding of the four—geographic and metaphoric—worlds. It is reflected in the four parts of this volume.

This model of integral economics, development, research and enterprise has been elaborated and its case studies commented upon in a whole series of books in the former *Transformation and Innovation* collection for Gower-Ashgate-Routledge. In those volumes, the Trans4m community uncovered the ways in which this GEN*E*alogical process has operated and GEN*E*rated many

5

social innovations. More recently, this work has taken the form of indicating the processes by which societies and cultures can learn to adapt this model, through *The Idea of the Communiversity* (5), our first book for Beacon Academic.

In this book, *Integral to Islamic Finance,* we now seek to reposition our understanding of money and accounting, placing the rediscovered—at least for the Western world—ancient system of 'Islamic finance' centre stage. As such, we are revisiting the Golden Age, when the Arab world played a centring role in the world at large, pivotally lodged in between Africa, Europe and Asia. In that age it spanned ancient Egypt and Greece, Persia and India, from its centring vantage point in Baghdad and thereafter, Andalusia. In the 21st century, it is high time to revisit the Golden Age and the role that the Arab world played in co-creating an intellectual order, reflecting, in our terms, its GEN*E*-ius.

Equally, it is time for further evolution of this work in integral economics, as we develop the theories, methodologies, methods and practices of Semiotic Economics. In subsequent volumes, we will examine issues such as how spiritual models, from some of the world's great faiths, signify alternative economic systems. Indeed, we introduce some of that practice in this book, in relation to money and financial systems.

Other topics will cover the application of semiotics theory to economics in general, the alternative economics of reconstructing war-ravaged cities in the Middle East, the variety of community and *ubuntu*-based indigenous economies in sub-Saharan Africa, the impact of ecological economics on addressing the greening of markets, and the role of women's co-operatives in utilising feminist economics for transforming many cultures in the two-thirds world. These themes provide the underpinning for the chapters in this opening volume of the series on *Insights in Semiotic Economics*.

Introducing the Chapters

The four parts of the book represent an evolution, indicated above, from integral to Semiotic Economics. In **Part One** we consider the nature of money and finance, when viewed from the standpoints of psychological and well-being perspectives. These two chapters help to ground the book in a range of humanistic meaning-systems, signifying alternative ways in which finance can be viewed, when contrasted with the conventional neoliberal model.

In the opening chapter, Robert Dellner—a Swedish-German-British ex-banker and counselling psychotherapist who works in the impact investing sector—has combined his economic and psychological insights to consider the nature of money. He follows this preface and introduces this series by taking up the story of how money acts semiotically to confer meaning on both itself and ourselves, and to even act as a signifier of moral agency.

Thereafter, in Chapter 2, Canadian social economist Mark Anielski, an internationally renowned expert on the economics of happiness and real prosperity, takes us from money to capital, from wealth to well-being. In Anielski's first book *The Economics of Happiness: Building Genuine Wealth* (6) and his new book *An Economy of Well-being* (7), he presents a new economic framework for measuring progress as well as governing monetary policy, banking and investment. As a well-being specialist, Anielski has been a senior economic advisor in the US, Canada, China, Singapore, Tahiti and Bhutan, as well as to the First Peoples of Canada indigenous movement, whose recent work in Indigenomics is gaining global traction.

Anielski's thesis is that, at least since the Second World War, the Western economic model has been based on a flawed accounting system that measures progress and welfare based simply on the monetary transactions of goods and services (using GDP or Gross Domestic Product as the measure). In this, he is following a venerable line of commentators, including US Senator Bobby Kennedy who famously commented that GDP 'measures everything except that which is worthwhile'. By contrast, Mark proposes a new economic system and national accounting standard (i.e. Genuine Wealth) that would measure and report on the conditions of well-being.

This utilises an integrated five-capital asset accounting system: human (people), social (relationships), natural (ecological), built (infrastructure) and financial (money) constituting the five capital assets of any organisation, community or nation. The methodology for doing this is introduced in his chapter, reliant, as it is, on the creation of a money system controlled by public rather than private banks, with the alternative meaning-making, compared to conventional capitalist banking that this conveys.

Part Two of the book presents the emergence of a more fully integral four worlds and GEN*E*alogical model of finance. In Chapter 3, Ronnie 'Samanyanga' Lessem introduces the theme of integral finance via the Trans4m four worlds model. Previously, together with Alexander Schieffer, he was the originator of *Integral Research* (8) as the re-GEN*E*-rative means, for interpreting *Integral Economics* (9) and *Integral Enterprise* (10), which are outcomes of that process.

The four cases that Lessem presents, representing the semiotic meaning-systems of Trans4m, cover Nature-Power in the Southern world; Spiritual Soulidarity in the Eastern world; Co-operative Organisation in the Northern world; and a remarkable mixing of Chaos and Order in the Western world. Together, these serve to point to the diversity of financial systems that contribute to the transformative rhythm from local **G**rounding to global-local **E**ffect. Financial systems vary enormously across the four worlds, as these cases indicate, building on the preceding models of financial well-being introduced by Robert Dellner and Mark Anielski.

In the following Chapter 4, Lessem turns his attention from integral finance to integral accounting. Over forty years, since Lessem first worked in an accounting firm and wrote on the need for a more holistic model of accountancy, there has been a patent lacuna in the ability of the profession to develop a more integral approach and methodology. As such, in this chapter, Lessem sets out to remedy this lamentable picture. In doing so he turns to the social philosophy disciplines of phenomenology, hermeneutics and—through the lens of Tony Bradley, the other editing author of this series—semiotics, to construct a way of developing an integral approach to accounting.

That said, the Southern (phenomenological), Eastern (hermeneutical) and Northern (semiotic) worlds need to be completed by the Western positivist and empiric(al/ist) perspective. But, as seen in the preceding chapters, this approach overshadows all the others to the extent that, if anything, it needs to receive diminished significance, semiotically-speaking, until the other approaches are given their correct position in the field of accounting. Lessem concludes Part Two of the book by indicating a series of tenets, drawn from each of the four worlds of the integral model, which offer that more holistic (static) and GEN*E*alogical (dynamic) procedure.

From these transformative cases—connected to both distinct cultural financial instances and an integral approach to accounting practice—**Part Three** navigates towards a theory of integral-semiotic economics, incorporating specific, practical cases of Christian and Islamic finance, structured around the integral four worlds model of Southern to Western dimensions. As such, we turn from the principles of integral finance and accounting to the developing practice of such. In Chapter 5, Anselm Adodo (Christian) and Jubril Adeojo (Muslim) offer a somewhat unconventional, integral approach to finance and accounting, which takes the local culture of Western Africa seriously and semiotically.

Adodo and Adeojo begin with the wisdom of the late, great African Islamic philosopher Ali Mazrui and his seminal work called *The Africans* (11). In it, he introduced the notion of Africa's 'triple heritage: indigenous, Christian, Islamic'. As such, Chapter 5 starts out in this Southern orientation to community, economy, and finance. For Adodo, it is the rhythm of the African drum and dance that directs the way in which the economy is conceived, as a response to Nature-Creation. This means that the abstract world of money, largely derived from the Northern and Western worlds, is recast in communitalist terms as a way of GEN*E*rating an economy of sharing.

Thence, Adeojo picks up this beat in response to the climate pandemic in Africa. He indicates, through the lens of his climate advisory firm, how strategic financial partnerships have mobilised public and private sector institutions, in order to fund commercially viable and socially responsible climate-resilient infrastructure projects and enterprises. He shows how the communitalism that Adodo writes about is practically awakened, in the areas of climate mitigation and adaptation, through an African dance of finance.

Having immersed ourselves in the South—naturally and communally—finance and enterprise are construed as woven into the relational fabric of society. As we turn to a uniquely Eastern perspective on such, through Islamic philosophy and theory, we examine, in some detail, one of the cases of principle that Ronnie Lessem introduces in Chapter 3; namely, the remarkable pan-societal institution of Akhuwat in Pakistan. Aneeqa Malik, one of the authors of such, is a spiritual explorer, a community activist and businesswoman, straddling Eastern and Western cultures, in Pakistan and the UK. For Malik, the Holy Qur'an is a book of revelation, which has over 6,000 *ayahs* (signs) presenting the criteria for a distinctive Islamic financial institution, purposefully seeking to eradicate poverty through mobilising the *mawakhat* (brotherhood of Islam).

In Chapter 6, Aneeqa Malik presents the integral Islamic philosophy that undergirds Akhuwat's remarkable story of transformation, both in Pakistan and, subsequently, being applied amongst other Muslim communities across the world, including the UK. The picture she presents is one which seems to collapse time between the era of the Holy Prophet (blessings be upon him) and today's 21st century world. Of course, the model is not as simple as that. But, through the work of Dr. M. Amjad Saqib, Akhuwat has taken the spiritual principles of Islamic teaching on how to support the community, and turned these into practical solutions for increasing the prosperity and support of millions of people across Pakistan.

Following this, we turn to the critical North in Chapter 7, to the first of two chapters, which introduce the principles and methodological background to Semiotic Economics through the work of Tony Bradley. Whilst the discipline of semiotics has hardly been applied to economics, Bradley indicates just how vital this application is, as the late 20th century assumptions of neoliberalism become increasingly challenged. He shows how, in line with the integral model, semiotics needs to develop a fourfold methodology, which takes seriously the GEN*E*alogy of the transformative approach.

In particular, Bradley identifies the missing element of semiotic theory and practice, which builds on the spiritual principles outlined by Adodo (Southern world) and Malik (Eastern world), to indicate how the deep structures of alternative systems, once uncovered, point to ways of recasting the meaning(s) of economics. In this pivotal chapter, Bradley introduces an evolution, in theory, to influence practice that develops integral economics to incorporate semiotics. Through this, he points to ways in which the spirituality of Islam, the great faiths and the values of humanistic philosophy need to be understood as fundamental sources for alternative economic systems, in practice as well as in theory.

As such, in Chapter 8, Basheer Oshodi takes relay hold of the critical baton from Bradley, by examining the actual practice of much Islamic finance as currently operated in global financial markets, representing the world of the West, which builds on the rest. Except, as Oshodi is able to trenchantly demonstrate, the institutions of much Islamic finance have singularly failed to emerge a new spiritually-based financial system. Instead, all too often, they have used the language of the *Shariah* (Islamic law) to operate in financial markets which retain an embedded basis in debt-related investment. Furthermore, as a banker and a Muslim, Oshodi is well-placed to present the critical history of Islamic finance, from the 1960s to the present day, pointing to its inadequacies as well as its potential prospects.

This turns us full-circle to the *e*ffecting Western, and **Part Four** of the book. In this final section, the previous two authors, Bradley and Oshodi, move from a critical Northern perspective to one which, in Western vein, indicates the effectiveness of semiotic and integral, alternative and Islamic, economics and finance. Bradley takes the Semiotic Economics methodology, introduced in Chapter 7, and applies this to Christian (kingdom), Islamic (Akhuwat) and humanistic (impact investment) economic models. Through this analysis, he shows the significant actualisation and potential of these contrarian—so far as neoliberalism is concerned—systems of economy and finance.

Thence, Oshodi builds on his critique of current Islamic finance practice (Chapter 8) by introducing a new, multi-billion dollar Bahraini and Saudi-backed investment fund, AmeenArthur, which is seeking to restore the full principles of classical Islamic teaching into the sphere of 21st century investment banking. As the Chief Impact Officer for the AmeenArthur fund, it is his responsibility to arrange and monitor funding arrangements that are fully Shariah-compliant. He points to the ways in which this new institution is tackling very real, contemporary challenges, concerned with poverty, inequalities in education and health and women's access to work in sub-Saharan Africa, doing so by reference to models of Islamic finance that take Muslim spirituality and teaching as normative and definitive.

Through these final two chapters, the volume completes its stated aim of indicating a new approach to Islamic finance, derived from the integral model, which adopts a semiotic approach, pointing to the meanings of authentically alternative economic systems. Even so, each of the authors of this book is acutely aware that all they have been able to do is present some initial signs towards the full meaning of an integral Islamic financial system. That, of course, is only to be expected. It is one of the tenets of semiotics that as soon as any representative sign (representamum) is revealed, it will signal the production of a range of new effects (interpretants). Those will be for future commentators and books to introduce.

How to Read This Book

When opening a collection such as this one, there is often the temptation to only read the chapter, section or part that most immediately appeals. Nevertheless, we have edited the book to reflect the integral GEN*E*. Part One grounds the book in the territory of money and finance, pointing to the ways in which culture, nature and community can recast the entire semiotic approach to these practical economic concerns. In Part Two, we take a circulation around the Four Worlds, but from the standpoint of emergent values, meanings and philosophy, exploring from phenomenology to positivism. Thence, in Part Three, we offer a genealogical navigation, recircling the four worlds, to consider the theory of semiotics and the practice of Islamic finance. Finally, in Part Four, we look to the effective development of both Semiotic Economics—the underpinning discipline of this new book series—and the possibilities for a more integral version of Islamic finance. As such, the chapters follow the GEN*E* logic.

Consequently, we do encourage you to read the book in a sequential way, recognising how the pattern rhythm of the GEN*E* permeates the whole. Or, if you wish to start with your own interest—whether it is with mainstream Islamic finance, albeit with a twist; the Eastern perspective on finance which may come as a surprise; the theory and philosophy of Semiotic Economics; or to take a fresh look at accounting procedures—we suggest that you identify how your particular focus fits into the GEN*E* and ripples out to other chapters from there. In this way, we trust you will have a fuller and more satisfying engagement with the themes of the book. Equally, we feel sure that this will assist you in orientating yourself for exploring each of the further volumes, which will be published in this series on *Insights in Semiotic Economics*.

It will be an important aspect of subsequent volumes in this series to enumerate many of the alternative economic meaning-systems, both Islamic and emerging from other values-based beliefs. As we indicate in our Epilogue, by doing so, we will be helping economics and finance to find their true homes within human consciousness. In this regard, we can do no better than to leave the last words of this introduction to Islamic philosopher Anwar Ibrahim (12):

> Recapturing the meaning of the *umma* would necessitate that Muslims engage with other people, nations, worldviews, religions and ideologies to work for a set of moral objectives that we can and must define together. But it takes us much further. It requires that we accept the umma of other people... the history of the umma has shown exemplary, almost unique models of multi-racial, multi-cultural, multi-religious, pluralist societies. If ever we had the need of recovering such an imperative it is now.

And nowhere is this more urgent, if we are to address the current existential crisis of humanity, than in the spheres of economics, finance and our relations with the worlds of Nature-Creation, the human psyche, science and our creative institutions. To harness these together, integrally and with new meaning, will deliver hope for societies and cultures in the 21st century, freeing us from the imprisoning power of money as we know it.

Bibliography

1 **Coratelli**, G, **Galofaro**, F and **Montanari**, F (2015) Introduction on Semiotics of Economic Discourse. *Ocula*, 16, 1–9. December

2 **Galbraith**, J K (2017, republished) *Money: Whence it came; Where it went*. Princeton. University Press

3 **Doorman**, F (2015) *Our Money: Towards a new monetary system*. Creative Commons. Lulu Internet Publishers

4 **Jackson**, A and **Dyson**, B (2012) *Modernising Money: Why our monetary system is broken and how it can be fixed*. London. Positive Money

5 **Lessem**, R, **Adodo**, A and **Bradley**, T (2019) *The Idea of the Communiversity: Releasing the natural, cultural, technological and economic GENE-ius of societies*. Manchester. Beacon Academic

6 **Anielski** M (2007) *The Economics of Happiness*. Gabriola Island. New Society Publishers

7 **Anielski** M (2017) *The Economy of Well-being. Commonsense Tools for Building Genuine Wealth and Happiness*. Gabriola Island. New Society Publishers

8 **Lessem** R and **Schieffer** A (2008) *Integral Research: A global approach towards social science research leading to social innovation*. Geneva. Tran4m Publishing

9 **Lessem** R and **Schieffer** A (2010) *Integral Economics: Releasing the Economic Genius of your Society*. Abingdon. Routledge

10 **Lessem** R and **Schieffer** A (2009) *Transformation Management: Toward the Integral Enterprise*. Abingdon. Routledge

11 **Mazrui** A (1986) *The Africans – A Triple Heritage*. London. Guild Publishing

12 **Ibrahim** A (1996) *Asian Renaissance*. New York. Times International Books

PART ONE

Introducing the Meaning of Money and Capital

CHAPTER 1

The Nature of Money: A Semiotic and Psychological Perspective

Robert Dellner, I3 Partners, UK

Money systems, from their prehistoric origins onward, were attributed primarily to the Great Mother archetype. As Western societies were characterised by a systematic repression of such, they developed financial systems that embodied what Jung describes as the 'shadows', or repressed part, of that archetype. These shadows turn out to be none other than the collective emotions of greed and fear of scarcity. As all professional operators, brokers, fund managers, financial experts will confirm, financial markets are primarily driven by these two collective emotions.

Bernard Lietaer, *The Soul of Money*

The word integral means comprehensive, inclusive, non-marginalizing, and embracing. Integral approaches to any field attempt to be exactly that: to include as many perspectives, styles, and methodologies as possible within a coherent view of the topic. In a certain sense, integral approaches are 'meta-paradigms' or ways to draw together an already existing number of separate paradigms into an interrelated network of approaches that are mutually enriching.

Ken Wilber, *Integral Spirituality*

Despite its original character as a desert tongue, Arabic displayed a remarkable potential as a medium of sophisticated and complex communication. It could create new words out of existing verbal forms, and its ability to compress shades of meaning into a single dramatic expression made it a vivid and exact language. Elaborated by its grammarians and stimulated by the challenge of new horizons it became a tool for thought and scholarship. As Latin did in medieval Europe and English did in British India, Arabic in the new state overarched local languages and literature to create a new and universal intellectual realm where Persian philosophers, Arab theologians, Jewish and Christian physicians, and Indian mathematicians could not only speak a common language but also have a sense of sharing in a common intellectual order.

Jean Badeau, *The Genius of Arab Civilization*

1.1. Introduction

1.1.1. The Changing Concept of Money: A Swedish History

The concept of money has changed significantly over the years—considering its functionality as a unit of account, storage of wealth and as a means of exchange—in terms of how it is held in the minds of its users, as symbolic representations, together with how it is created and managed by governments. In other words, the *semiotics* of money has been evolving. Over the centuries, money has taken various forms, depending on cultures and context—which determined aspects such as scarcity or cost of production—from Cowrie shells to carved stones, etc. This was overlaid by periods and cycles where either trust was broken and more universal forms of value had to be added, intrinsically, such as precious metals, to facilitate trade across borders using an acceptable means of exchange. This worked very well for long periods of time across the world. But this concept was heavily reliant on the availability of chosen raw materials, such as gold, silver or copper. Equally, it depended on trusting the issuing entity and government, for example, The Royal Mint, to remain honest in terms of weights and purities to preserve value; something which history has proven is more difficult than might be expected.

My home nation, Sweden, introduced the copper standard for minting coins in 1624, given its abundance of copper with the Falu copper mine. To give some perspective, at the time this mine accounted for two thirds of all of Europe's copper supplies during the first half of the 17th century. Not long thereafter, Sweden had problems in finding demand for all its copper and when the price declined domestically, currency inflation set in, requiring the Mint to issue larger and larger coins. This culminated in 1644 when the Mint issued the 10 Daler coin, weighing in at a hefty 19.72 kg (c. 43½ lbs) which literally and physically meant people having to go to the markets carrying the coins they needed in wheelbarrows.

In such circumstances, money had lost its practical value as an efficient means of exchange and the copper standard was abandoned as a result. However, as necessity is the mother of all inventions, this gave rise to the first banknotes being issued in Europe. The Stockholms Banco issued the first paper money, with government coins deposited in exchange for notes, which could be reversed for the same kind of coin on demand. Despite their practical attraction and success, this ended in a now predictable and classic bank failure.

By 1660, the central government had begun to mint new coins of a lower weight than the older ones to make them practical, once again. This meant that many depositors who had made the paper exchange now wanted their old, heavier coins back, as they had a higher metal value. This led to a run on the bank. The founder, Johan Palmstruch, then began to issue deposit certificates. These were promissory security notes, which gave the owner the right to withdraw the deposited amount in paper cash.

The special thing about the deposit certificates, which were called credit notes, was that the bank was no longer dependent on having money deposited to be able to lend. The new thing about Palmstruch's banknotes was that they were not linked to any actual physical deposit. Instead, they were based on the general public's confidence that the bank would pay the value of the note in cash, upon demand. Instead, the new certificates were handed out as loans from the bank and could be used to purchase anything. In effect, these were the first banknotes in Europe to be born based on institutional *trust*.

During the following years, in 1663, both the Crown and the Chancellor at the time, Magnus Gabriel De la Gardie, also took large loans and the bank duly obliged by printing more and more notes. This, of course, led towards their collapse in value, a phenomenon we now know as currency inflation.

Confidence was finally lost amongst the general public and many people demanded that their notes be redeemed. But as Stockholms Banco did not have enough coins, they began calling in the loans that they had previously granted. This ended in a classic bank failure. The world would witness such collapses time and again over the centuries. The Council of the Realm—the government of the time—decided in 1664 that the loans would be repaid and that the credit notes would be withdrawn. Palmstruch was ordered to appear before the Svea Court of Appeal in 1668 and was sentenced to death for mismanagement of the bank. He was later reprieved and remained in prison until 1670, but died in the following year.

After this experience at the Riksdag of the Estates in 1668, the nobles pushed through a proposal to form a new institution from the ruins of Stockholms Banco, but now with the nobles, the clergy and the burghers as principals (excluding the peasants), to create common ownership and interest. What was then called The Bank of the Estates of the Realm, Riksens Ständers Bank, today known by its current name, Sveriges Riksbank, was established. So, the world's oldest central bank was created again out of necessity to re-establish trust and functionality in the political and economic exchange system. This is a tale of which the principal dynamics could be retold in many countries over the coming centuries, up into modern times. What may surprise many people is how such scenarios are allowed to be played out over and over again, despite the knowledge of how to prevent them being readily available.

1.2. The Nature of Money

1.2.1. The Psychology of Money

The nature of money, as Lietaer (1) has intimated, embeds all our economic hopes and fears and is highly susceptible to the shifting psychology of the time. One could even argue that money shares many of its aspects with world religions in that whilst based on trust and faith, it also needs to be grounded in the soils of a belief and value system which creates its reality. Money, like a religion, also contains the aspiration and need for future salvation, one economic and the other spiritual.

Also, akin to religion, money can be highly political and open to many different views and interpretations of its management, value and stewardship. It has a multi-valent semiosis. Consequently, the nature of money needs grounding and rooting deeply into the soils of its functional context. Some of these roots have started to disintegrate, as many argue today.

1.2.2. The Monetary Challenges We Face

In many respects, we are at a threshold in how money functions, as technology and digital variations are taking over the more traditional means of using money. Also, governments have lost much of their control over national money creation and management, with potentially significant implications for us all, both positive and negative. These transitions need to be navigated somehow, both politically and economically.

Some of these core challenges are:

- The move to fiat money and how to maintain the value of money through trust as its only reference.
- The money supply mainly being created by increased debt, as issued by banks, which has reached such levels to question the validity of capital valuations.
- Technology creating and enabling digital currencies to emerge as substitutes to regulated money.
- The relational change in capital as we enter the 'integral age' and its connection to money.

Equally, we need to consider this as a journey of the self. When working with capital and money, we cannot exclude any part or dynamic of ourselves, because the very thing that we are studying is both an extension and a mirror of ourselves. Money, as such, is both technical and psychological and the two need to meet and synthesise for money to function. As we know, most of our problems as a species stem from our incapacity to see things as complex and natural holistic systems. When we do so, we are better able to make the necessary changes.

1.2.3. So What is 'Integral' in Relation to Money?

On a Journey From a Story of Separation

So why do we need the 'integral'? In large part this is because of our need for cognitive binary fragmentation; that is, seeing things through reduction into separate parts, in order to aid us with our numerous limitations for understanding, together with our search and need towards certainty. As renegade contemporary economist Charles Eisenstein (2) suggests, 'Individually and collectively, we are on a journey from a story of Separation to a new yet ancient story of Reunion: ecology, interdependency, inter-being.' He goes on to say that 'Separation is not an ultimate reality, but a human projection, an ideology, a story… It is a story of the separation of the human realm from the natural, in which the former expands and the latter is turned progressively into resources, goods, property, and, ultimately, money.'

The purpose, then, of this opening chapter is to introduce to the reader how to become acquainted with looking through the integral lens, as a means of semiosis, to build and create a full systems approach to understanding the nature of money. This means that at the same time as attempting to create wholeness, our actual understandings come from simplification, splitting, creating and symbolically labelling contrasting metaphorical visualisations. In this way, we are helped to build simple relationships and meaning which can be cognitively stored. One such metaphor is a concept of money that we can use to interpret its personal nature. However, we and our governments often create limitations to this endeavour. In combination with polarised politics and a need to be right, this model often keeps us static and without any real change or progress.

This lack of moving with the times is one among many reasons why some parts of the economy has splintered off, enabled by technology, to create new concepts of money such as Bitcoin. At one level, there is probably no actual real need for new currencies such as Bitcoin. However, an opportunity arose to embed certain features, such as anonymity, which proved highly attractive to parts of the economy. Nevertheless, as a direct consequence, the energy requirements to run the global digital currency market are estimated to be equivalent to the energy consumption of the entire country of Belgium. So, the cost implications of creating and maintaining a digital currency is not only highly related to the extraction of value from any exchange rate movement, but also to the market's willingness to pay such transaction costs.

These costs can only be covered by willing participants who find additional value in its use elsewhere. The value of anything is ultimately in the eye of the beholder but, also, in relation to any market. As such, money, as we know it, relies almost entirely today on market valuations and its collective psychology, together with its use-value. Therefore, the nature of money is a moving and shifting construct, the meaning of which is represented symbolically and semiotically, both through our culture as well as its economic exchange value.

Money Does Not Grow on Trees

> It's not the creation of wealth that is wrong, but the love of money for its own sake.
>
> Margaret Thatcher

> For the love of money is the root of all evil.
>
> 1 Timothy 6:10. King James Version

Like many, in my youth, I was often told that *'Money does not grow on trees'*. Over time this becomes a construct that feeds into many of our values and beliefs. We develop an intimate relationship with money, so that its importance is evident in terms of lifestyle and needs, but which can also assume pathological proportions to the detriment of other relationships. Money is a key component of our identity, in terms of how we see and value ourselves, as well as how we believe others may see and value us, in terms of property and possessions, etc. This leads to our understanding of meaning and purpose for ourselves, partly ascribed in relation to wealth and money. This can be fundamentally positive but it also contains a shadow.

Money is, of course, not evil in itself. The driver in this case is the word 'love', which for each of us has a different meaning. In this case, St. Paul derives the word for 'love of money' (φιλαργυρια) from the word for 'fondness for', essentially meaning 'covetousness'. Thus, the root of evil rests in the person, not in the money itself, which, being inert, has no intentionality or objective. Any tool, for example, a knife, can be used for good, with the skill of a surgeon's hand to save lives, or for bad, by a murderer who takes someone's life. Money has a similar characteristic to a battery, acting as a repository of static energy, which, when activated and attached to something, generates movement and action.

Finance at the Threshold

Here we need to distinguish between the features of money, capital and wealth, as they are all related, given that the word 'money' particularly becomes an exercise in semiotics (meaning-making). Christopher Houghton Budd (3) of the Centre for Associative Economics in Britain, who wrote 'Finance at the Threshold' in the *Integral Transformation and Innovation Series*, noted that money is a semiotic creation, the meaning and creation of which is shared by agreement, which has no intrinsic value:

> The most important thing about money… is that men consciously agree on its purpose. Something non-economic is thereby introduced. The Greek word for money means custom, consensus, convention. When men arrive at consensus, they are not involved in economic processes, but in 'rights' processes. Money belongs to the rights life, it enables the rights lore to permeate economics. The question is: to what purpose? Money in itself—a coin, a note, a cheque—in no way determines what is to be done with it. Money is utterly emancipated from the economic processes that give rise to it. What happens with money is up to the user. The past cannot live on in money. Money by its very nature belongs to the future. The only way of knowing what can happen to money is to observe the use it is put to. Moreover, the use will reveal the intention of the user and thereby reveal the user also.

In other words, money is fundamentally *semiotic*. It is a sign, pointing to its use-value. Money travels well beyond just its functionality and, as such, is a highly personal psychological construct, the representation and meaning of which can only be known symbolically to its owner. Money can be and mean nothing, or everything, depending on the lens you are looking through. But what is undeniable and independent is the market valuation and its legal status and conversion rate into goods and services. Currently, it is the nature of its legal status and its creation which is being challenged and redesigned by alternatives.

Equally, in the quote above, Budd introduces the idea that money is a forward-on economic output. It is essentially a bearer contract that has been closed, based on a value exchange in the past, but carries within itself a universal future right of claim or conversion into something else. It is fungible. This concept becomes abundantly clear when we think about the idea behind our pensions and savings, for those who have them.

Intrinsically, of course, money has no value in itself. As 'fiat', no longer made from precious metals, it carries a separate and semiotic valuation. In effect, it has zero intrinsic value. Its value lies in the trust we have, to be able, at some future date, to receive in exchange something of equal value to the sign-value it represents and points towards. It is not without some irony that when we read 'In God we trust' on American money, a possible double meaning occurs: of blind faith intimating 'God help this poor currency' versus a real faith and understanding, in which all things are rooted and, therefore, from where it derives its ultimate value. Fiat means 'let there be'. Truly, this is a *sign* of faith, with money as a spiritual object.

A further important distinction is to understand that money and its other static and accounting forms, for e.g. wealth, capital, assets, etc. only have value based on their ability to generate a return/yield. But, due to inflation, money does depreciate with time. As such, money seems to have created for itself a perpetual contractual and institutionalised right to increase, not necessarily sufficiently in value itself, but in accounting terms, whilst being subject to the basic laws of thermodynamics and entropy, so far as its sign-value is concerned. When, on 19 November 1967, British Prime Minister Harold Wilson announced the devaluation of the pound sterling (£) by stating, 'It does not mean that the pound here in Britain, in your pocket or purse or in your bank, has been devalued', no one seriously believed what he said. A £ note still signified it was worth a pound, but it had reduced in future sign-value by 14%.

If money is a construct of our collective imagination and, like language, acts as a symbolic translation mechanism, what is it then that gives money its nature and value? For us the answer lies in nature and natural systems itself, from which all economic and financial activities ultimately derive their value, namely: Human capital, Nature/Environmental capital, Cultural & Spiritual capital and Intellectual capital, which also include the realms of finance and economics—that is to say, each of the capitals related to the integral GEN*E*.

The Future of Money

> For where your treasure is, there will your heart be also.
>
> Matthew 6.21 NIV

The recently late Bernard Lietaer (1), an ex-Professor of International Finance at the University of Leuven in Belgium, economist, former banker, one of the architects of the euro (and who US magazine Business Week proclaimed as the world's best currency dealer) describes money as an agreement, like a marriage or a business contract or an agreement within a community, to use something as a means of payment. According to Lietaer, it is important to realise that money is not a living thing. As it is an agreement with no intrinsic value, we can always make a new and different agreement, which is the basis and foundation for all social, local, digital and virtual currencies that we see today.

The functionality of money is well-known (i.e. unit of account, store of wealth, means of exchange, etc.). Wealth, on the other hand, has many possible meanings, with conversion to and from money being one. Equally, it can signify our social, human, intellectual, cultural and built capital, all of which are interconnected. The actual etymology of wealth is that it comes from the Old English words 'weal' (well-being) and 'th' (condition), which taken together means 'the condition of well-being'. This semiosis may surprise some, but it indicates why we need to include well-being inside our social frame: to build real 'wealth' through the functions of money creation. This subject and area can be highly contentious and political, but it is only when we acknowledge the existence of other capitals such as human, social, intellectual and natural that we can begin to see how we may have deliberately excluded those from any sort of reciprocal measurement and accounting system, such as money.

Capital, however, like money, is measured in units on which returns (such as interest) are expected. So, whilst money, like currency in circulation, does not need to generate a return, electronic money, on account, has the expectancy to create a return by its very nature. In this way, money functions as an intermediary step, digital translator and fungibility agent between all areas, acting as a flow mechanism. However, the main consideration in all of this is our relationship with value and its creation. To see money from this perspective we need to turn the lens 180 degrees and always remind ourselves that most money derives from the creation of value originating in some natural phenomenon which someone has been willing and able to part money for, or at least, appropriate. In this sense, the semiosis works in reverse. Money signifies value backwards in time, to the natural capital on which it is based.

So, the creation of value always comes first. Following this, the value is transformed, by a transaction, into something else—examples of which could be:

1. Money (barter, Bitcoin, cash, credit)
2. Innovation (knowledge and IP in its different forms)
3. Competitive advantage (perhaps more valuable as an engine for money)
4. Speed (outflanking the competition)
5. Collaboration (better integration, economics of trust, cohesive values, closeness to customer, etc.)

Money and capital are highly political—not intrinsically, but by the very nature through which they are used and allocated across and throughout our economic system. As such, the use of capital and money follows neurological, psychological, cultural and political paths through the human mind, the output objectives of which form into one singular decision and outcome expectation: utility. Wisdom tells us that one worships either heaven or hell and one will eventually become the servant of one or the other through our own decisions and consequences.

One of the possible dangers of working with money creation through investment instruments such as debt and equity, is that it may become a removed abstraction, which only has symbolic value to represent what it means for us personally. In other words, it detaches itself from its source of origin, which we are separated from. In consequence, our entire focus and locus of operation is what it can perform for us. As a tool for either good or evil this has profound implications, as to how seriously we take our own development, morals and ethics in relation to money, and as a result, how we behave towards ourselves and others. Money can become a signifier of moral behaviour.

This aspect is very important for each of us to consider carefully. It lies on the cornerstone of our capacity to understand what money signifies within our integrity. Whatever our personal understanding and capacities are, we constantly swim in multiple myth streams of life and money, finance and their related background areas, which have been explored in many pre-eminent books. However, a part of me wishes that the 'money tree' was real. If it was, I could fulfil one of my long term dreams and have my own orchard, sit on my veranda and enjoy the 'fruits' of 'my' capital (land) and labour (planting and tending) after the prerequisite investment in 'patience' for the yield to appear before my eyes…

I like to believe that the 'Money does not grow on trees' phrase came about after a wise person had contemplated, over many years, the link between money and nature. More likely, it came about from a frustrated parent who needed to break the incessant demands of their children, an issue which surely has existed since time immemorial and from the time 'money' first appeared. Whatever its origins, it acts as a sign pointing towards a 'truth' about scarcity within one economic meaning-system. The deep irony within our contemporary world is that the sign has come to point in reverse, so that we may say that 'Money is more common than trees'.

In this respect there is an underlying link and deeper meaning to the saying:

1. Money is part of a natural system.
2. Financial returns are rooted and need to be grounded first in its nature.
3. All 'yields' are natural outcomes from organic ingredients, processes and systems.
4. 'Capital' is recycling material that has an inbuilt potential, a life-force where it originated.
5. Too much financial 'capital' (i.e. money on its own), like any imbalance, can be detrimental to its host and its offspring, by removing and robbing from him or her real experiences; necessary ones that have true meaning and lead to development.

As such, stewardship of any natural resource requires a balanced approach, which every farmer knows and cannot ignore. If the world (and our orchard) was run by accountants, we could not allow them to pull the trees up every quarter (or even yearly to prepare the annual report) to check, measure and report on the progress of the root system, as the 'operating engine' and predictor of our expected 'yield'. Insane as this may sound, many organisations and investment companies are unaware of the organic root system that feeds and nourishes the 'yield' of our metaphorical 'money tree'. However, it is up to each one of us to understand fully how we hold and differentiate between concepts of money, capital and wealth, so we can build and create some clarity for ourselves in the management, stewardship and impact of these signs of value on our own lives. In our world, which is deluged by irrelevant and conflicting information, clarity is required to provide the power and emphasis for us to act decisively.

Unlike a natural system, money/capital by itself multiplies through compound interest within the function of cost of capital and risk. Interest on money, as such, always contains a return for the opportunity cost based on its use, in combination with risk, both in time and type. Albert Einstein once commented that compound interest was 'the eighth wonder of the world' and said, 'He who understands it, earns it… He who doesn't, pays it.' The cost of capital is hidden and embedded in everything we purchase without many of us being aware of it.

Economic Responsibilities for our Grandchildren

Unfortunately for some, too much money can create the ability to remove or shield a person from the very lessons and experiences we need to learn, so as not to fall into these traps and prevent natural personal growth, development and individuation, which working deeply with impact may alleviate. Moving the interpretative meaning-making from psychology into economics, the highly famed economist John Maynard Keynes (4) wrote the following important statement in his 1930s essay entitled 'Economic Responsibilities for our Grandchildren':

> There are changes in other spheres too which we must expect to come. When the accumulation of wealth is no longer of high social importance, there will be great changes in the code of morals. We shall be able to rid ourselves of many of the pseudo-moral principles which have hag-ridden us for two hundred years, by which we have exalted some of the most distasteful of human qualities into the position of the highest virtues. We shall be able to afford to dare to assess the money-motive at its true value. The love of money as a possession—as distinguished from the love of money as a means to the enjoyments and realities of

life—will be recognised for what it is, a somewhat disgusting morbidity, one of those semi-criminal, semi-pathological propensities which one hands over with a shudder to the specialists in mental disease. All kinds of social customs and economic practices, affecting the distribution of wealth and of economic rewards and penalties, which we now maintain at all costs, however distasteful and unjust they may be in themselves, because they are tremendously useful in promoting the accumulation of capital, we shall then be free, at last, to discard.

So here we are today, staring at these lines and wondering why things in many realms are the same with little visible change and in some areas, inequality for example, where the dial in some areas has shifted dramatically towards the negative.

Money: Whence it Came, Where it Went

The great Canadian economist, John Kenneth Galbraith (5), in his 1971 book *Money: Whence It Came, Where it Went?* maintained that:

The process by which banks create money is so simple the mind is repelled. Where something so important is involved, a deeper mystery seems only decent.

1.2.4. Money: A Few Numbers

Each and every time a bank makes a loan, new bank credit is created—new deposits—brand new money.

Graham Towers, former Governor of the Central Bank of Canada

Much has been written in recent times about how governments and their respective central banks have lost control over the printing presses and the increase in money supply. Most money today, not unsurprisingly, is in electronic formats (ca. 97%) with the rest (ca. 3%) being held as notes and coins in circulation, with the vast majority of electronic money supply being created by banks in the form of loans.

In March 2014, the Bank of England (the governor of which is Mark Carney, a Canadian originally from Edmonton, Alberta) released a report called 'Money Creation in the Modern Economy', where they stated that:

Commercial [i.e. high-street] banks create money, in the form of bank deposits, by making new loans. When a bank makes a loan, for example to someone taking out a mortgage to buy a house, it does not typically do so by giving them thousands of pounds worth of banknotes. Instead, it credits their bank account with a bank deposit of the size of the mortgage. At that moment, new money is created. And in the modern economy, those bank deposits are mostly created by commercial banks themselves.

Sir Mervyn King, the Governor of the Bank of England from 2003–2013, recently explained this point to a conference of business people: 'When banks extend loans to their customers, they create money by crediting their customers' accounts.' In this, he was confirming that it is the responsibility of private banks to create the majority of our modern money system. Martin Wolf (6), who was a member of the Independent Commission on Banking and Chief Economics Commentator for the *Financial Times*, put it bluntly in his review of *Modernising Money*:

> The essence of the contemporary monetary system is the creation of money, out of nothing, by private banks' often foolish lending... Money is a social invention, indeed among the most important of all social inventions. At present the right to create money has been handed over to the private businesses we call banks. But this is not the only way we could create money and, as recent experience suggests, it may be far from the best one. Read this book with an open mind and you will understand why.

As such, every new loan that a bank makes creates new money. This may at first sight not appear to be a bad thing per se as on one level, this is how governments have in effect 'designed' and allowed broad money supply to increase, to keep up with economic growth. It is the nature of how we hold money. However, whilst notes and coins in circulation carry no cost, money, if originated as debt, carries annual and compound interest charges. For many of today's debt-based economies these charges are beginning to outstrip their intrinsic capacities to generate sufficient economic growth to sustain the ever-increasing interest levels. The big difference, also, is that whilst money itself is free to use as a 'facilitation agent', it is you and me who pay interest to the banks, either directly as mortgage payments or indirectly through the pricing of goods and services. Returns to capital is the one factor that always gets paid.

We estimate that ca. 50% of all consumer prices in the US economy and in most other Western debt-based economies are made up of commercial banks' interest cost of capital, which is being passed on and embedded in our goods and services. Our decisions and choices, as such, may seem limited in how we can avoid these. Nevertheless, they are highly personal. An equally important and political question is how we have allowed banks to monopolise the creation of money from thin air and, at the same time, get away with charging the economy at large for the privilege of its use.

In the UK, by creating money in this way, banks have increased the amount of money in the economy by an average of 11.5% a year over the last 40 years. This has pushed up the price of houses and priced out an entire generation. In the US the amount of total debt money created, primarily by private banks, has increased on average by 8.2% pa over the past 40 years (1976–2016).

Only 1.4 trillion dollars is US cash or currency created by the government of the United States. This means that only 2.2% of the total US money supply is paper currency created free of charge by the government.

At the time of writing, the debt of the US government exceeded $19.8 trillion or 106% or more of the US GDP, the highest in history compared to a rate of only 32% in 1974 and in 1981. The total amount of outstanding debt (private, government, household, foreign) exceeding $65 trillion amounts to 357% of the US GDP in 2016. While there are no official statistics on the interest costs associated with the $65 trillion in outstanding debts, we estimate that interest costs in 2016 were about $3,551 billion, or an average interest rate of 5.5% of total debt.

Interest costs alone would, therefore, amount to 19% of US GDP in 2016. Since households shoulder a significant cost of debt money in the goods and services they purchase, we estimate that the cost of interest charges associated with total household, business and government debt amounts to $28,815 per household: $6,325 interest payments on household/consumer debt, $6,592 interest per household on government debt and $15,897 interest costs per household associated with business sector debts. Therefore, about $0.51 of every dollar of median American household income ($56,516 in 2016) is taken up for debt service. The thin, green sliver is the amount of interest-free currency that is created on our behalf by the government.

1.3. Conclusion: Where Do We Go From Here?

1.3.1. From an Integral Perspective

The integral perspective does not purport to create simple answers to complex problems. Even so, if you look through the integral lens you can and will create a framework through which you can develop and own your own solutions within your own context. The integral perspective will help you to build the necessary knowledge realms to enable an organic and natural order to develop, which will lead to a more robust and sustainable outcome. Let us begin by looking at two aspects through this lens and we will explore two fundamental issues with the current state of money and its creation:

1. The conversion over time from free currency into debt money creation, exerting a heavy cost on society and our economy.
2. Can innovation and new technology provide solutions whilst maintaining the integrity, value and functionality of money?

1.3.2. Rooting, Resonance, Relevance, Rationale

Money now and future money, enabled by technologies such as block-chain, will take new and varied forms. From our integral perspective, we see all successful and sustainable new monies as rooted in nature capital and real economic activities. In addition, trust capital will be added from the social and cultural realms and create resonance with the systems and intellectual capital that sustains functional values. In turn, this will create relevance for its user community and be held as a repository of all the symbolic representations the money is referencing. If we are able to do so, we will have created the rationale for the economic realm to adopt and generate value through its use.

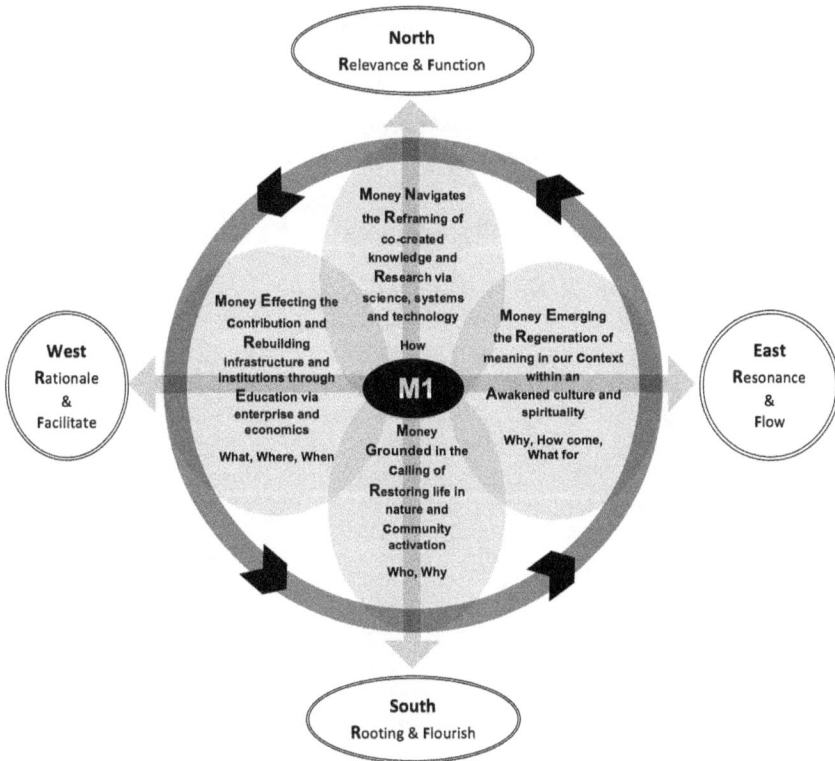

Figure 1.3 Four R's and F's of Money

Money, integrally speaking, needs to build on, contain and embed certain ingredients to flourish (South), flow (East), function (North) and facilitate (West) the economic functions and have extrinsic value; the extrinsic value now being the social and psychological constructs on which its credibility, trust and capital sustainability depends.

In the following chapter by Mark Anielski, we turn from money to capital, from wealth to well-being, and, while remaining within the Anglo-Saxon world, from the UK to Canada.

1.4. Bibliography

1 **Lietaer** B (2004) *The Future of Money*. London. Century Books

2 **Eisenstein** C (2011) *Sacred Economics*. Berkeley. California. Evolver

3 **Houghton Budd** C (2011) *Finance at the Threshold*. Abingdon. Routledge

4 **Keynes** J M (2017) *The General Theory of Employment, Interest and Money: with The Economic Consequences of the Peace*. Ware, Herts. Wordsworth Editions

5 **Galbraith** K (2017) *Money: Whence it Came, Where it Went*. Connecticut. Princeton University Press

6 **Jackson** A and **Dyson** B (2013) *Modernising Money: Why our monetary system is broken and how it can be fixed*. London. Positive Money

Chapter 2

The Nature of Capital: A New Financial Order Based on Economic Well-being

Mark Anielski, Anielski Management

Islam is not so much a religion as an integrative worldview: that is to say, it integrates all aspects of reality by providing a moral perspective on every aspect of human endeavor.

Inayatullah, S. & Boxwell, G. (1)

The verb 'to grow' has become so over-laden with positive value connotations that we have forgotten its first literal dictionary denotation, 'to spring up and develop maturity'. Thus the very notion of growth includes some concept of maturity at which point physical accumulation gives way to a steady state. While the psychic dimension of wealth, then, its want-satisfying capacity, may forever increase due to increasing knowledge and technical improvement, the physical dimensions are limited.

Herman Daly (2)

2.1. Introduction: Towards Economic Well-being

2.1.1. Well-being Conditions: Towards Genuine Wealth

Genuine Wealth is based on the etymological roots of the word 'wealth' which comes from the 13th century Old English 'weal-th' meaning 'well-being conditions', as Robert Dellner commented in the opening chapter of this collection. The word 'happiness' comes from the Greek *eudaimonia* meaning well-being (*eu*) of the spirit or soul (*daimonia*), as per Aristotle. The word 'economy' comes from the Greek *oikos* (household) *nomia* (stewardship or management). As such, I am proposing a new accounting system (see Chapter 4 on Integral Accounting) for measuring progress that integrates the five capital assets into an integral holistic system that measures and tracks the physical and qualitative conditions of 'well-being' of society or organisations.

This new well-being accounting system is based on the 500-year-old double-entry bookkeeping system developed in the late 15th century by the Franciscan monk and mathematician Luca Pacioli and his colleague Leonardo da Vinci. Pacioli was advising the Medici banking family of Florence as well as guild-society merchants of Venice, on how to be better business people by maintaining an inventory of the assets (in ledgers) organised into a 'balance sheet' where assets = liabilities + equity. Pacioli's accounting system was based on the principle of the Golden Mean, of debit = credits, as well as the Fibonacci sequence, the numerical natural progression found throughout nature (e.g. in the patterns seen in a sunflower or Nautilus shell).

Five Capital Assets Model

Financial Capital

Financial assets (Money, cash, stocks, bonds, derivatives), liabilities (debt) and equity.

Built Capital

Infrastructure, buildings, roads, houses, factories, machinery, equipment, and manufactured goods, and intellectual property (patents, copyright) that make up the material structure of society.

> ASSET:
> any tangible or intangible economic resource that is capable of being owned or controlled to produce value and that is held to have positive economic value.

Human Capital

Individual skills, education, knowledge , capabilities, and health (mental, physical, emotional and spiritual) of individuals that make up households, organizations and communities.

Social Capital

The web of interpersonal connections, relationships and networks, including trust, institutional arrangements, rules, and norms that facilitate human interactions. Also, the set of values, history, traditions and behaviours which link a specific group of people together.

Natural Capital

The land and natural resources, including soils, forests, water, air, and other species and life forms, and the services which the earth and its atmosphere provide, including ecological systems and life-support services.

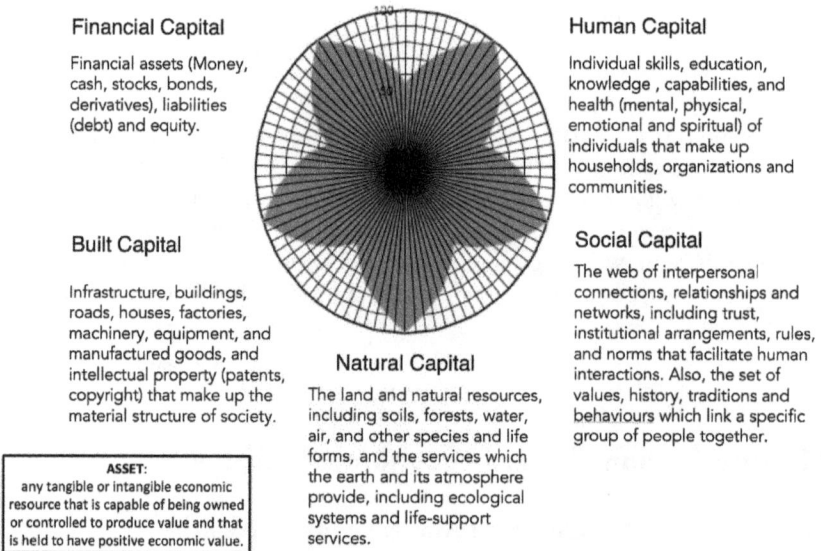

Figure 2.1. Five Assets Capital Model

Pacioli argued that since 'all wealth comes from God' it is important to 'account' to God for the wise stewardship of the wealth (real assets and well-being conditions) under the stewardship of business. Pacioli's accounting system became one of the main reasons the Medicis became the dominant banking power of Europe in the 16th century. At that time in history, guilds were a form of co-operative business association. Pacioli never defined the word 'profit' and to this day, accountants still lack a clear definition. Where Pacioli gained his genius and insights and wisdom into double-entry bookkeeping is unclear; he may have studied the ancient economic systems of Sumeria, who developed sophisticated economic models, including unique monetary policies and structures.

But in the Western—or the domain of the North (European, North American)—economies, the roots of great wisdom find parallels in both South, East and West according to the Integral Model and GEN*E* developed by Trans4m (see Chapters 3 and 4). The issue is one of renewing the wise applications of these tools which may have been forgotten or poorly applied. My supposition is that one of the reasons that the West has seemingly forgotten its own history is due to the dominance of a debt-money-focused financial order, which has been dominated by the Anglo-American and North (Western nations), with roots going far back. These have their origins in the merchant banking dynasties of the Medicis, the House of Rothschild and, later, the establishment of privately-held central banks. These arose with the founding of the Swedish central bank (see Chapter 1), the Bank of England in 1694 and, ultimately, the US Federal Reserve (a private-bank-owned central bank) in 1913.

As such, our work is based on a renewed understanding of Luca's 500-year-old system of accounting. This asserts that a wise business and wise society must keep accounts of the physical, qualitative and monetary conditions (assets, liabilities and equity or distribution of well-being) of its total wealth, using an integrated accounting system. We apply the Genuine Wealth model in many cases. These range from the macro scale of China's Xiaokang (Well-being) Societal Indicators system, through the Canadian Index of Well-being, to the Genuine Progress Indicators/Index for the US, Alberta and the City of Edmonton. Equally, they are evident in the City of Santa Monica's Sustainability Index and in examining the well-being impacts and Well-being Return on Investment (W-ROI) of policies and programmes, both in the public and private sectors.

Application of the Genuine Wealth accounting model demonstrates the practicality of measuring well-being conditions across all spectrums of the five asset classes (including the subjective or perceived well-being of citizens using well-being and happiness surveys). This new accounting system is meant to ultimately replace the current limited national income accounting systems that give us GDP. Indeed, that was developed by John Maynard Keynes in England and Simon Kuznets in the US at the end of World War II, for the very narrow but vital purpose (at the time) of assessing the effectiveness of post-War reconstruction programmes, such as the Marshall Plan. But, it was never intended to assume the global significance it has, as a supposedly universal measure of effective economic development and prosperity.

By contrast, Figure 2.3 shows the architecture of a Well-being Economy using the Genuine Wealth and Well-being Accounting system to guide decision making. Using currently reported statistics from central statistics agencies, the physical conditions of well-being of the five capital assets can be inventoried and tracked. Other subjective well-being indicators, drawn from regular perceptional well-being surveys, conducted in a population, can be used to qualitatively augment these quantitative measures of well-being.

2.2. Money and Well-being

2.2.1. Dominated by Private Bank Created Debt Money, with Ruinous Consequences

The second focus of our work has been to explore the financial architecture and monetary systems dominated by Western economies for at least 500 years. We trace the history of banking and money in our first book *The Economics of Happiness* (3), and propose a new financial architecture that would align all macro-monetary policy, banking and investment towards explicitly improving the well-being conditions of society.

For too long the Western financial system has been dominated by private bank-created debt money, with ruinous consequences. Historically, going back to the ancient Greeks (Aristotle, Plato), usury or the charging of interest on money was considered reprehensible and unjust. The Greeks understood that the creation of money as a means of exchange in an economy should be a *public* good. Money is to be treated as a public utility. The teaching that usury was unacceptable was upheld by the Roman Catholic Church for centuries, until the mid-1800s when the laws against usury were relaxed and forgotten. So, we see that for at least 2,500 years, in the West (Greeks, Romans, Jews, Holy Roman Empire), there was an understanding that charging interest on money, created as debt, could ruin societies. The question is, therefore: how is it that the West rejected this ancient wisdom, to the extent that, at least over the past 100 years, usury (the charging of interest on debt money creation) has become completely justified as normal?

The late economist John Maynard Keynes in his essay entitled 'Economic Responsibilities for our Grandchildren', as cited in our opening chapter, was unequivocal in stating that 'usury is a misdemeanor' and that the West would have to pretend to itself for another 100 years that 'fair is foul, and foul is fair', to quote Shakespeare's *Macbeth* (Act 1, Scene 1). We find in ancient Jewish economic ethics the rejection of usury amongst Jews, as we shall also find is the case in Islamic teaching and, to a large degree, practice (see Chapters 3, 6, 8 and 10). The ancient Jews had in place Jubilee laws where financial debts would be forgiven every 7 years and the original wealth of the 12 tribes of Israel would be redistributed every 49 years (7 x 7). These laws were, in effect, prior to the Israelites' exile in Babylon, though it is unclear whether the laws were ever practised following their liberation from captivity.

2.2.2. Further Truths About Money Creation

Continuing a theme raised in the Introduction and first chapter of this book, what many people don't realise is how 97% of money is created when private banks issue loans. These, then, are simply bookkeeping entries, creating brand-new money out of thin air to help finance mortgages, student loans, car loans and lines of credit. As we have already seen through Robert Dellner's analysis, debt grows exponentially over time and, in theory, can never be re-paid. The total US debt to GDP ratio is now 354% (and growing) compared to 150% just after World War II.

In principle, governments could create the money needed in an economy without the cost of interest if it was to treat money as a public utility, within the power of sovereign central banks. ATB Financial is Canada's largest and most important public bank that has this capability, though they behave no differently in their lending practices to other private commercial banks.

Banks justify charging interest to cover the risks they face with lending to borrowers, as well as to cover operating costs. However, if you think about the fact that a bank creates new money out of thin air, then each time they issue a loan, what is the risk to them if the credit they created for a mortgage defaults? Other than having to cease and then sell the asset (the house) at a reduced value, there are no other costs to the bank. Therefore, a bank is akin to a counterfeiter, creating money with a stroke of a pen.

2.2.3. The British Tally Stick as Money

In fact, the dominance of debt money in today's world is rather recent so far as Western economic history is concerned. Historically, nations (including England) used alternative systems of money creation without using bank-created debt. The British tally stick was the most important form of money in England dating back to the Norman Conquest, initiated in 1068 and in circulation until about 1840. The founding of the Bank of England, the world's second privately-funded central bank, in 1694, saw the beginning of the end of the tally stick.

As such, it was the most important and stable form of money in the Western world for over 800 years. The tally was a wooden stick made of oak that represented the money necessary to buy goods and services and pay taxes in England. Semiotically, it was a sign in wood of both financial need and the ability to pay. It was issued by the King and the King's Treasury as sufficiently supplied to meet the needs of the nation. No interest was charged by the King's Treasurer. Rather, it was the power of the sovereign to create as many or as few tally sticks as was necessary for a healthy economy and the payment of taxes to the King. The era of the tally stick was the most stable economic period in British history, with no inflation.

The wisdom of the tally stick system ended with the founding of the Bank of England, under the kingship of William of Orange from Amsterdam. The Bank of England was effectively a privately-owned bank which was deemed necessary to help finance England's war efforts. With its founding began the era of debt money and fractional reserve lending by private bankers. The Bank of England became the model for other central banks around the world including the US Federal Reserve, established in 1913.

Few people know about the tally stick including the curators of The Bank of England Museum in London. How strange that a system of money that was based on something in nature (an oak tree), and which lasted almost 800 years, similar to the Magna Carta, would be forgotten in a matter of the last 100 years in the West.

The same story of a nature-based money system is also true of North America (once referred to as 'Turtle Island'), where indigenous peoples used sea shells as the basis of money in their mutual exchange economy (known as the *Pehonen* in Edmonton, Canada). Ancient Polynesians, originating from Taiwan, first established a shell economy, which expanded throughout the South Pacific, Hawaii and North America in the form of wampum belts (shells sown on deer buckskin representing the wealth of a tribe or nation). Imagine a modern form of a natural asset-based money system. What might this look like?

2.2.4. Earth Dollar: Natural Capital-Based Monetary System

A promising initiative that I was asked to advise on in Canada was the creation of a natural-capital, asset-backed cryptocurrency called the 'Earth Dollar'. The Earth Dollar would be a digital currency created in parallel with the natural assets of the Ottawa watershed in the province of Quebec, ancestral lands of the Algonquin Nation in Canada. The premise is that sufficient working currency could be created in direct relationship with the ecological integrity and functions of the watershed (an area of 16 million hectares) such that a living wage for all 1.2 million residents of the watershed could be secured in perpetuity, while also ensuring an optimum economy with optimum

GDP output for a sustainable economy. The Earth Dollar would trade on par with the Canadian dollar but would of course be stronger and more stable, in some sense, since it would be linked directly to physical assets, including land (and its natural capacity for generating food and other yields), forests, rivers, wetlands and the 20 unique ecological functions or services attributed to the watershed ecosystem.

The governance of the Earth Dollar would be under a shared asset management system, guided in part by the elders of the Algonquin Nation. Unfunded ecological liabilities—including historical damages to the watershed and its ecosystem functions from industrial development (forestry, mining, hydro-electricity, etc.)—would be financed with sufficient cryptocurrency creation (Earth Dollar), thus eliminating the ecological liabilities of the watershed that should be on the balance sheet of the Ottawa Watershed governance model.

The entire system of cryptocurrency creation would be guided by a fulsome balance sheet of the human, social, natural and built assets of the 16 million hectare watershed and the various human communities, including Canada's capital city of Ottawa. The Earth Dollar concept was well-conceived; however, it was poorly executed by its founder, who lost the trust of the First Nations communities which he aspired to serve. This is an example of what the Trans4m community refers to as the 'recursive GEN*E*alogy', wherein those who act on behalf of the community (S) turn West to chase the money, rather than following the GEN*E* logic of turning East, to embrace the consciousness awakening capacity of the economic system's spirituality. Nevertheless, whilst such practical cases of failure to operate genealogically need to be identified, this doesn't change the fact that investment based on well-being lies at the heart of economic well-being.

2.2.5. Well-being Based Investment

The world of finance and investment is primarily focused on making money and financial profitability. In turn, this is based on the (usually unchallenged) belief that the purpose of corporate business is to maximise financial returns to owners and shareholders. Yet, if you were to examine the legal documents that are the DNA of a corporation in North America, you will find no mention that the legal responsibility or purpose of the enterprise is to make money. Indeed, section 3 of a corporate charter, namely 'Best Interest', is generally silent regarding what the primary purpose and responsibility of the corporation is. In fact, I challenge any businessperson to ask their lawyer or check their legal documents of incorporation to find any statements which itemise the meaning of the best interest of their company. This is a matter of semiotics, to identify the meaning of 'best interest' and 'good business'.

In the absence of a clear and definitive statement of the purpose and best interests of the corporation or enterprise, there is room to add the various attributes of well-being. These should include the impacts that the corporation has on employees, shareholders, communities, economies and the natural environment or ecosystems. If the best interests of the corporation were directly and legally bound to these stakeholders, it would change the nature in which enterprises operate and how the financial world of banking and investment would view them. Well-being is a crucial aspect of stakeholder value; even though it is not usually seen as fundamental to shareholder value.

As such, we are proposing a new era in capitalism; one that would make net positive well-being impact the highest aspiration of any enterprise or organisation that has been given a social licence to operate. This will require new means of calibration, for assessing impacts across a wider spectrum of well-being domains, as indicated above. These well-being returns on investment and on assets (W-ROI) would complement the existing financial performance measures that are used in the banking and investment world. Indeed, using a broader approach to accounting and reporting would strengthen the due-diligence of investment portfolio managers and improve their capacity to choose companies in their investment portfolios that are resilient, sustainable and even flourishing. We believe that a well-being impact investment and banking approach could well be the greatest opportunity in the 21st century banking and investment world. Of course, supplementing money maximisation with a well-being bottom line will be a challenge. But, what if investment decisions were based on well-being impacts? What kinds of analytic frameworks would be required?

What we are proposing is no less than a new form of capitalism which makes well-being the fundamental bottom line of asset management. Financial institutions and banks today are governed by the notion of leverage of assets. However, most financial institutions, including the accounting firms that support these violations of assets, fundamentally ignore the value of intangible assets, including relationships, trust and natural capital assets. So long as these intangible assets are not valued in the sense of their importance to society, our investment decisions, as well as credit decisions, will be blind to the real value of these assets, as far as our well-being is concerned.

Impact investment has become a new buzzword. This is an out-growth from the corporate social responsibility (CSR) culture that has arisen in the last 20 years. But, as we see throughout this book, impact investment may not have gone as far as it can in the current investment climate. If impact investment were to look at this broader suite of assets, then decisions to invest in them would change as well.

Financial Capital
Money, cash, stocks, bonds, derivatives, and other financial assets (and liabilities).

Built Capital
Built capital includes machinery, equipment, buildings, and intangibles (copyright, patents and others).

Integrated Five Capital Asset Balance Sheet

Human Capital
People: Mental, physical, emotional and spiritual well-being conditions of individuals in an organization that include, health, skills, knowledge, capabilities and aspirations.

Social Capital
Social networks, relationships, trust, reciprocity, and cooperation between the organization, its customer, suppliers, investors and other stakeholders.

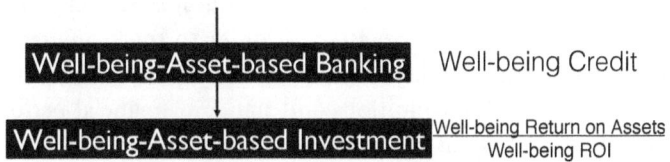

Natural Capital
Natural resources, land, water, air, and ecosystem assets.

Well-being-Asset-based Banking Well-being Credit

Well-being-Asset-based Investment Well-being Return on Assets
Well-being ROI

Figure 2.3. Well-Being Based Impact Finance
Source: Anielski, M (4)

If what we measure is what we manage, then what we look at, as interest on assets, is how we will make decisions for credit and investment. We don't have to change the tools we are using now but we do need to expand our asset valuation methods, to re-GENErate a new era of well-being capitalism. Our focus would be on asking the question: will this investment improve the well-being conditions of an enterprise, the community, society and nature? How we answer this question is based on analytic protocols, including quantitative and qualitative tools to assess impact. Impacts can be positive, negative and neutral. So, we need to look at the impacts on a much broader range of asset classes.

2.2.6. Well-being Based Risk Management and Investment Decision Making

How would well-being metrics work, how would they reduce risk and how could we gauge results? A well-being perspective, utilising alternative investment analytics, would use the various well-being related forms of accounting for each of the five classes of assets. These would need to both project and assess progress, results and risks to the well-being of the five assets. As with quarterly financial reporting protocols, the state of well-being, using the suite of enterprise well-being indicators, would be assessed on a regular basis, as required by management decision-makers and investors.

Both quantitative and qualitative protocols and accounting standards would be adopted. In the case of qualitative or subjective measures of well-being, survey tools have been developed by Anielski Management Inc., supplemented (see Chapter 4) by Trans4m's integral approach. These are able to track changes in human and social assets, using both workplace well-being and customer-value survey tools. These metrics are based on subjective ratings of well-being in the workplace and measures of customer-value, which are used as standard by marketing firms. The Genuine Wealth model uses the best of these analytic tools for evaluation.

For each asset class, an assessment of trends in quantitative and qualitative well-being is made. Evaluation of the drivers of these trends is made, together with projections of future well-being conditions. Well-being Indices are prepared for each of the five assets in order to track progress. Furthermore, an examination of the relationship between key human, social and natural capital asset well-being conditions and standard financial performance indicators are conducted, so as to derive robust well-being ROI, ROA and ROE estimates. Each asset would be described in terms of how it is currently delivering well-being benefits, as well as identifying potential risk to assets, which can be attributed to current business practices and the relationships that the firm has with various stakeholders. It is vital to manage these relational risks, to ensure the enterprise's long-term resilience and sustainability.

The following measurement protocols need to be used:

1. Identify the human, social/cultural, natural, built and financial assets (sub-asset classes) being impacted by an enterprise or investment and develop a well-being asset balance sheet related to it.
2. Assess and score the positive, negative or neutral expected impact (both objective and subjective metrics) on the five-capital assets, for the enterprise or the investment.
3. Develop a Well-being Impact Index and Rating/Score based on the five-capital assets assessment.
4. Estimate a Well-being ROI and Well-being ROA of the enterprise or investment, using the Well-being Impact Index.

In concluding this chapter, we turn to a form of public banking in my home country of Canada, which is in tune with the well-being approach outlined here.

2.3. Conclusion: Banking on Well-being

2.3.1. The Public/People's Bank of Alberta Canada

ATB (Alberta Treasury Branch) Financial is Alberta's most important financial asset. Founded 80 years ago in 1938 under a Social Credit government during the Great Economic Depression, ATB is North America's largest public bank, with over $47.673 billion in assets, 6 times larger than then the only other public bank in North America, the Bank of North Dakota and 3.6 times larger than Servus Credit Union in Alberta (with $14.2 billion in assets). What does it mean to have our own public bank? How could the natural advantages of a public bank like ATB Financial help build a new economy of well-being for Alberta and be a model for the rest of North America and the world?

2.3.2. ATB Financial Is Different from Other Financial Institutions

First, ATB Financial is not a private bank but a bank with full financial services that is literally owned by Albertans, backed by 100% of the assets of the Province. In other words, ATB Financial is a Public Bank.

Second, ATB Financial is governed by a special act of legislature called the Alberta Treasury Branch Act (2000) which sets out the terms of financial services that ATB Financial can provide, on behalf of the needs of Albertans.

Third, ATB Financial has the legal powers to operate just like any other bank, but has a significant number of Albertans as its members. In fact, all operations that are shareholders in ATB Financial should, equally, be members. In some ways, ATB Financial is like a credit union such as Servus or Vancity, with members, yet ATB Financial already has every Albertan as a member, by virtue of being a resident citizen of the Province. ATB Financial is so safe that the only way it can fail is if the entire Province of Alberta fails, which is highly unlikely.

Fourth, ATB Financial can never go bankrupt as long as the Province is solvent and remains asset-rich. ATB is 100% backed by the assets of the Province which total in the multiple trillion dollars. Ironically, these have never been measured or placed on a proper balance sheet for the Province.

Fifth, ATB Financial does not pay any federal or provincial income tax. This is because ATB Financial is an asset of the Government of Alberta and is exempt from paying income taxes. No other bank in Canada has such benefits. ATB Financial is required to pay a levy in lieu of not paying taxes. For the three months ending June 30 2016, ATB Financial paid the Government of Alberta (Minister of Finance) a mere $7,466 for payment in lieu of taxes.

Sixth, ATB Financial has one of the healthiest balance sheets of any bank in the world. Healthy bank balance sheets have strong equity to asset ratios.

The assets of ATB Financial include loans to Albertans, which totalled more than $40 billion in 2016. Liabilities include the deposit accounts of Albertans, which totalled $30.8 billion as well as $12.4 billion in other liabilities (wholesale borrowing, collateralised borrowings and some derivatives, representing a mere 1.2% of ATB Financial's assets, which is very small for a bank). The difference between the assets and liabilities constitutes net equity, which in 2016 amounted to $3 billion, or an equity to asset ratio of 6.4% (7.2% in 2015). These are signs of a very healthy and vibrant bank.

Seventh, ATB Financial could serve as Alberta's public financial utility, creating money and credit for Alberta households, business and even governments at competitive rates. In truth, ATB could create sufficient credit for all citizens and businesses of the Province, as well as debt for the provincial government, without charging interest on loans. This is because it has a mandate simply to operate by recovering its operating costs with no need to generate a profit. In this regard, ATB would in principle be compliant with Islamic financial laws that forbid charging and paying interest on mortgages and other loans (see later chapters).

However, in truth few people (including the executive of ATB Financial and the provincial Finance Minister) understand the true potential of ATB. They fail to recognise that it could create sufficient credit for the entire province of 4.3 million citizens without the unnecessary burden of interest charges that prevail in Canada's current economy.

Our public banking colleagues in the US, who are part of the American Public Banking Institute, are amazed at what Alberta has in terms of its own public bank. There is growing interest in the creation of public banks in the US, in places as diverse as Los Angeles, New Jersey and Philadelphia. Many Americans have heard of the Bank of North Dakota (BND) as the only US public bank, but which has only a fraction of the financial services that Albertans enjoy with ATB Financial. However, BND does have one unique advantage over ATB Financial, which is that it provides low-cost interest financing to the State of North Dakota for infrastructure capital investments, as well as low-cost student debt financing.

2.3.3. A Genuine Wealth Interest-Free Bank

Moreover, anticipating what our Pakistani colleague Aneeqa Malik describes regarding Akhuwat (see Chapter 6), we can imagine the creation of new bank charters for a Genuine Wealth bank. Genuine Wealth banks would be legally licensed to operate in a community's best interests. A Genuine Wealth banker would facilitate financial wealth exchange within a co-operative banking environment just like the Caja Laboral at Mondragon in the Basque Country (see Chapter 3), together with serving as a financial coach or steward to clients. This new bank could also make use of the Genuine Wealth accounting system and well-being inventories maintained by municipal or local governments to determine bank lending policies that help support Genuine Wealth development in the community. They would operate on a 100% reserve system, thereby eliminating fractional reserve banking and, ultimately, eliminating usury.

Imagine if ATB Financial was directed by Alberta Treasury Board on behalf of all Albertans, to provide near-zero interest loans and credit to help fuel investment in the undervalued assets of Alberta? What if these loans were tied specifically to a well-being bottom line for Alberta, using full cost-benefit accounting protocols to evaluate the potential risk for all businesses and households? What if the provincial Treasury Board was guided by a well-being economic impact model that required all decisions to be analysed through a well-being impact lens, so as to empower our capacity to demonstrate true value for our investment and tax dollars?

Banking is about leveraging the underlying value of assets. ATB Financial could play a key role in unleashing the full potential of billions of dollars in undervalued human, social and natural capital assets acting as a public utility. This would include financing a green energy future for Alberta, through energy efficiency investments in our homes and businesses, building renewable energy capacity and reducing Alberta's carbon liability to the world. The benefits from the cost savings from energy use savings and reduced carbon liabilities alone would offset the costs of administering these programmes.

2.3.4. The Cost of Money (Loans) Could be as Low as 1% of the Value of Loans

The beauty of ATB Financial is that it can create money by issuing loans to households, farmers, businesses and even to other governments (municipal) and the Government of Alberta itself (in principle) at a more competitive rate (low cost of capital) than commercial, publicly traded banks. Why? First, because a public bank can operate on a non-profit basis, since its beneficiaries are the citizens of a Province (Alberta: ATB Financial) or State (North Dakota: Bank of North Dakota), and it can, simply, operate on a cost-recovery basis. Second, in the case of ATB Financial, being a corporation belonging to the Crown or Government of Alberta, it pays no corporation tax. Therefore, the only thing a public bank must ensure is that it covers all of its operating costs, plus having sufficient provision against loan losses or defaults by its customers.

Therefore, in principle, a public bank does not need to charge the same interest rates on loans as other conventional banks, if it is simply operating on a cost-recovery and loan loss-risk management basis. These various features anticipate several of the cases included in Parts 3 and 4, where we allude to Islamic finance, of one kind or another.

2.3.5. Towards a Community Well-being Asset Fund

Anielski Management has proposed the development of a new impact investment fund for community asset development in the US city of Cincinnati. The fund's mandate would be to improve the well-being conditions of depressed neighbourhoods in Cincinnati, which exhibit large-scale household and personal poverty, low levels of economic activity, lack of full employment and, unsurprisingly, lack of happiness and well-being. Similar to a community fund, which many cities have, this well-being fund will invest in neighbourhood assets including skills, capacities, competencies and other personal household and community assets that are currently being underutilised, resulting in conditions of poverty and lack of hope.

The approach to managing this fund is to look at the inventory of existing community assets, whether this is housing, land, people and social networks or relational capital. An audit would be done to examine the conditions of well-being of these assets. Once the audit is complete, investment opportunities in strengthening or building up these underutilised assets in the neighbourhood would be identified. These would include the need for business planning, feasibility studies and investment dollars to establish these community assets. The fund would be governed by well-being analytic protocols. In a similar way to the methods of financial analysts, who currently look at companies in terms of their financial sustainability, the well-being fund would be managed by well-being impact analysis experts from across various disciplines. These would include finance and accounting, as well as psychologists, sociologists and biologist-ecologists, who understand how to measure and manage the integrity of ecosystems and natural capital assets. The rules governing the management of the well-being fund will emerge, just as we have seen the emergence of accounting rules and financial analysis protocols over the last 500 years.

One of the challenges people face when thinking about investment is that they assume that the funds required for investment must come from outside of the community. Yet, few stop to think that the basis of investment funds originate with the households resident in a community. Millions of dollars leave communities every day to be invested in companies (stocks and bonds) that do not operate in their communities, or which have no relationship with the community other than perhaps the sale of goods and services.

Another conventional belief is that any credit required must come from standard loans provided by banks or credit unions. The truth is that the money necessary to invest in communal assets resides in the community itself, through disposable income and investment income dollars that are available from households. However, currently, our investment decisions cause us to invest outside of our communities through stocks, bonds and guaranteed investment certificates that are sold to us by financial brokers, mutual fund managers and banks. This is equally true of community foundations, which most cities have. Millions of dollars in these community portfolios are managed by fund managers who typically will buy stocks and bonds and other financial instruments that do not actually benefit the local community or city in which they operate.

Ask any community foundation what percentage of their portfolio is invested in local assets or local equity and you'll be met by blank stares or no response at all. What if even 5–10% of these community foundation portfolios were invested in local assets, including entrepreneurs, local sustainable businesses or organisations like Habitat for Humanity, who provide zero-interest mortgages to low income families? What if you and I could invest our own after-tax earnings in the local community foundation with returns that typically range from 5–8% per annum? Currently, there is no opportunity to invest in community foundations unless we are wealthy and dead; community foundations benefit from family trusts or endowments gifted by wealthy families of their deceased loved ones.

A well-being based approach to investment portfolio management would use the same analytic tools currently used for sound and sustainable management. We would add a number of well-being impact criteria and analytic tools to assess and verify the relative impact of the companies in a portfolio for the local community, workplace and employee well-being, together with the integrity of the watershed or ecosystem in which these companies operate. Measures such as trust, belonging and meaningful work can also be used to assess the resilience of companies.

In the case of the well-being fund, we would also look at the financial resilience and sustainability of any prospective business or enterprise in which we think an asset can be further developed. However, this fund would also examine the potential well-being impacts as positive, negative or neutral on the community as a whole, in harmony with the importance of financial sustainability or resilience of the enterprise.

A new set of metrics for well-being W-ROI (return on investment) and a well-being W-ROA (return on assets) would emerge. Return on assets would look at the returns on investment to human, social, natural and built assets, as well as a conventional financial return on these assets, in terms of profitability and financial sustainability. W-ROI would be constructed of quantitative, qualitative and monetary metrics of impact. Qualitative ROI impacts would look at the expected quality of life impact of an investment in a community asset, from the perspective of the beneficiaries of the investment.

2.3.6. What is the Ultimate Path Forward?

What is the path forward that takes an integral view of finance, weaving together the wisdom, practices and meaning-making of the last 3,000 years?

We have sought to show how debt money and the need to service the debt with interest charges is the key driver for more GDP growth. Our analysis of the US economy, as of 2018, estimates that total debt outstanding now exceeds $70 trillion with annual interest charges that make up at least 35% of US GDP and 48% of the expenditures of the average American household with a median income of $62,500 per annum. The nature of debt money creation is that it is exponential. In truth, the debt can never be repaid from current economic growth. Hence, debt money is a form of terminal cancer on the economies of *all nations*, not just the US.

By eliminating debt money and returning to a sovereign money system we could reduce the average work week by 50% and reduce greenhouse gas emissions that are correlated with GDP. What is the solution to this intractable, cancerous stage of capitalism? Some say only collapse, which is mathematically inevitable, will solve this disastrous situation.

Even so, alternatives to debt money systems—which are dominated by private banks that control 98% of all money created—are available, including as recent as the US monetary policies of Abraham Lincoln of Greenbacks and Benjamin Franklin's Philadelphia experiment, of tying money to the natural productivity of land. Equally, we can refer to the tally stick system in England that operated for 600 years. It will require collective international actions to move to a state of the ending of debt slavery and debt-based, private bank money. This is unlikely so long as the current money power dominates or money is understood according to the semiotic economics of neoliberalism.

Nevertheless, alternative models of interest-free banking such as Akhuwat, in the following chapter and Chapter 6, are useful models but remain relatively unknown and are anathema to the existing usury banking system, where interest charges are rationalised and most people are unaware of alternative meanings and practices. Of course, Christian Church leaders, led by Pope Francis, could re-establish the laws against usury, despite the reputational damage that has been inflicted on the Vatican Bank in recent years.

Even so, there is clear evidence that the debt-based money system is both unjust and unnecessary when there are alternatives. These include the return of money power to the governments of nations. We have shown that money creation tied to real assets can be a public utility when such money supply is tied to well-being goals and the highest and best use of all societal assets.

Eliminating the burden of interest costs, now hidden in all economic transactions, would alleviate much of the pressure that leads to so much human and ecological suffering.

The establishment of new public banks in the US is gaining more interest. ATB and BND serve as successful models that have been operating for more than 80 years. These public banks have the power to create credit at cost, without the need to charge interest and without the need for profits. These are, essentially, the people's banks that would be 100% backed by the total assets in the state, including natural capital. The path forward in fact, as we shall see throughout this book, is through current and future experiments. These include the best practices in both Muslim and non-Muslim nations and communities, in the South and East, as well as the North and West. We now turn to our integral approach, which accounts for all those diverse worldviews, before revisiting Islamic finance and economics in that light.

2.4. Bibliography

1 **Inayatullah**, S & Boxwell, G (2003) *Islam, Postmodernism & Other Futures: A Ziauddin Reader.* London. Pluto Press
2 **Daly**, H (2016) *From Uneconomic Growth to a Steady State Economy.* Cheltenham. Edward Elgar
3 **Anielski** M (2007) *The Economics of Happiness.* Gabriola Island. New Society Publishers
4 **Anielski** M (2017) *The Economy of Well-being. Commonsense Tools for Building Genuine Wealth and Happiness.* Gabriola Island. New Society Publishers

PART TWO

*Integral Perspectives on
Finance and Accounting*

CHAPTER 3

Integral Finance: A Four Worlds Perspective

Ronnie Lessem, Trans4m Communiversity Associates

The collapse of the Berlin wall within the Germanic heartland of Europe heralded, three decades ago, the re-birth of a continent, if not of the whole of the world. The sudden demise of communism called for—in prospect if not yet in current reality—a newly variegated economic, integral and dynamic, worldview, born out of variety rather than duality. For both capitalism and communism were born out of partial, monolithic views of our humanity. Each being European, and respectively Scottish and German in origin, as we have seen, neither doctrine, despite the seminal nature and scope of each, attempted to capture the cultural richness of the European continent, not to mention the whole globe.

Ronnie Lessem, Managing in Four Worlds (1)

Trans-locality can be theorised as a mode, one which pertains not to how people and cultures exist in places, but rather how they move through them. Trans-locality is hence a form of travel. It involves studying what flows through localities rather than what is in them. The political implications of such resultant hybrid spaces will become evident as we go on to look at Muslim trans-locality today. The same forces which have brought about trans-local spaces have also given rise to phenomenal increases in the extent to which people communicate and encounter each other across boundaries of cultures, ethnicities, nations and communities.

Peter Mandaville, Transnational Muslim Politics:
Reimagining the Umma (2)

3.1. Introduction

3.1.1. Re-GENE-rating Finance

Finance, as a business and economic function, and as a management discipline, is considered a creature of the West. It is no wonder, then, that our two introductory chapters were written by Dellner and Anielski, in the UK and in North America respectively. In Mark Anielski's previous chapter, he highlighted many of the inherent limitations in the conventional model, making the case for a more broadly-based financial system of *integral* 'well-being', in our terms.

It is no accident that Wall Street and the City of London, in the USA and UK respectively, are considered to be the financial capitals of the world, and that the UK has more financial accountants, per capita, than any other part of the globe. However, given that our focus in this book is on *integral* finance, we not only revisit finance, capital and money from a 'four worlds' perspective, but we represent a 'West that builds on the rest', with the 'rest' being a now visible South (Africa, as well as South America), East (Asia) and North (Europe).

To that extent, unusually, with a view to re-GENE-rating finance, we start with nature and community, our local **G**rounding in the African South via Providence Human Capital. We then **E**merge locally-globally through culture and spirituality in the East via Akhuwat in Pakistan, in south-east Asia. Thereafter, we **N**avigate newly globally via Mondragon, the renowned co-operative movement in Northern Iberia, the Basque Country. Finally, we turn to the unusual global-local case of VISA, at least in its formative period, born and bred in California, **E**ffecting the American West. We start in the birthplace of humankind: that is, in the African South, specifically in Zimbabwe where I was born and bred, and thereby, as we shall see, choosing the Abrahamic path.

3.1.2. Choosing the Abrahamic Path

My father, Abraham Lessem, was an accountant by profession, though he had a passion for literature rather than finance, prior to emigrating as a Jew escaping the Russian pogroms. Specifically, he migrated from Lithuania to what was Rhodesia, in the early part of the last century. Interestingly enough though, when reminiscing seven decades later on his work and life, he declared that his greatest passion had been for what in the native Zimbabwean Shona language were called *mombies*, meaning cattle, from which the term 'capital' is derived.

As such, Abraham, whose father was a lay Rabbi, had a passion for nature and the land, which is perhaps why he started out in Africa as a farmer and a trader. Living and working in the African bush with the local communities, adopting their rhythm of life, he built up a company called African Trading, which thereafter became a great financial success story. Indeed, theologian, economist and ecologist Dirk Van Hoogstraten (3), comments:

> The choice facing us is between Abraham's Oriental path and the Occidental Oedipus tradition. Choosing the latter meant accepting the present global inequalities as fate. To take this occidental path means making an effort to reduce birth rates and accepting the process the process of 'natural selection'. Human rights violations and large-scale economic violence are condoned as unavoidable, albeit unfortunate, results of living in a 'survival of the fittest' world. Choosing the alternative oriental tradition, Abraham's path, offers a different set of possibilities, whereby taking this path would mean rejecting the free-market economy's 'fatal attraction'. This fatal attraction is defined as the sacrificing of part of the world's population and nature's richness in the interest of the remaining part's wealth and well-being. Abraham's faith means not letting the children die off (passive) but feeding and nurturing them instead (active). This path requires a change in the distribution of wealth and inclusion in global economic activities.

Furthermore, Van Hoogstraten goes on to say:

> In the first creation story, humans were created on the last day of creation; hence the biosphere was already there. In the second creation story, humans are supposed to consider nature in general and the beautiful garden in particular as their home. Their lives start as an invitation: feel at home, use as much as you need. It is as if there is a host trying to make people feel comfortable and at home in the new environment. Feel free to use what you need, just as other creatures do. Every species and creature here takes what is needed (Genesis 1:29–30).

As such, in our own Zimbabwean context, we (4) have coined the term 'integral *kumusha*' (the latter word meaning 'homestead' in the indigenous language), as constituting the source of origination of business and enterprise, especially in a rural setting. Indeed, the origins of enterprise in the South lie not in Europe—whereby the French terms *entre* (in between) and *preneur* (taking hold of) denote entre-preneurship—but in an altogether different African rhythm, from which finance and enterprise are derived.

3.2. Finance in the South: Providence Human Capital – A Rhythmical Living Force

3.2.1. Internal Dynamism That Gives it Form

Souleymane Bachir Diagne (5), Professor of Philosophy and Francophone Studies at Columbia University in the US, cites the work of the Senegalese poet-statesman Leopold Senghor, in the 1960s:

> The ordering force that constitutes African style is rhythm… What is rhythm? It is the architecture of being, the internal dynamism that gives it form, the system of waves it emanates towards others, the pure expression of Vital Force. Rhythm is the vibrating shock, the force that, through the senses, seizes us as the root of being.

For Senghor, African philosophers shared the ideal of a *becoming-person*. The 'vital forces' constitute the fabric of the world, animated by a dialectical movement. This movement is towards the creation and continual reinforcement of a collective, i.e. a community of persons. There is, therefore, in the end, something tragic in the way that Marx was able to express a thought so metaphysical and even religious—that is, socialism—while repressing the 'vital rhythm' that it implicates.

3.2.2. Aliveness and the Unfolding of Time

Contemporary Senegalese-American philosopher Cheikh Thiam (6), now based at Ohio State University's Department of Philosophy, also quotes Senghor:

> A fluid Negro 'logos' then serves to question the supremacy of the rigid Western 'ratio'. Senghor defines the African 'logos' as a divine 'elan vital' (aliveness).

Senghor understands time differently from the standard Western notion of a unit of measure, which transforms the fluidity of life into mechanistic snapshots. For him, it is duration, the attribute of the object, which causes its constant and permanent becoming. This implies an understanding of the subject as participating in the unfolding of time, rather than being out of time, measurable and definable. As such, *roots, tradition, or places of origin reinvent themselves and evolve*. In other words, despite the change, becoming and movement that Negro cultures have gone through, they have not lost their fundamental particularities. Being is not outside of the existence of the spirit of God, but is manifested through His vital force, precisely because all things, animate or inanimate, are emanations of His/Her Being. This is the concept of panentheism: God animating all things and everything rhythmically vibrating with the presence of God.

3.2.3. Individuals Are Related to Each Other Through Their Vital Force

Furthermore, individuals are ontologically related to each other through their vital force and each vital force develops towards the ultimate manifestation of communal life.

African society is a community. Indeed, this community goes beyond even the human members, since it involves communion with all beings in the universe: stones, plants, animals, men, ancestors and God. The colonial experience of African cultures cannot, moreover, be considered an extraordinary moment of acculturation, the solution of which would be a return to an imagined pristine past. For Senghor, it is constitutive of the ongoing transformation of African cultures. However, he conceives that there is nothing strange about being mixed, because cultures and races are fundamentally nomadic. They are constantly in contact with other cultures and other modes of defining the world, and, consequently, permanently changing. Yet hybridity is not just a synonym of in-between/ness; it entails a perpetual becoming.

Each of these understandings—of vital force, perpetual becoming, communion with others—is a far cry from the Western world of free enterprise, entrepreneurship and the like, to which we are constantly being reduced by the 'West leading the rest'. Of course, Abraham Lessem never completely let go of his European, Jewish heritage, but he was young enough when he migrated to Africa, at the age of 17, to imbibe that African rhythm. Twelve years later, he departed from the rural area to establish himself more, once married, in the capital city. Then, the accountant in him came to the fore. This brings us on to Providence Human Capital, whose founder, Chipo Ndudzo, was also an accountant.

3.3. Providence Human Capital: Towards a 'Chitupu' Gift Economy

3.3.1. Sacred Economics

Providence Human Capital (PHC) has emerged out of the Western financial fire in Zimbabwe and created its own new spring: *chitupu,* meaning 'fountainhead' in the local Shona language. It is the source of 'wellness', as grounds for its ongoing renewal, or *rumuku*. In other words, it is grounded in natural well-being, rather than in economic wealth, and as such is culturally building up 'Providence' Human Capital, over and above, though inclusive of, technological and financial capital.

Its founder, Chipo (meaning 'gift' in the Shona language) Ndudzo, is thereby a source of Providence. This resonates with the American social philosopher Charles Eisenstein (7) in *Sacred Economics*:

> If money did not arise from the economists' imaginary world of calculated, interest-maximizing barter, then how did it arise? It arose as a means to facilitate gift giving, sharing and generosity, or at least that it bore something of that spirit. To recreate a sacred economy, it is necessary to restore money to that original spirit. By facilitating trade, motivating efficient production, and allowing the accumulation of capital to undertake large-scale projects, money should enrich life: it should bestow upon us ease, leisure, freedom from anxiety and an equitable distribution of wealth... The fact that money has become an agent of the opposite—anxiety, hardship, and polarization of wealth—presents us with a paradox.

The word Providence comes from the Latin *providentia* (foresight, prudence), an amalgam of *pro-* (ahead) and *videre* (to see). The current use of the word has the sense of knowledge of the future or prescience, understood as an attribute of God. If we relate such, in turn, to Eisenstein's (8) perspective, what we recognise is:

> The social dividend, the internalization of costs, de-growth, abundance and the gift economy, all take us away from the mentality of struggle, of survival, and therefore of utilitarian efficiency, and towards our true state of gratitude: of reverence for what we have received and of desire to give equally, or better from our endowment. We wish to leave the world more beautiful than we entered it. The history of civilization, in the final analysis, of growing separation and imminent transcendence in a long age of growing reunion, is also a journey from an original abundance to the extreme of scarcity, and then back toward abundance at a higher level of complexity.

So, we are back—and forward—to the theme of 'sustainable abundance'.

3.3.2. Sustainable Abundance: Wealth to Well-being

PHC started out as the payroll division, emerging out of a Western-style Zimbabwean corporation, before Chipo Ndudzo extricated herself from such alien terrain, by dint of the *ntu* (vital force) within her. Gathering together a group of kindred spirits, she started out by creating her own 'payroll' company, which was soon recast in terms of *Goho*, a Shona word for 'harvest'. At the same time, the newly termed Providence 'Human' Capital needed to ground itself in more fertile, indigenous soils, than such a Western-style, depersonalised 'pay-role'.

Thereby its Wellness Centres were established—*Chitubu CheHutano*—as a 'wellspring' from which the harvest is reaped. Interestingly, this chimes with the perspective on well-being and happiness presented by Mark Anielski in the preceding chapter. As Providence understood it, such well-being was enhanced by human development (*Chitubu CheHungwaru*) most specifically through what was termed 'Staffing Solutions'. This entailed employment opportunities being sought for thousands of Zimbabweans who had lost their permanent jobs. Payroll, then, the *goho* harvest, was what subsequently ensued, from prior wellness and subsequent opportunities.

Overall, in Southern guise, it is to natural, social and human capital that PHC has turned, in order to generate built and financial capitals, when examined in relation to Anielski's '5 Capitals' model. The financial West for the gifted and gift-bearing Chipo, truly builds on the 'rest', starting in the natural and social South. We now turn to the cultural and spiritual East.

3.4. Finance and 'Soulidarity' in the East: Akhuwat

3.4.1. Creating Virtuous Circles through Ihsan

Akhuwat (meaning 'brotherhood') based in Pakistan (see also Chapter 6), is conventionally known as the world's largest interest-free, microfinance enterprise. In effect, it is much more than a financial institution. Akhuwat identifies 'virtuous circles' of borrowers and lenders that it serves, which deeply resonates with a foundational Qur'anic verse: 'Truly those who believe and perform righteous deeds—for them the Compassionate One shall appoint love' (19:96). The key to strengthening beneficial love for something that is good is to perform righteous deeds (*amal*) and, hence, to behave virtuously (*akhuwah*). For Akhuwat, then, virtue (or goodness, *ihsan*) is truly its own reward.

This all sounds very simple. Yet, in the profit-and-growth-centric societies we have all formed and live in, this could be the most challenging task, albeit one of the most pressing needs, to result in communal co-existence. For Trans4m fellow and Akhuwat research associate Aneeqa Malik (9) (further elaborated in Chapter 6):

> From an initial stage, and from my standpoint of perceiving Akhuwat as not 'just' a microfinance organisation, this was my enthrallment with Amjad's 'virtuosity' and the Mawakhat—Brotherhood—social movement. By and by, as I immersed myself deeper into its philosophy, it started unfolding as all the hidden layers of its Ihsan/virtuous paradigm—the virtuous circle (*silsilah*) in motion, creating other virtuous circles (reciprocal endowment) for what we call barakah rounds that keep on replicating naturally.

3.4.2. Virtuosity Generates a Community's 'Solidarity Capital'

Akhuwat has a long list of accomplishments to its credit. For the reward of goodness (ihsan) could only be goodness. As such, virtuosity generates a community's 'solidarity capital'. Much like the spiral of downfall and degeneracy, known as a vicious cycle, there is also a spiral of ascent and accomplishment, understood as a virtuous cycle. Then countless avenues begin opening up (virtuous circles). The journey leads to more journeys, some due to the grace of a generous grant, some as the result of prayer.

Through 17 years of existence, besides generating its own 'solidarity/circular economy', by rekindling the spirit of ihsan, Akhuwat has successively created its own 'community of Akhuwateers'; that is, multiple virtuous circles. For Akhuwat's leader, Amjad Saqib, brotherhood (*bhai-chara/akhuwat*) is an unmatchable feeling of compassion that promises to empower people. By virtue of solidarity, the cyclic reverberation has spiralled through Akhuwat's many community initiatives. It also gives expression to *khalifa*.

3.4.3. Virtuous Communities, Virtuous City and Cultivating Solidarity: Khalifa

According to our Trans4m colleague, Professor of Technology Management at the Gulf University in Bahrain, and Trans4m Senior Fellow, Odeh Al-Jayyousi (10), one of the three fundamentals of the Islamic faith is Trusteeship. In Arabic, this is khalifa, analogous to *utariri* in Shona. Each human being, as vicegerent on earth, has been endowed with all the spiritual and mental characteristics, as well as material resources, to enable him/her to live up to his/her mission. Since the human is good by nature, (s)he feels psychologically happy so long as (s)he stays in, or moves closer to, inner nature. The resources with which God has endowed the world are not unlimited. But they are sufficient to cater for the needs of all, if used efficiently and equitably.

In the same vein, Al-Farabi (11), the renowned 10th century Persian philosopher, thought of a perfect human being (*al-insan al-kamil*) in his virtuous city, as the one who has obtained theoretical virtue, thus completing his intellectual knowledge, and has acquired practical moral virtues, thus becoming perfect in his moral behaviour. This thinking represented a cross-over from West to East, from the writings of Aristotle BCE and Augustine CE. Thus, crowning these theoretical and moral virtues with effective power, they are anchored in the souls of individual members of the community when they assume the responsibility of political leadership, thus becoming role models for other people.

Al-Farabi unites moral and aesthetic values, in line with the Greek tradition: good is beautiful, and beauty is good; the beautiful is that which is valued by the intelligentsia. So, this perfection which he expects from education combines knowledge and virtuous behaviour, is happiness (Aristotle's *eudaimonia*, as referenced by Anielski, in the previous chapter) and goodness, simultaneously. Theoretical and practical perfection, moreover, can only be obtained within society, for it is society that nurtures the individual and prepares him to be free. If he were to live outside society, he might only learn to be a wild animal. Thus, one of the goals of education is the creation of the ideal community, 'the one whose cities all work together in order to attain happiness'.

We can see then, in Akhuwat's case, how cultivating the seeds of solidarity created a ripple effect of 'goodness as a reward for goodness', thus, practically, reflecting the virtues of ihsan being cultivated in the community of Akhuwat, through its borrowers, replicators and partners.

3.4.4. The Soulidarity Multipliers: Members' Donation Program

The kindling of any spark in the darkness, for Saqib and Malik (12), bears evidence that darkness will inevitably come to an end. However, there are some conditions that must be honoured before embarking on this path. Whoever wishes to do this work must first surrender their being (ego) to service. It is this surrender that stands as the greatest manifestation of his devotion. Of course, this principle is contained in most spiritual traditions, but it has been enshrined very particularly within Akhuwat's programmes.

Over the period of one decade, Akhuwat has grown from a small initiative to a large movement fighting against usury and exploitation of the poor. The trust and honour of the borrowers have helped them with their members' donation program (MDP), which relies entirely on the philanthropic spirit within their borrowers. Their eagerness to donate for the cause of Akhuwat along with their monthly payments increased their confidence as it developed a new foundation within the organisation, which is supporting Akhuwat's operations to create more virtuous circles.

Their support for replications is purely based on Saqib's dream of building an interest-free *mawakhat* (solidarity) community throughout Pakistan and extending this to the entire (Muslim) world. Thus, without any interest in capitalising on market shares, they invest their energy and resources into helping develop other organisations without detracting from their objective. This contributes to Amjad's ultimate vision of a poverty-free society. In a period of over a decade, several organisations have implemented 'The Akhuwat Model' and added *Qard-al-Hasan* as one of the tools for their community services.

3.4.5. Orders of Love – Silsilah – The Soulidarity Chain

Akhuwat's community-building ihsan (excellence) is an economic multiplier, in the form of creating a chain (*silsilah*) that emanates from love for humanity and one's community. This love originates in the form of universal love, i.e. love for the Creator and consequently His creation, which forms the basis of mawakhat (solidarity) in this case. Silsilah, an Arabic word, also used in Persian, Malay and Urdu, means chain, link, connection, and is often used in various senses of lineage. In particular, it may be translated as '(religious) order' or 'spiritual genealogy', which has been evolved into our GEN*E*-alogy.

For mystics (13), the state of ecstasy (perfect happiness) is reached after losing one's 'self' and ascending vertically to the state of the 'I am the UNI-VERSE' state! This is where the '*ishq*/love' orientation reaches its highest pitch: that is, union with the God-reality. The journey back from that state is the purified state of God-realisation in all one does afterwards. For Saqib, prayer is a form of love too, as it involves surrendering one's will to Allah. He strongly believes that the power of prayer can move the earth. He usually credits Akhu-wat's success to those heart-felt prayers of both his close associates and also his ancestors. Thus, he (14) writes, in his Urdu book *Kamyab Loug*:

> It was the love of Allah and his profound love and reverence for the Prophet (may peace be upon him) that transcended into love (Ishq) and compassion for the people of his land, which made him travel beyond the age he is living in—the soul resonance of Mawakhat.

We now turn from South and East to North, specifically from Zimbabwe in Africa and Pakistan in Asia, to Mondragon in Europe; from Chipo Ndudzo and Amjad Saqib, to Father Don Jose Maria Arizmendi, as the Northern source of inspiration.

3.5. Finance in the North and the Basque Caja Laboral: Co-operativo Mondragon

3.5.1. Founded on Christian Humanist Values

Don Jose Maria Arizmendi, a Catholic priest based in the Basque Country in the Northern Iberian peninsula as well as co-founder and the major source of inspiration for the Mondragon Co-operatives in the 1950s, never developed his ideas systematically in a book, but he spoke and wrote constantly. Joxe Azurmendi in his 1984 work on *El Hombre Co-operative: Pensamiento de Jose Maria Arizmendiarrietta* (15) made an exhaustive analysis of his writings and placed them in the political and economic context of his times. Azurmendi describes the evolution of his thinking:

> In his first writings, in the early 1940s, the crisis of the times is seen as a crisis of faith, although seen in terms of a specific system of Chris-tian-humanist values… By about 1945–50, Arizmendi was centering his attention on the social question. The nucleus of the crisis was no longer

one of faith but that of property. After this epoch distinctly religious themes seem to disappear from his writings.

Along with this evolution of ideas, Don Jose Maria shifted his attention from the family to the factory. In his first years at Mondragon, he had been grappling with issues of housing and health, but now he focused ever more on the workplace. Among secular authors, meanwhile, Don Jose was a close student of the writings of the leftist Catholic French social philosophers Jacques Maritain (16) and Emmanuel Mounier (17). He was also influenced by Brazilian pedagogue Paulo Freire (18) and, curiously, by the sayings of Mao Zedong.

3.5.2. Political Ideology and Religious Faith

Arizmendi (19) had several close friends and admirers amongst the clergy, but the Catholic Church did not provide institutional support for his work or for the Mondragon Co-operative movement. He was highly critical of formal religion in general and of his church in particular:

> In the name of religion, what barbarities have been committed. We must be on guard against any form of dogmatism... Religion has been well marketed, but what good has it done? It has led us to feel the importance of the universal and the abstract. Theologians, sociologists, philosophers have operated from the top down, when the correct way to think is in the opposite direction.

He was allergic to all isms. 'Isms imprison and oppress us', he wrote. By contrast, he (20) had a far more positive view of co-operativism:

> The third way distinct from egoist capitalism and from depersonalizing socialism. We want co-operatives, which constitute a new social potential and, thus, are built by those who are not impelled by a myopic and limited egotism or by a simple gregarious instinct. Co-operativism seeks to create a new state of conscience, of culture, through the humanization of power, through democracy in affairs, and through solidarity, which impedes the formation of privileged classes. Here and now it assigns a functional value to property. That is, property is valued in so far as it serves as an efficient resource for building responsibility and efficiency in any vision of community life in a decentralized form.

On another occasion, he (21) wrote:

> It is a monstrosity that a system of social organisation is tolerated in which some can take advantage of the work of others for their exclusive personal profit... The co-operativist distinguishes himself from the capitalist, simply in that the latter utilises capital in order to make people serve him, while the former uses it to make more gratifying and uplifting the working life of the people.

He (22) described his political philosophy, which sounds like an early interpretation of an Open Society, as pluralist:

> In the minds of the co-operators is the idea that future society probably must be pluralist in all of its organizations including the economic. There will be action and interaction of publically owned and private firms, the market and planning, entities of paternalistic style, capitalistic or social. Every juncture, the nature of every activity, the level and evolution of each community, will require a special treatment, but not limited to one form of organization, if we believe in and love man, his liberty, justice and democracy… Co-operation is one organizational option among others, that for effectiveness and spontaneous acceptance should be achieved with its own characteristics, but without challenges and tensions with other entities present in the economic field.

3.5.3. Education for a New Social Order

While teaching, Don Jose Maria continued his own education at the Escuela Social Seminary of Vitoria, where his interest extended from economics and sociology to philosophy and pedagogy. He saw the co-operatives as being built on a foundation of education, and in turn providing education for economic progress toward a new social order. He (23) defined the co-operative experience as:

> An economic effort that translates itself into an educational action… an educational effort that employs economic action as a vehicle for transformation. One is not born a co-operator, because to be a co-operator requires a social maturity, a training in social living. For one to be an authentic co-operator it is necessary to have learnt to tame one's individualistic instincts, through education and the practice of virtue.

He (24) believed in learning from experience:

> Life is a fabric of relations between the past and the present, and the future is not built in a vacuum; experience, that of others as well as our own, is enriching, a positive resource… we build the road as we travel.

The last phrase, *'se hace camino al andar'*, quoted from Spanish poet Antonio Machado, recurs again and again in Arizmendi's (25) writings. It has been important for the people of Mondragon to recognise that they are building the road to the future by reflecting on their past:

> We are realists. Conscious of what we can and cannot do we concentrate on those things that we have hopes of changing within ourselves more than on those things we cannot change in others. The idea is to do the good that we can and not that of which we dream.

Arizmendi believed in revolution, but the revolution he sought would come gradually and peacefully. He spoke of Jesus Christ as the greatest revolutionary in history: 'Daily revolution consists of effective transformations built upon new structures. It is like growing a chain which can reach beyond that which we can imagine.' In 1966, he wrote (26):

> We are totally in agreement with the revolutionary formulation of the clear-sighted Christian thinker, Mounier. The moral revolution will be economic or it will not take place.

One of Arizmendi's close friends described (27) the founder's conception of revolution:

> Many times I have heard him attack the obsession with the political for polarizing the revolution in terms of political power. Any group, he would say, that considers itself revolutionary must overcome this mentality, or its revolution will be simply a taking of power to install another tyranny of a different complexion. For him the revolution had to be based on other perspectives, taking more into account the cultural infrastructure. The revolution that the cooperators must bring about is primarily a cultural revolution.

Arizmendi (28) warned against the complacency that often comes with success and stressed the need for constant re-evaluation of the co-operative experience:

> Let us move ahead with criticisms and self-criticism more than with criticisms of others... Water which does not flow becomes stagnant... To live is to renew oneself... We must emphasize the fact that the firm is a peculiar entity in permanent process of evolutionary change: it must renew and revitalize itself at all times due to the inevitable consequences of the changing technology and economy of our world.

This brings us to the heart of the Mondragon Co-operative matter and as far as we are concerned, namely, the Caja Laboral Credit Union.

3.5.4. The Caja Laboral Credit Union

Stakeholding and democratic governance apart, the success of the Mondragon Co-operatives is also largely due to the unique system of secondary or support co-operatives, from which the primary co-operatives (manufacturing and retailing) source key specialist services. Arizmendi realised, at a very early stage in the life of the co-operatives, that expanding the existing businesses and creating new ones would require reliable access to capital on affordable terms. 'A co-operative', he wrote, 'must not condemn itself to the sole alternative of self-financing.' His insight led, in 1959, to the establishment of the Caja, in order to mobilise capital from the local and regional communities. It was to become not only the financier but also the driving force in shaping development and holding the co-operatives together.

The slogan used by the Caja (29) in the early stages was 'savings or suit-cases'. Its real attraction to the local population was that they knew the money would be working on their behalf, to bring about development from which they could directly benefit. The Caja, in its original form, was also the means whereby the co-operatives managed the capital held in their permanent reserves. They were able to borrow, moreover, at interest rates 3 to 4 per cent below the conventional market rate, freeing themselves from capital constraints, which would have drastically curbed their development.

From functioning purely as a source of capital for the co-operatives, the Caja became the mechanism through which their association with one another was formalised and their activities integrated. Each co-operative was required to invest in the Caja, including holdings on behalf of the members, such as pension funds and workers' share capital. Each co-operative was also required to adopt a five-year budget and report on it at monthly intervals.

3.5.5. A 'Factory Factory': New Kind of Economic Development

Finally, the Caja had a key role in developing new co-operatives and advising and helping out existing ones that were experiencing difficulties. These latter services were performed by the Empreserial Division as 'factory factory'. The division consisted of 7 departments: advice and consultation; feasibility studies; agricultural and food promotion; industrial promotion; intervention; urban planning and building; auditing and information.

Together with the Caja Laboral Popular as a whole, it is the prototype of a new kind of economic development organisation, which institutionalises the function of the small business entrepreneur. Where new co-operatives were concerned, a group of workers who were interested in establishing a new venture, together with a manager, first had to find a product or service for which they believed there was a market. They were then in a position to approach the so-called Empreserial Division of the Caja. If the division believed the proposal was sound they assigned an advisor or 'godfather' to the group. The group, in turn, registered as a co-operative and accepted a loan to cover the manager's salary while feasibility studies were being undertaken.

These studies lasted up to two years, during which time a new product might emerge from the Division's 'ideas bank', and after which design, production and marketing issues would be addressed. The completed study would then be presented to the Operations Committee of the Banking Division of the Caja, which determined whether the venture should be approved. If approved, the 'godfather' continued to be seconded until a break-even point was reached, after which the Division continued to remain in touch through the monthly reporting.

When an existing co-operative experienced difficulty, there were various categories of intervention available. Overall, no more than a handful of the more than one hundred co-operatives started, to date, have had to go out of business, although the situation with Fagor, its white goods manufacturer, when it collapsed in 2013, has provided one of the greatest shocks to Mondragon. In all other instances of co-operatives finding themselves at risk, the Intervention Department was successful in putting them back on their feet. Just as the systematised innovation of the modern scientific research laboratory represented a major advance over the garage inventor, so the institutionalisation of entrepreneurship in the Empreserial Division represented a quantum leap over the isolated small business entrepreneurs of the capitalist world.

Fourth and finally we turn to the USA, to Dee Hock, the founder of VISA, to reveal the largely hidden story of VISA in its early days, under his inspirational leadership.

3.6. Finance in the West: VISA Card and a 'Chaordic' Alliance

3.6.1. Self-Organisation With Close-knit Others

There was a compelling need for a new financial organisation in the 1970s. While Dee Hock was based at the National Bank of Commerce, he attempted an audacious bid to generate a new form of payments card. He was sponsored by an enlightened CEO, who afforded him the liberty to try. Equally, Hock (30) suppressed his own perspective on what the future might be, and tried to create the conditions by which new concepts could emerge. How that would happen, he did not know.

His learning would have to evolve in concert with others. He thought long and hard about each member of the national executive committee that he had formed, which served to link up a number of banks. He ultimately settled on three, each of whom seemed to have a good sense of who he was: an open, curious mind, generous spirit, with a keen sense of humour. More importantly, no one seemed inclined to either follow or lead a mob. Each moved to a rhythm of his own making.

Sam Johnson was a big, bluff Boston Irishman with a ready smile and thousands of ideas that spilled from him, as Hock put it, 'like iridescent marbles from a bowl'. His enthusiasm was contagious, and his huge capacity for friendship 'had wrapped me in his arms'. Jack Dillon was a veteran of World War II, who loved to talk of army life, though long removed from it. A 30-year employee of the Bank of America, raconteur extraordinaire, connoisseur of fine food and wine, he was delightful to be around. Fred James, finally, from Memphis, Tennessee, was a fine storyteller 'in the droll southern manner'.

This collective group asked themselves that if anything imaginable was possible—if there were no constraints—what would be the nature of an ideal organisation to create the world's premier system for the exchange of value? In the process they needed to master four perspectives—how things were, how they are, how they might become and how they ought to be—synthesising them into a compelling concept of a constructive future. But this would require a lot of forethought.

3.6.2. What If a Financial Institution Could Be Established Jointly?

Hock's shift in organisational perception was indeed profound. He knew that no bank, no nation state or organisation could create the world's premier system for the exchange of value. Hock, therefore, wondered: what if a fraction of the financial resource of all the financial institutions in the world, and a fraction of the ingenuity of all the people who worked there, could be applied jointly? But how might this occur? Dee Hock came up with some organisational principles:

- it should be equitably owned by all participants
- participants should have equitable rights and obligations
- it should be open to all qualified participants
- power, function and resources should be distributed to the maximum
- authority should be equitable and distributive
- no participant should lose out to any new concept of organisation
- to the maximum degree possible, everything should be voluntary
- it should induce, not compel change
- it should be infinitely malleable yet extremely durable.

Had we powers, capital, position or influence (as senior management) Hock maintained, we would undoubtedly have used them in the command-and-control style in which we have been so admirably indoctrinated. Without them, we were forced to a change of consciousness; to conceiving larger, better ideas that could transcend and enfold existing institutions and practices. Four vice presidents of the four modest banks involved, to begin with, could not dominate or compel anyone. They could only persuade and induce. And so they did. Bit by bit. Though they did not know it at the time, they were, in fact, building a foundation on which an extraordinary enterprise would self-organise and evolve, unfinished to this day.

No one thought that banks in America would voluntarily surrender a portion of their autonomy and act together for a common purpose. No one believed that such a horizontal grouping of competitors could exist within the spirit and constraint of anti-trust laws. And no one dreamed that the emerging ideas would bring together, in common ownership, an enterprise, people and institutions of every race, language, custom and culture—every economic, legal, philosophical and religious persuasion in the world. Perhaps the same combination of institutional and cultural forces is needed around us, to inaugurate sustainable development.

Each time, Hock tells us, that he fell into despair and wanted to give up in the face of the enormity of this enterprise—and it happened often—something softly whispered 'Not now'. For there was an inexpressible, compelling sense that in some profound way, existence would lose its meaning if he didn't persist. To what end, analogously we might ask, is each of us driven? What, then, is our spiritual quest?

3.6.3. The Theology of Chaordic Organisations

In what Dee Hock terms 'the theology of chaordic organisations', heaven is purpose, principle and people. Purgatory is paper and procedure. Hell is rules and regulations. Inspired, then, by the sense of purpose that was conveyed, and the principles being served, hundreds of talented, dedicated people from subsequently more than one hundred banks to begin with, self-organised. They worked assiduously to understand and anticipate legal, marketing, operating, financial and technological problems and opportunities.

It was an impressive group that met in February 1970 in New York, in an awesome boardroom, near the top of a towering bank headquarters. They greeted one another as old friends, comparing notes of private jets, golf scores and banking deals made. It was an intimidated sheep of a person who sat, silently, wondering if they were people who bloodied the hide of obstreperous sheep. Incredibly, Dee had never been in a corporate boardroom before. Little more than a year ago he had been sorting trash in the basement of a bank branch.

So he, silently, repeated to himself a mantra he had devised years before: 'I am as great to me as you are to you, and you are as great to you as I am to me, therefore we are equal.' At the end of the board meeting they wanted Dee's (31) commitment—as a condition before going ahead with the proposed scheme—that he would move to San Francisco and head up what was being termed the 'NBI'. As he put it:

> They were asking me for a commitment to a job they could not offer (the terms were derisory), working for a company not yet fully structured, for owners yet to be determined, and governed by an unknown board. No commitment no commitment. I was gibbeted, swinging in the wind.

What foolish logic, then, would rationalise becoming president of NBI, Hock thought to himself. It meant giving up grass, rain, trees: all the natural living things. It meant dirty air, city jungles, confinement in steel and concrete boxes, conniving people and fussing work.

Reflecting on the kind of organisation he might be heading up, Hock was aware that like all organisations, corporations have no reality, except in the mind. They are no more than mental constructs; specific modern manifestations of the ancient idea of community. The original idea of a corporation was that of a collective entity intended to attract people and resources, needed to realise a desired social objective beyond the ability or resources of a single individual.

As such, the for-profit, monetised shareholder form of corporation has recently demanded and received perpetual life. It has demanded and received the right to define its own purpose and act solely for self-defined self-interest. It has demanded and received, according to Hock, release from the revocation of its charter for inept or anti-social acts. The roles of giant, transnational corporations and government have slowly reversed. Government is now more of an instrument of such corporations than vice versa. They are no longer, not even indirectly, an instrument of the populace they affect, but an instrument of the few who control the ever increasing power and wealth they command. The use of the corporate form—for the purpose of social good—has become incidental.

3.6.4. VISA: Quasi-Governmental, Quasi-for-Profit, Quasi-not-for-Profit

Deciding to take the role of CEO on, Hock (32) over and over again explained the purpose, principles, concept and structure to his colleagues:

> No member of any class will have greater or lesser rights than any other.
> No director will have a greater or lesser voice. You, the participants and
> you alone will make all decisions through the most open and equitable
> structure that hundreds of participants could devise.

In 1968 the VISA community was no more than a set of beliefs and a vague concept. In 1970 it was born. By the turn of the millennium its products were created by 22,000 owner-member financial institutions and accepted at 15 million merchant locations in more than 200 countries. In 2000, three quarters of a billion people use VISA products to make 14 billion transactions, producing an annual income of $1.25 trillion: the single largest block of consumer purchasing power in the global economy. Ten years later VISA Inc connected 1.9BN cards, and that did not include the newly separated company of VISA Europe.

VISA was, in effect, a quasi-governmental, quasi-for-profit, quasi-not-for-profit, quasi-consulting, quasi-franchising, quasi-educational, quasi-social, quasi-commercial, quasi-political alliance. The financial institutions that created its products were, at one and the same time, its owners, its members, its suppliers and its customers. VISA spawned new industries and new ventures in tens of thousands, creating conditions by which members can connect with one another without permission or limitation. Since it had no interest in controlling or owning technology or participants, the unlimited ingenuity and creativity of thousands of external entities was freely brought in to bear on the needs and opportunities of the system.

The entirety, like millions of other 'chaordic' organisations, including those we call body, brain, forest, ocean and biosphere, was largely self-regulating. The word 'chaordic' had been coined by Hock, to indicate an organisation that was a mix of order and chaos. It was represented, in VISA, by a staff of fewer than 500, scattered across more than a dozen countries, on four continents, who coordinated this system of ordered chaos, as it skyrocketed past a hundred billion dollars, providing product and systems development, global advertising and electronic communication systems. If only, in the final analysis, the likes of Facebook was constituted in this chaordic way, we would not see the calls for 'external' regulation that are currently being made.

3.6.5. Evolving Diversity and Complexity

Such products, services, and organisations—in which the value of the mental content begins to dwarf the value of the physical content—require wise people of deep understanding, like Dee Hock. To endlessly add to the quantity of mechanistic information, knowledge and technology, as per 'e-commerce', without similar evolution of values and wisdom, he reckons, is not only foolish; it is dangerous. In a complex, changing world, a clear sense of direction, a compelling purpose and powerful beliefs about conduct are required. These are more significant and seemed to be infinitely more sensible and robust than mechanical plans, detailed objectives and predetermined outcomes. It seems to be a principle of evolution, perhaps the fundamental principle, that the greater the capacity to receive, store, utilise, transform and transmit information, the more diverse and complex the organism must be. What, then, does this mean in nature?

Information in the form of DNA is endlessly replicated at little apparent cost, distributed in seeds. A process of replication, driven by the power of the sun, begins. Molecules and cells assemble on the spot into unknown patterns from atoms of surrounding air, soil and water. In the case of animals, it happens not only on the spot, but on the move. When such creations are no longer viable, nature breaks them down into atoms once again for recreation into something new and useful: a never-ending, effective, non-polluting chain of events of ever-evolving diversity and complexity. No factories, no waste, no despoiled resources or pollution, no mechanistic organisation and no command and control. Nature does it all, for Hock, with chaordic organisation: a complex, diverse flow of information that 'chaordically' mobilises physical materials into both animate and inanimate forms. The same principles applied to VISA.

3.6.6. A Story of Material Success and Spiritual Failure

Judged by orthodox measures of objective measurement—growth, size, profit, market share and volume—VISA has been a phenomenal success. By standards, though, of what VISA might have become, and what it ought to have been, Hock admits to a strong sense of failure. As a small team of staff with limited resources, Dee and his team faced incredible industry problems and insatiable demands on their time. Legal depositions were long and wearing, causing stress and depression. At the same time, though, Hock could not free himself of his obsession with information and its effect on institutions.

Reductive data, at one end of the spectrum, is separable, objective, linear, mechanistic and abundant. Wisdom, at the other end, is holistic, subjective, spiritual, conceptual, creative and scarce. Science has traditionally operated in the provinces of segmented data, information and knowledge, where measurement particularly, specialisation and rationality are especially useful. It has, largely, ignored the provinces of holistic understanding and wisdom.

Traditionally, this has been delegated, albeit imperfectly, to theology, philosophy, literature and art, where subjectivity, spirituality and values are deemed to be appropriate. When there is an explosion in the capacity to receive, utilise, store, transform and transmit information, it first creates an immensity of new data, thus transforming the ratio of higher cognitive forms to the lower, drowning wisdom and understanding in a flood of data and information. This is what is often termed the DIKW pyramid, where data and information are plentiful, but knowledge and wisdom are scarce.

In the age of the internet, we are drowning, Hock maintains, in a raging flood of new data and information, and the raft of wisdom to which we desperately cling is breaking beneath us. Native societies, which endured for centuries, with little capacity to receive, store, utilise, transform and transmit information, had time to develop a very high ratio of understanding and wisdom to data and information. They may not have known a great deal by today's standards, but they understood a very great deal about what they knew. They were enormously wise in relation to the extent to which they were informed, and their information was conditioned by an extremely high ratio of social, economic and spiritual value. By contrast, our society understands very little about what it knows. It has a reducing command of wisdom in relation to the information it controls. The immensity of data and information that assaults our cognitive capacity is also conditioned by a very small ratio of so-cial, economic and spiritual value. One of the objectives of our development programme, therefore, is to help to balance out the data-wisdom ratio; to flat-ten the pyramid, by increasing the apex compared to the base.

3.6.7. Distributed Knowledge

The result of the current imbalance is vast technological power unleashed with an inadequate understanding of the systemic propensity for destruction, or sufficient wisdom to guide its evolution in holistic, creative and constructive ways. It leaves us locked within our separatist, linear, mechanistic institutions, confined at the university within our ever more isolated specialities, constricted by ever narrowing perspectives, while in millions of rational, insular, isolated acts we pour billions of tons of manmade chemicals into the biosphere that it cannot recycle. We, thereby, allow chemicals to accumulate with little percep-tion of how they are systematically combining to affect all living things: punch holes in the ozone layer of the atmosphere, dissipate and alter genetic materials and destroy species by the tens of thousands. This is the actual meaning of car-bonising the atmosphere and generating anthropogenic climate change.

Meanwhile, in the financial world, it is becoming conceivable that two or three payment systems may straddle the earth. If that be so, Hock maintains, it is better they be distributed behemoths such as VISA rather than single stock companies, or an extension of some government entity. In fact, by late 1972, the international committee of the NBI (thereafter to become VISA), requested that its senior management undertake the formation of a worldwide organisation. As such, it became necessary to organise regional committees with representatives from every licensee: in Europe, the Middle East, Africa, Asia-Pacific, Latin America and North America. Each committee contained representatives from countries with long histories of bitter commercial, ethnic and cultural conflict, including warfare and periodic subjugation of one anoth-er. How, then, did Hock and his team establish unity amongst such diversity?

Those with the greatest power and wealth, for Hock, and the most promi-nent place in the old order of things have the most to lose. It is understandable that they seek one another out and merge the institutions they control, there-fore, to amass more power and wealth in order to perpetuate what they cling on to. It is understandable, Hock asserts, that they blind themselves to the fact that they are attempting to preserve the form of things long after that form no longer serves a function. This is a certain formula for failure. For the closest thing to a law of nature, in the organisational world, is that form has an affinity for expense, while function has an affinity for income. What, though, if the old order were to cage the Four Beasts—ego, envy, avarice and ambition—and take a lead in the new order of things?

3.7. Conclusion: The West Is Failing to Follow the Rest

3.7.1. An Archetype From Which to Learn

When VISA International came into being, its behaviour was neither traditional nor merely innovative. It was 'chaordic' and open to surprise. It was, for example, impractical to compose a board composed of people from a dozen countries more than quarterly. Each meeting was held in a different country to familiarise directors with different cultures. In an effort to broaden the perspective of members, Hock began inviting world-class speakers and entertainers from a variety of cultures to stretch people's imagination beyond the limited traditional world of banking payment systems.

For more than a decade, until he left the company he had founded in 1984, Hock was working in the midst of ever increasing complexity. At the end, he was reporting to more than 100 directors from dozens of countries comprising six boards, meeting on nearly every continent, as the sales volume rocketed past one hundred billion dollars, with virtual certainty it would increase eightfold each decade well into the next century. But such success was only part of the story. In spite of his pride in all that VISA demonstrated about the power of a chaordic concept of organisation, Hock does not now believe that VISA is a concept to emulate. It is merely an *archetype* to learn from and improve upon. It represented a process of semiosis, making a chaordic meaning-system.

3.7.2. From Commercial Terrain to Ravaged Land

Early in 1984, by his own decision, the curtain came down on Dee Hock's reign as CEO of VISA. The business costume went into the closet and he went directly from the commercial theatre to life on 200 acres of remote, ravaged land. The lifelong dream of pioneering a new concept of organisation had been realised. There was pride and gratification in knowing that it had been done, what it now was, and what it might become, but there was a deep sense of failure about what it ought to be.

In fact, Hock's story, if you like, is our story. The South Providence, the East Akhuwat, and the North Mondragon are all alive and well, as altogether integral financial enterprises, building on nature and community, primarily, technology and enterprise only secondarily, as 'financial' instutions, albeit with different degrees of Southern, Eastern, Northern and altogether Western emphases. VISA, in the West, started out in that guise, setting an integral example for us as such, but has since patently failed, as finance in the West is today failing, abysmally, in our integral terms.

Moreover, as we reflect on the nature and scope of a PHC, and Akhuwat or a Mondragon, they are a long way from your conventional, financially-based enterprise, because they are explicitly grounded in local soils, before emerging locally-globally, thereafter constituting, each in turn, a newly global enterprise.

3.7.3. Travelling Theories: A Cultural Politics of Becoming

That which 'is' in one place then, for Peter Mandaville (2) whom we cited at the outset, elsewhere becomes undone, translated, re-inscribed; this is the nature of trans-locality: a cultural politics of *becoming*. But, what does it mean for theory and culture to travel? Far from representing the universality of Western culture, trans-locality serves to open up new spaces of discourse and semiosis, in which travelling theory, hybridity, and shifting idioms of identity are the most salient characteristics.

'Travelling theory' is, in fact, the title of an essay by the late Palestinian-American Edward Said (33) that first appeared in his 1983 collection *The World, the Text and the Critic*. For him, cultural and intellectual life is dependent on the circulation of ideas. In this sense, the movement of theory is often a precondition for intellectual creativity. Said's main concern was with ways in which theories change when they become trans-local. They, necessarily, undergo processes of semiosis, representation and institutionalisation, different from those at the point of origin.

Said identifies four stages which he believes are common to the way all theories travel. The first of these he calls a point of origin (our **g**rounding), where a set of ideas are first elaborated. In the case of travelling Islam, the point of origin can be understood in two ways: the 7th century *ummah* or the socio-cultural context from which the idea is derived. The second component of Said's scheme (our **e**mergence) is the 'distance traversed'—the act of travelling itself—in which the theory or set of ideas moves from the point of origin to a different time and space. 'Vessels' for such include migrants, exiled intellectuals and transnational publishers, or even electronic media.

In the case of trans-local Islam, all of these, for Said, have played a role in bearing tradition across great distances. Third, our itinerant theory would necessarily encounter a set of conditions (as per our **n**avigation) that mediates its acceptance, rejection or modification in a new time and place. For travelling Muslims, this is usually the European and North American societies in which they settle, but, there is also the Muslim 'Other'—competing interpretations—to take into consideration. What finally effects (our GEN*E*), in the fourth stage of Said's process, is an idea which has been transformed by its new uses; in short, a new (well-travelled) theory has undergone semiosis. It is that final stage which seemed to have most interested Said.

In Chapters 4 and 7 we introduce Tony Bradley's methodology of semiotic economic analysis, which evolves the GEN*E* and displays many points of contact with Said's fourfold schema. At this point, we turn from integral finance to integral accounting, again spread across South, East, North and West.

3.8. Bibliography

1 **Lessem** R and **Palsule** S (1997) *Managing in Four Worlds: from Competition to Co-creation*. Oxford. John Wiley

2 **Mandaville** P (2000) *Transnational Muslim Politics: Reimagining the Umma*. London. Routledge Research in Transnationalism

3 **Van Hoogstraten** D (2001) *Deep Economy: Caring for Ecology, Humanity and Religion*. Cambridge. James Clark and Co

4 **Lessem** R, **Mawere** M, **Matupire** P and **Zongololo** P (2019) *Integral Kumusha: Aligning Policonomy, Nature, Culture, Technology and Enterprise*. Mazvingo. Africa Talent Publishers

5 **Diagne** S.B. (2017) *The Ink of the Scholars. Reflections on Philosophy in Africa*. Dakar. Codesiria

6 **Thiam** C (2017) *Return to the Kingdom of Childhood: Re-visioning the Legacy and Philosophical Relevance of Negritude*. Columbus. OH. Ohio State University Press

7 **Eisenstein** C (2011) *Sacred Economics: Money, Gift and Society in the Age of Transition*. Berkeley. Evolver Editions

8 **Eisenstein** C (2011) *op cit*

9 **Saqib** A and **Malik** A (2018) *Integral Finance: Akhuwat – A Case Study of the Solidarity Economy*. Abingdon. Routledge

10 **Al-Jayyousi** O (2012) *Islam and Sustainable Development: An Islamic Perspective*. Abingdon. Routledge

11 **Al-Farabi** A N (1959) *In the Perfect State*. Beirut. Imprimerie Catholique

12 **Saqib** A and **Malik** A (2018) *op cit*

13 **Al-Farabi** A N (1959) *op cit*

14 **Saqib** A (2016) *Kamyab Loug*. Lahore. Sand-e-Meel Publications

15 Joxe **Azurmendi** (1984) work on El Hombre Co-operative: Pensamiento de Jose Maria Arizmendiarrietta. London. Sage

16 **Bird** O and **Sullivan** R eds (1996) *Collected Works of Jaques Maritain*. Notre Dame. University of Notre Dame Press

17 **Mounier** E (1989) *Personalism*. Notre Dame. University of Notre Dame Press

18 **Freire** P (2000) *Pedagogy of the Oppressed*. London. Continuum

19 **Azurmendi** J (1984) *op cit*

20 **Azurmendi** J (1984) *op cit*

21 **Azurmendi** J (1984) *op cit*

22 **Azurmendi** J (1984) *op cit*

23 **Azurmendi** J (1984) *op cit*

24 **Azurmendi** J (1984) *op cit*

25 **Azurmendi** J (1984) *op cit*

26 **Azurmendi** J (1984) *op cit*
27 **Azurmendi** J (1984) *op cit*
28 **Azurmendi** J (1984) *op cit*
29 **Whyte** W and K (1991) *Making Mondragon.* Ithaca. Cornell University Press
30 **Hock** D (2002) *Birth of the Chaordic Age.* San Francisco. Berrett Koehler
31 **Hock** D (2002) *op cit*
32 **Hock** D (2002) *op cit*
33 **Said** E (1983) *The World, the Text & the Critic.* Cambridge. Harvard University Press

Towards Integral Accounting: Phenomenological, Interpretive, Semiotic, Positivist

Ronnie Lessem, Trans4m Communiversity Associates

Islam envisages an economic system that is fundamentally different from the prevailing ones. Having its roots on shariah, from which it derives its worldview, its goals are not primarily materialist. They are based, rather, on concepts of human well-being (*falah*) and good life (*hayat tayyibah*) which give utmost importance to brotherhood and socio-economic justice, to balance the material and spiritual needs of all human beings.

Umer Chapra, Islam and the Economic Challenge (1)

In the same obstructing way that economic measures like GDP force us to privilege monetary transactions, income, and corporate/industrial activity by discounting the non-monetary practices of caring what happens in small places, or the contributions of trees to weathering the planet or well-being, carbon metrics reduce climate change to the amount of carbon in the atmosphere and the ability of emissions markets to meet sustainability goals. As part of the climate imaginary that is produced by neoliberal agendas of progress, linear time, anthropocentric control, separation from nature, and technological optimism, today's carbon discourse and activism obfuscate other ways of thinking about the weather.

Bayo Akomolafe, These Worlds Beyond our Fences:
Humanity's Search for Home (2)

4.1. Introduction

4.1.1. Accounting for an Enterprise's Well-being

We have now articulated how an integral approach to finance; one that emerges from the South, East, North and West respectively, indicates how the West builds on the 'rest', rather than by-passing or overwhelming them. At this point, we wish to focus on the specific implications for *integral accounting*, taking a leaf out of Pakistani-born, Saudi-based development economist Umer Chapra's (1) *Islam and the Economic Challenge*, whereby brotherhood and social justice take centre-stage.

In the 1970s and 1980s, I was heavily engaged in the field of so-called social auditing, social reporting and indeed social accounting. This was at least in part a reaction to the sterile experience of having being an articled clerk to a firm of Western accountants in the City of London, in the 1960s. For there, I had become bored to tears by all the figures, all the numbers, which for me represented a very impoverished representation of the firms I 'audited' around the UK.

So, a decade later, now in my thirties, having joined Matrix Consultants, whose focus was on corporate 'social affairs'—perhaps anticipating my lifetime integral focus—I was given the opportunity to develop a richer form of 'social accounting and reporting'. In my first published article entitled 'Accounting for an Enterprise's Well-being', I (3) wrote in the 1970s:

> Business enterprise today is being called upon to exercise significantly wider 'social responsibility' than has traditionally been the case. As a result, individuals, communities and national governments are beginning to call for statements of 'social account' which reflect a company's performance in the eyes not only of financial shareholders, but also of other stakeholders in the community at large. As a result herein I attempt to extend fundamental accounting principles, which have traditionally embraced only monetary stocks and flows, towards physical, social and psychological exchanges. I therefore provide a foundation both for the development of the accountant's/auditor's traditional role and for a means of communication between interest groups within and without the enterprise. As such I do not attempt to develop thoroughgoing quantitative measures to the same degree of specificity as conventional financial accounts; rather I aim to develop a novel framework, to which both management practitioners and theorists may apply their own specific refinements.

To my knowledge, crude as this opening account may have been, there had been little attempt to apply such 'double-entry' principles to environmental, social, and psychological, as well as to financial transactions, until the recent work of people like Mark Anielski, the Impact Investment movement and ecological economists (see Chapter 2; also Campbell, 2004 [4]). Yet for the young Ronnie, such 'double-entry' (asset and liability, credit and debit) accounting involved 'life principles', rather than exclusively financial ones. For example, for every asset acquired by a mining company, in terms of gold or iron ore, there is a liability incurred, at least as far as the earth is concerned. Such a liability, at the time of writing (May 2019), is more likely than not a partial cause, together with climate change, of the horrendous fires raging in both northern and southern California, together with Australia, ultimately 'debiting' billions of dollars to the state's financial accounts, not to mention the monumental loss of personal lives and nature.

4.1.2. Corporate Social Reporting

We now turn to corporate social reporting more generally. A year later in 1975, I (5) turned to the more broadly based field of *Corporate Social Reporting*, following up on my previous work. The particular field in which I requested documentation, in a letter sent out to 400 companies, was corporate social responsibility in general, social and/or human resource accounting, consumer programmes and activities, pollution control, energy conservation, recycling, community affairs, volunteer programmes, race relations, corporate contributions and manpower lending.

As I ascertained, Corporate Social Reporting could be categorised:

- By a particular *channel*: newsletter, annual report, composite social report.
- Through the particular *medium* of words, number, pictures.
- Including a specific *mix* of activities, policies, results, standards, achievements.
- Conveying specific *information* about physical and human resources, products meeting social needs, distribution of finances, internal and external stakeholders.
- Employing a particular *form* of presentation: scorecard, inventory, balance sheet.
- Conducted by the company itself or by an external *source.*
- *Focused* on a mere account of what is, or an account of what should be in relation to a potential standard or comparison.
- *Concentrated* around the company's main product, and/or market, or on peripheral stakeholder interest.
- Finally in varying *degrees* of breadth or depth of concern.

However, by the end of the decade, I had abandoned the whole social accounting/reporting/auditing field to move on to broader and deeper managerial and intellectual pastures. In fact, for all the rich potential that I uncovered, I discovered that most, if not all of the accounting practitioners in the field (there were very few academics engaged in such) became mesmerised by numbers—physical numbers, financial numbers, statistical numbers—to the extent that I began to feel, as Nigerian social philosopher Bayo Akomolafe (2) has so eloquently stated (see above) in *These Worlds Beyond our Fences*, the whole exercise was becoming self-defeating.

Instead of getting closer to the environment, to the person, to the community, the 'social accountants' were putting more and more distance between such phenomena and themselves, not to mention also the practising, managerial others. The trouble is, though, I only had a general intimation as to where to go from there, as I was not yet a social science 'researcher' in its purest sense (see below), nor had I yet discovered an *integral* way. In fact, I had to wait over three decades before I began to see that integral economic light, which would thereafter pave the way for *integral research*.

Fast forward three decades, now early in the new millennium, in my article on *Managing in Four Worlds* (6), written for the UK journal *Long Range Planning* (my MBA thesis at Harvard Business School had been on corporate planning), I was beginning to develop our 'integral' approach, encompassing South, East, North and West:

> The world of economics and business has become dominated by one cultural frame of reference—'north-western'—to the point that the hidden strengths of other cultures, even those of China and India which are pursuing a strongly 'westernised' economic course today, are being ignored by individuals, organisations and societies, alike. Before the demise of communism there was at least an alternative approach, albeit one in opposition. Now, the post-modern age of the information society is almost universally capitalist and even in its latest manifestation, that of globalisation, it exploits difference (market and consumer segmentation) rather than differentiating and integrating between and within cultures and economies. No ecology, including the modern university, can thrive for long when one element, propositional knowledge for example, is rampant.

Yet, truth be told, the world of accounting, like that of business and management, is almost as strongly 'Westernised' today as it was in the 1970s, notwithstanding decades of social reporting, social accounting and social auditing. This is despite the fact that today, social enterprise and social entrepreneurship abounds, not to mention also the advent of the 'triple' or 'quadruple' bottom line! Yet it would take another decade still before I would have any substantive idea as to what could be done. Such an idea emerged through an unlikely *research* route.

4.1.3. Integral Research and Innovation

Indeed, having devoted several decades to uncovering the cultural and so-cio-economic variety that underlie *integral* enterprise (7) and *integral* econom-ics (8), now together with my Trans4m partner—the NGO based in France we had formed—Alexander Schieffer, I took a leap into what is called 'ontological' (theory of being) waters.

In the process of setting up a new PhD programme in Transformation Management in the UK, having now left City University Business School to join Buckingham University, I coincidentally came across a heterodox Cam-bridge University economist Tony Lawson (9). He told me at an academic research seminar that 'ontology' (equally, theory of reality) is everything. This was exactly what I needed to hear. At the time I was establishing the method-ological basis for our programme, also given my growing sense of despair, that Africa, his continental birthplace, as originally that of humankind, was habit-ually—ontologically—ignored by the economic, managerial and accounting world he had been pursuing. As I wrote (10), in 2010:

> Most of the research in the social sciences, particularly in business, man-agement and economics, has lost touch with its 'social essence'. It is guided by rationalism and pragmatism, while humanism and holism have been left out of account. As a result it is seldom contextualised for a particular society. Moreover, it does not contribute to the resolution of the burning social issues of our time. As a result, we tend to look to governments and to corporations, but not to universities and to research establishments to help resolve our social, political and economic prob-lems.

What I did not realise at the time, but have come to recognise more recent-ly, is that exactly the same could be said of management generally, but, also, of both national and business accounting, reporting and auditing, specifically. For today, as indeed yesterday, what we may call 'social' reporting specifically, or now so-called 'impact' investing (see our opening chapter), is as severely stuck in the pragmatic and rational 'North-West' as is financial accounting, generally. The fact that we may call such reporting 'social', or that we may now purport to serve the *quadruple*—purpose, planet and people as well as profits (4 P's)—bottom line, makes little odds. The same outlook, or 'ontology' (the-ory of reality) prevails. So, the key to open up the fully integral door, as much for management or social accounting as for impact investment, was actually *integral research.* More specifically then, for Lessem and Schieffer (11):

> … the major differences between research in the natural, and that in the social, sciences, is that in the former case there is considered to be a scientific method, albeit duly incorporated into an R&D trajectory from invention to commercialisation. In the latter case, however, there

are many such social, scientific paths. In fact, because there are so many, the social researcher usually ends up not being able to see the wood for the trees. For that reason we have grouped such research methods, and methodologies, into four overall paths: relational, renewal, reason and realisation.

These four respectively Southern (relational), Eastern (renewal), Northern (reason) and Western (realisation) paths then, as I came to see it, potentially, though not actually, underlie the worlds of accounting and reporting, as much as they do, in their view, the worlds of research methodology, epistemology or ontology, or indeed economy and enterprise. Moreover, each of these paths has a particular foundation, or 'classical' research methodology, that is phenomenological (relational), interpretive (renewal), rational (reason) and empirical/positivist (realisation) respectively, to which intellectual giants have contributed over the past two to three centuries, and to which we now turn, starting with relational, life-like phenomenology.

4.2. Integral Accounting

4.2.1. Phenomenological Accounting: Relational: Community Building: South

The Rise and Fall of Management Accounting

The crisis in the sciences (and for Lessem in accounting as a management and social science), for the founding father of phenomenology, Moravia's Edmund Husserl (12) early in the last century, is mirrored by a crisis in the social and natural world. Indeed, for Husserl, who was a mathematician, the prevailing rational and empirical worldview, and market-based economy, so pervasive in the West, had lost touch with 'real' phenomena, lodged in a particular context, enterprise or life world.

Similarly, for two American accounting academics, Johnson and Kaplan (13), who wrote their now renowned book *Relevance Lost: The Rise and Fall of Management Accounting* in the 1980s, the profession of management accounting had lost its way. It had, for them, become a servant of number crunching with no clear picture of how to serve management's fundamental responsibility to build a healthy business. Thereafter, however, the two authors went in totally different ways. Robert Kaplan, also now renowned for his subsequent work (14) on *The Balanced Scorecard*, became a Professor at Harvard Business School. The new customer, people, process and money-oriented 'scorecard' he developed, as now an illustrious professor at my alma mater, retained its number-crunching credentials, even if different ones to the previous accounting norm. Meanwhile, Johnson took up an academic post at the much lesser known Portland State University in the US. Then, having become much less visible than his prominent Harvard ex-partner, he (15) turned to *profit beyond measure,* and to 'management by means' as opposed to conventional 'management by results'.

Profit Beyond Measure: Managing by Means

For Johnson (16), accounting had lost its relevance to nature, to community and to physical and human *life* in our Southern integral terms:

> Business leaders can now choose to either fashion organizations that trespass against nature's pattern or create organizations that blend harmoniously and constructively with the rest of nature, thus enhancing life... a company that manages by means will profit only by nurturing fundamental human and natural relationships, in contrast to the conventionally managed company that drives people to meet profit targets by sacrificing these relationships.

More specifically for Johnson, 'profit beyond measure' is oriented towards the health and long-term survival of the ecosystem that supports all human life. Relentless economic growth has a negative impact on the natural ecosystem—global warming, mass extinctions, loss of soil and so on—that threatens human existence in the long run. In this respect he was following the eminent ecological economist Herman Daly, who had warned, since the 1980s, that continued economic growth was entirely unsustainable in a final planet (17).

Management by means proposes a way to organise work that is slower, quieter, and more likely to ensure human survival in the Earth's ecosystem, while being sufficiently profitable to ensure the long-term survival of companies. Instead of viewing business as an institution that commercialises human technology, at any cost to human and natural relationships, management by means views business as a living system, through which humans use and transform technology to achieve a fuller life in harmony with other forms of life and with the system that sustains life on earth.

What, then, has this got to do with so-called 'phenomenology'?

The Spell of the Sensuous

For noted American phenomenologist and anthropologist David Abram (18) 'phenomenology' returns to the taken-for-granted realm of subjective experience, not to explain it, but simply to pay attention to its rhythms and textures. The true task of phenomenology, then, as he writes in *The Spell of the Sensuous,* lies in its careful demonstration of the way in which every theoretical and scientific practice grows out of, and remains supported by, the forgotten ground of our directly felt and lived experience. It has value and meaning only in reference to this primordial realm.

For Providence Human Capital in Zimbabwe, and its founder, Chipo Ndudzo, as we saw in the previous chapter:

> PHC has evolved to become a builder of relations tying together our family members in a culture of empathy and care that in turn supports the well-being of employees and the health of the societies we serve. As PHC health centres we have evolved to 'CHITUBU CHE-HUTANO'—fountain of well-being—that seeks to provide a holistic approach to Wellness. Awareness of grooming, reproductive health, general cleanliness, healthy eating and tips on healthy living are communicated to our clients at all times.

Key Relational Tenets: Unique, Natural, Moral, Authentic

Relational Foundation: Now, we turn to the key 'phenomenological' tenets of *relational* accounting. For the founder of phenomenology, Husserl, there is not one single life world, but a set of overlapping worlds. This 'home-world' extends to other worlds further away, the worlds of other cultures.

Uncover **Uniqueness**
Reveal **Natural** and Communal Essences
Go Beyond Surface 'Facts' to Underlying **Moral** Values
Locate what is Particular to the Place that makes you **Authentic**ally Who You Are?

Table 4.2.1 Tenets of Phenomenology – Relational Accounting

Besides rejecting objective accounts of reality, phenomenologists such as Husserl, were also critical of the narrow, reductionist models of human experience found in empiricism. What are the key tenets of their approach?

Uncover Unique Origins: Husserl, as we have seen, viewed a particular life world as the universal framework of human endeavour, including, for us, the fundamental basis for accounting. To that extent, it is foolhardy to focus on the financial results of Facebook, in isolation from the study of the unique 'life world' of Mark Zuckerberg, specifically, and of social media, generally. The same applies, as we shall see, to Saqib in relation to Akhuwat (Chapter 6) or to Oshodi in relation to CISER (Chapter 10).

Illuminate Essences: Secondly, for Husserl, phenomenology is concerned with what you experience or feel directly, not what you think about empirically or do practically. As such, it seeks to avoid all preconceptions placed on such experience, in advance, whether these are drawn from religious or cultural traditions, or indeed from science itself. Explanations are not to be imposed, externally, on you, before the phenomena have been understood, internally, by you. They are to be experienced, by you, from within. So the natural way to manage, for Johnson, would be to discover and nurture appropriate relationships and wait for results to emerge spontaneously, like a skilled gardener who knows that properly caring for the soil is enough.

Tap into Underlying Values: Thirdly, for Husserl, true science, including social 'science' generally, and accounting, specifically, comes from a very special attitude: one of detached playfulness and curiosity. Each of us has the potential to be a Saqib (Chapter 6) or an Oshodi (Chapter 10), for example, because of the love we have for what we do. Our passion to be authentic to who we are, individually and communally, is the source of our ability to act with integrity. Accounting, for such, involves a rich description of the nature and scope of things, just as we see in a chapter of a powerful novel or short story.

Be Authentic to Who You Are: As such, every unique person, culture, community and indeed 'life world' needs to be authentic to the stories (s)he/ we are historically, and prospectively, becoming. To that extent, for example, Akhuwat's story is its own story, part of Pakistan's story, and the world's story. To the same extent, Ndudzo's story is part of PHC's story, and is part of Zimbabwe's story.

An Overall Southern Relational Enterprise Perspective

Black Consciousness: Indeed, for the late Steve Biko—the architect of *Black Consciousness,* in 1970s South Africa—Africans, being a pre-scientific people, do not recognise any conceptual cleavage between the natural and the supernatural. They experience, or become deeply involved with, a situation rather than face a problem. This means that they allow both the rational and the non-rational elements to make an impact upon them. Hence, any action they may take could be described more as an engaged response of the total personality to the situation than the result of some mental or rational undertaking by a purely 'economic man', or 'profit maximising' business (wo)man. For Biko (20) then:

> In rejecting western values, therefore, we are rejecting those things that are not only foreign to us but that seek to destroy the most cherished of our beliefs—that the cornerstone of society is man himself—not just his welfare, not his material being, but just man himself with all his ramifications. We reject the power-based society of the westerner that seems to be ever concerned with perfecting their technological knowhow while losing out on their spiritual dimension.

Biko believed that in the long run, the special contribution from Africa would be in the field of human relationships. The great powers of the world may have done wonders in giving the world an industrial and military look, but the great gift, still, has to come from Africa: giving the world a human face. This is close to Edmund Husserl's perspective, philosophically, in entering wholeheartedly into the 'life world' of self and other, despite the fact that he and Biko were far apart, in terms of place and time. Husserl (21), in fact, writes in '*ubuntu*-like' terms:

> Personal life means living communalised as 'I' and 'we', within a community horizon, and this in communities of various forms—family, nation, supra-national community. It involves purposeful life, the term life in this context not having a physiological sense, but in the broadest sense creating culture in the unity of a historical development of a particular life world, and person-in-community.

At this point, we turn from South to East and from phenomenology to interpretivism. In integral terms, this involves a shift from the relational path to the path of renewal, and, thereby, from Africa to Asia.

4.2.2. Interpretive Accounting: Renewal Path: Conscious Evolution: East

The Management of Flow

According to the eminent Japanese organisational sociologists Ikujiro Nonaka and Hirotaka Takeuchi (22), Japan's comparative advantage lies in the Eastern way it views knowledge. I began to understand this more fully during the three years that I was fortunate enough to work closely with Nonaka. As they see it, in the West, the theory of organisation has long been dominated by a paradigm that conceptualises the firm as a system that 'processes' information, 'solves' problems, or 'trains' leaders. This paradigm points towards an 'input–process–output' sequence of hierarchical information processing, familiar to management accountants and auditors alike.

A critical problem with this approach is its rational and pragmatic, as opposed to holistic and humanistic, view of the world. Information processing is viewed as a problem-solving activity which centres on what is externally given to the organisation, without due consideration being accorded to what is internally created by it. Such a Western or Northern approach emphasises the absolute, depersonalised, and non-human nature of knowledge. As such, it is typically expressed in propositions and formal logic. By contrast, Nonaka and Takeuchi (23), as Japanese 'Easterners', consider knowledge to be a dynamic human process of justifying personal belief, with a view to finding the truth. Any organisation that dynamically deals with a changing environment ought not only to process information efficiently. Rather, it must also creatively transform information into knowledge, in support of a meaningful purpose.

Rather than existing as self-contained, atom-like statistics or data, we exist, or come into being—from such a processual, Eastern flow perspective—as interdependent with the world (for us 'worlds'), through our interactions with others. As such, we are active beings, seeking to define, redefine and ultimately *renew* ourselves. Equally, we reform the environment through our interactions with it, by asking the question: what is the *purpose* of our life? Interestingly, the originator of double-entry accounting in the 16th century, the Italian polymath Luca Pacioli, a close friend of Leonardo da Vinci (see Chapter 2), wrote a seminal work on *Divine Proportion*. He recognised that being in close touch with harmonic forces in the world required accounting to become 'double-entry', which was integral to these harmonic forces. Even so, it is hermeneutics which provides a basis for accounting for renewal.

Origins of Hermeneutics

Hermeneutics may be described as the interpretive study of places, of people, of texts, with a view to their further evolution. Essentially, it involves cultivating the ability to understand things from somebody else's point of view, and to appreciate the cultural and social forces that may have influenced their outlook and prospects.

The leading 20th century hermeneutic philosopher Hans-Georg Gadamer (24) argued that people have a 'historically effected consciousness'. They are embedded in the particular history and culture that shaped them.

> In fact, history does not belong to us; but we belong to it. Long before we understand ourselves through the process of self-examination, we understand ourselves in a self-evident way in the family, society and state in which we live. The self-awareness of the individual is only a flickering in the closed circuits of historical life. That is why the prejudices of the individual, far more than his judgments, constitute the historical reality of his being.

Thus, interpreting a text involves a 'fusion of horizons' whereby the scholar, or for us the interpreter of national or enterprise 'accounts', is thereby concerned with the meaning, significance, and prospective evolution, of a society or an enterprise, naturally and culturally, as well as socially and economically.

Key Tenets of Renewal: Originate, Empathise, Co-construct, Regenerate

More specifically, in the process, as below, you need to account for: how to reconnect with your source; give 'the Other' a voice; understand how your world is constructed; with a view to reconstructing, within your tradition, in the light of modernity, and vice versa.

Reconnect with your **Origins**
Empathise with 'the Other'
Understand how your World is **'Co-constructed'**
Regenerate Tradition in the Light of Modernity

Table 4.2.2. Interpretive Hermeneutics: Accounting for Renewal

Reconnect with your Origins: You are incomplete and, therefore, unable to adequately function—individually, organisationally and societally—unless embedded in a specific cultural matrix. Hence, the cultural matrix 'completes' humans. The material objects you create, the ideas you hold, and actions you take are shaped in a fundamental way by the social framework in which you are raised. Your task then, in such accounting, is to interpret the multitudinous and conflicting ways in which various worlds around you are constructed and human meanings developed, and co-evolve something new, and worthwhile, out of all of these.

Historically, you, your enterprise or society always becomes what it is by projecting itself out of your past, your lived inheritance. In Zimbabwe we call this your *nhaka*. Your 'destiny' is what comes out of yourself, individually and collectively. It is the prospects of your history and the possibilities of your generation. As such, in many 'developing' societies, if not also enterprises, accounting requires a 'return' to history, as a cultural and political recovery of the oppressed historic possibilities in the existence of the colonised. However, the 'return' is not meant to be a return to tradition or stasis. Rather, you are engaged in the affirmation of, and thereby accounting for, who you both are, and could be.

Empathise with the Other: The pursuit of interpretive accounting, secondly, serves to expand your awareness of the interconnectedness between different levels of activity—natural and social, individual and organisational, communal and societal—in what we term a developmental ecosystem. This incorporates an interpretive understanding of your context as a whole, trans-personally as well as cross-culturally, with a view to catalysing further development. As a result, it is especially suited for working across boundaries, and for the co-evolution of the local and the global, between culture and economy, between one enterprise and another.

Even so, such a pursuit poses an epistemic (knowledge-based) problem: if others live within their own framework and you live within yours, how can you understand them? Furthermore, how do you evolve the future (modernity) out of the past (tradition)? That is where hermeneutics comes in. As such, for the interpretively inclined, the basic question of such accounting ought to be whether understanding others—particularly others who are different—is possible, and if so, what does such understanding involve, and how can we account for, and co-evolve or renew, such, accordingly?

Understand your Co-constructed World: In such interpretive accounting, thirdly, the primary aim of such is to develop an understanding or 'account' of how your world is 'co-constructed,' in multifaceted, transdisciplinary guise. The notion of your individual or institutional world being constructed implies that it is complex, interdependent, and can be viewed from different perspectives. Hermeneutic accounting involves you in uncovering historical and cultural horizons of meaning—that is, if you like, interactive storylines—building, narratively, on what you individually, organisationally, societally are becoming, through what is mutually experienced.

This lived self-formation, of a fusion of horizons, becomes the practice of GENE-uine freedom. It involves emerging (locally-globally) from your prior (local) grounding, with a view to (globally) navigating towards a new (global-local) effect. This is the hermeneutical response to the emergent question, in the context of this book: what are the people of Africa through Providence or CISER, or in the Near East through Akhuwat, trying to free themselves from, in order to become? This brings us to tradition and modernity.

Renew Tradition in the Light of Modernity: The need to revitalise tradition by adding on new elements is the consequence of two main factors: internal criticism of the tradition, undertaken from time to time, and the appropriation of worthwhile exogenous ideas, values and practices. The causal factors of cultural change or transformations of tradition are, therefore, internally and externally induced. The success in moulding and appropriating the elements of an alien culture is determined by the adaptive capacity of the indigenous one. For Saqib and Malik (25), in respect of Akhuwat:

> Akhuwat's community-building *ihsan* (excellence) multiplier in the form of creating a chain (*silsilah*) then emanates from love for humanity and one's community. This love originates in the form of universal love, i.e., love for the Creator and consequently HIS creation, which forms the basis of Mawakhat (solidarity) in this case. *Silsilah*, an Arabic word, also used in Persian, Malay and Urdu, means chain, link, connection, and is often used in various senses of lineage. In particular, it may be translated as '(religious) order' or 'spiritual genealogy', which has been evolved into our GENE-alogy.

From general hermeneutics we turn to Eastern hermeneutics, as that is where we have positioned such interpretive accounting.

Eastern Hermeneutics

Bahraini educationalist, Zahra al-Zeera (26) writes, in the course of her own PhD studies in Canada, in her book *Wholeness and Holiness in Education:*

> The goal of locating my study in hermeneutics is to increase the understanding of how the East and the West came to misunderstand each other. Being the child of East and West I had learnt to compare languages and cultures, histories and personalities. My two selves were in continuous dialogue, even conflict. Since hermeneutics involved dialogue, and dialectical interchange, I came to realize that my own dialectic would involve love rather than hate. I realized that my longstanding struggle was rooted in my feelings of insecurity that I might lose my Arabic/ Eastern identity in the West.

Similarly, Ibrahim Abouleish (27)—the founder of Sekem in Egypt, which has become one of the most renowned 'ecovillages' in the world—reflected on himself as a young Egyptian doing his doctoral studies in Austria, in his book *Sekem: A Sustainable Community in the Egyptian Desert*:

> During my studies, I noticed inner changes taking place within me. I became thoroughly involved with European culture, getting to know its music, studying its poetry and philosophy. Somebody looking into my soul would have seen anything 'Egyptian' left completely behind, so I could absorb everything new. Because of my childhood and adolescent grounding in Egyptian culture, I could not leave such entirely behind. I now existed in two worlds, both of which were essentially different: the oriental, spiritual stream I was born into and the European, which I felt was my chosen course. But I was neither Egyptian nor European. I realised this particularly when I was experiencing art. For example I started hearing Händel's Messiah with Muslim ears as praise to Allah. The two differing worlds within me gradually began to dissolve and merge into a third entity.

In both cases, what is being accounted for, by al-Zeera and Abouleish, is interpretive in nature and scope, identifying a fusion of East-West horizons. For Abouleish, Sekem itself became a fusion of East and West, and South and North, as an integral enterprise.

As we rotate to the path of reason, we reach, what Tony Bradley (28) refers to as 'Semiotic Economics', which we apply to accounting, but starting from a well-reasoned, Northern theory of the firm.

4.2.3. Semiotic Accounting: Path of Reason: Knowledge Creation

Semiotic GENEalogy

To paraphrase Bradley's outline in Chapter 7, the 'rational' is not always sensible or meaningful. As he puts it, 'There are worlds of economic meaning that fall outside the narrow equations, econometrics and graphs of neoliberal economics.' Semiotics is the study of how meanings are made, interpreted, communicated and utilised, in a fourfold process. But, at least in the way 'rationally' laid out here, this is not a discipline that has often been applied to alternative economic models. This is the approach he has termed as 'Semiotic Economics'.

The point of semiotics (path of reason)—taking on from where phenomenology (relational path) and hermeneutics (renewal path) leave off, in a specifically economic and financial context—is to identify how the meaning-systems of economic models are cultural, dependent on local context and contingent on historical formations. The task of Semiotic Economics is to understand these specific cultural particularities, in terms of the meaning-systems that undergird them. One part of this enterprise is to recognise the singularity of neoliberalism, as well as the many alternative economic models that pertain in specific cultures and contexts. In the Table below, Bradley has related this to our four worlds, and to the GEN*E*, pertaining to alternative cultural models of accounting.

As we will see in Chapter 7, by applying semiotics to economics, using the integral rhythm, we are able to specify a precise fourfold methodology for semiotic economic analysis and, hence, accounting practice. This involves identifying the object of economic accounting, its 'subterranean' meaning-making archetype, the sign-system used to convey this meaning and (some of) the range of examples and cases in which this conveyed meaning is used. The following Table offers exemplars of this approach related to Southern, Eastern, Northern and Western worlds. Equally, in the subsequent chapter, we will see further examples that Bradley gives, including the way the Semiotic Economics methodology works out in respect of the pervasive model of 'Western-global' neoliberalism.

FOURFOLD SEMIOTIC ACCOUNTING	AN ECONOMIC OBJECT (G)	ARCHETYPE OF SIGNIFICATION (E) Meaningful question that the archetype conveys	SIGN OF ECONOMIC SIGNIFICANCE (N)	EFFECTIVE (E) EXEMPLAR INNOVATIONS
NHAKANOMIC ACCOUNTING (SHONA AFRICAN) (S)	Inheritance	Traditions and legacy What is developing our heritage?	Community holding	Communal land, property and resource holdings e.g. Zimbabwean Tribal Trust Lands, Mexican Ejidos
SOUL-IDARITY ACCOUNTING (SUFI ISLAM) (E)	Solidarity Capital	Ihsan How do we uncover the inner divine beauty?	Silsilah – Process of creating a chain of solidarity	Akhuwat - Pakistan and the diaspora community in the UK
CO-OPERATIVE ACCOUNTING (CATHOLIC ENCYCLICALS) (N)	Social health (real prosperity)	Love How do we create true wealth?	Social value	Mondragon Co-operatives and other such co-operative enterprises/ constitutions
IMPACT ACCOUNTING (W)	Impact Investments	Value How do we make a difference?	QBLA (quadruple bottom line accounting) Purpose, People, Planet, Profit	GIIN and IRIS Qualitative and quantitative accounting measures

Table 4.2.3a Semiotic Genealogy

Source: after Bradley (28)

Semiotic Accounting: Key Tenets – Object, Archetype, Sign, Innovations

<u>Objects, Concepts and Forms</u>: As Bradley indicates, the discipline of semiotics developed during the late 19th and early 20th centuries, as the study of meanings and how these are communicated through signs and symbolic processes. Its founding fathers were American pragmatics philosopher C.S. Peirce and the French semantics exponent Ferdinand de Saussure (29). Their disciplines—as Peirce referred to semiotics, whilst de Saussure to semiology—overlap with socio-linguistics, the philosophy of language and hermeneutics.

But, as Bradley emphasises, the specific focus of semiotics is on the ways in which understanding is shaped through the relationships of language, image and media to the objects, concepts and forms that they seek to represent. In this respect, my work on *social reporting* (see above) was undertaken anticipating this semiotic light. As such, the specific tenets of semiotic accounting are laid out below by Tony Bradley, and are exemplified in terms of Impact Investment, alongside the integral GEN*E*alogy.

Identify the **Economic Object**
Uncover **Signification Archetypes**
Specify the **Sign to be Addressed**
Effect **Local Material Innovations**

Table 4.2.3b Semiotics: Rational Accounting
See: Chapter 7, after Bradley (28)

To use Bradley's own words:

1. <u>Identify the economic object</u> e.g. for impact accounting or impact investments. The key grounding object for the economics of impact investing is the investment itself. But, drill down deeper into this object and a spectrum for leveraging enhanced standard financial returns emerge, for example, by a ROI of political or other forms of social capital, such as trust-building amongst clients. Even so, we may regard the investment as the basic economic object.

2. <u>Uncover the cultural/spiritual/integral/archetypes of signification</u> e.g. the (initial pre-conscious) emergent desire to effect change and make a beneficial difference in the world, as the practical financial objects become clear. The stated purpose of impact investing is to enable investors to intentionally provide capital to challenge some of the world's most pressing social

and environmental needs and concerns. The emphasis is placed on the emergence of intentionality. Indeed, until relatively recently, much debate about accounting practices, in this sphere, had been predicated on the idea of triple bottom line accounting, which takes people and planet into account, alongside profit. But, more recently, a fourth 'p' of *purpose* has been added, in quadruple bottom line accounting (QBLA), which gets to the heart of the question surrounding archetypes of signification. Notably however, and unlike the cases of phenomenological and interpretive accounting, the means of calibration has not come into question.

3. Specify the sign/symbolic question (signifier) to be addressed e.g. how do we develop quadruple bottom line accounting? As suggested above, the sign-relation of impact investing is QBLA, with its emphasis placed on the 'purpose' underpinning an investment and the accounting procedures used to measure this meaning-system and its outputs. Beginning to fully investigate this sign-relation, then, it will be necessary to construct a Table such as 4.2.3a above, with its differentiated categories.

4. Effect the co-creation of local material innovations e.g. of impact investing. This fourth, completing, aspect of the GENEalogical cycle—in respect of the methodology of Semiotic Economics analysis—requires the co-creation of particular local cases in which the specific signification is being effected.

We now turn, finally, to positivist-oriented, standard, empirical accounts.

4.2.4. Positivist Accounts: Realisation Path: Sustainable Development

A Financial Theory of the Firm

The traditional and positivist view of business and accounting, finally, as reflected in Bigg, Wilson and Langton (30), and cited in my (31) original article on *Accounting for an Enterprise's Well-being,* runs as follows:

> Business transactions comprise the exchange of value, either in the form of money, or of goods and services which are measured and expressed in terms of money. Book-keeping is the systematic recording of such transactions in a manner which enables the financial relationship of a business with other persons to be clearly disclosed, and the cumulative effect of the transactions on the financial position of the business itself to be ascertained.

Classically, the 'firm' is typecast as a purely economic enterprise, whereby financially-oriented, monetary transactions reign supreme. In fact, what has transpired in the four decades or so since this article was written, with the advent of the United Nations SDG—Sustainable Development Goals and the like—is that the financial 'bottom line', as such, has been replaced by a 'quadruple bottom line' (see above), that is People, Planet, *Purpose* and Profit, but the same overall empirical and positivistic, Western mentality has prevailed, in relation, still, to 'the bottom line'. No wonder there has been no fundamental progress, in my view, toward an integral form of accounting that combines phenomenological, interpretive and semiotic, together with empirical accounts.

An Account of Empiricism and Positivism

Empiricism has certainly been the single most influential force in modern science, and most notably for us, in business and economics, including of course, finance and accounting. Empiricism, as such, is a theory of knowledge emphasising the role of sense-based experience in the formation of ideas, while discounting the notion of innate ideas, intuition, or subjectivity. Moreover, it is closely related to positivism—that is, seeking the 'positive' facts, rather than relying on pure faith or indeed dogma. Positivism (32) incorporates a Western ontology of an ordered universe made up of atomistic, discrete and observable events, typified by the economic marketplace, and by management accountants.

Scientific theories, in such empirical, positivist guise, are regarded as law-like statements, specifying simple relations or constant conjunctions between phenomena. Value judgments and normative statements, as such, require a separation of objective 'facts' or verifiable 'evidence' and subjective 'values'. Yet today, the self-same empiricism, free markets, national and enterprise accounting, and indeed liberal Western democracy, have been riding roughshod over the rest. This has led, in a straight line, to such phenomena as the election of a Donald Trump in America or a Brexit from the European Union in Britain. Consequently, we turn to the key tenets of empiricism.

Positive Accounting – Key Tenets: Facts, Values, Data, Systems

Seek after the 'Positive Facts' – Quantitative and Qualitative: The empiricist, as a researcher or an accountant, firstly, seeks after the 'positive' facts, rather than relying on pure faith or indeed, dogma. In an accounting context, these 'facts' are reflected in specific measures, on the one hand based *quantitatively* by numerical statistics—be they financially, environmentally or socially based (e.g. SDGs or 'training days')—or, on the other hand, *qualitatively* based on surveys of 'happiness', 'morale' and the like. Only that which can be observed, that is experienced by the senses, can be regarded as real.

Seek after the **'Positive Facts'**
Separate Facts and **Values**
Collect Data and Build Inductive Theories
Control through **'Closed Systems'**

Table 4.2.4. Empiricism – Key Tenets

Empirically speaking, moreover, 'facts' need to be separated from 'values'.

Separate Facts and Values: Value judgments and normative statements, secondly, in this empirically based approach to national, social or management accounting, require a separation of 'facts' and 'values', whereby values are denied having an equivalent status of knowledge. The grounds for origination are lodged entirely and objectively in the external world 'out there', as, for example, financial, numerically documented accounts, rather than in the internal and subjective world of personal and interpersonal individual and communal, narrative accounts, on the path to realisation.

Collect Data and Build Inductive Theories: The logical positivist, moreover, uses induction, analytically, to collect observational data, and then build theories—indeed a set of trading accounts, national accounts or balance sheets—to explain the observations. The method of induction refers to a logical process of constructing knowledge about observed relationships between variables in specific instances. This can be taken as a basis for making universal generalisations, about, for example, the 'financial health' of a company, or the 'economic health' of a country in as yet, unobserved, particular instances. As such an accountant, you identify a limited number of numerical variables, such as GNP or GDP, financial profit or loss, and hence observe their behaviour and the changes of one in relation to the other. Therefore, you identify factors, which are significant—within this positivist framework but not necessarily in terms of *semiotic* significance, as above—so their effect can be observed. Through this method, you argue, factors are pinpointed, and directions of causation, in respect of the observed outcome, are identified.

Control through 'Closed Systems': With a view to such, economic or management accounting occurs finally within 'closed systems', enabling you to isolate the objects you wish to investigate from all other objects, which would confuse the picture. Such a 'closed system' means that in addition to the identification of variables and the observation of their behaviour, you avoid any interference from unexpected external forces, such as typically and problematically, today, environmental ones. Exclusion clauses ensure that the mass of possible influences are screened out (*ceteris paribus*). It is you who controls the situation by manipulating variables.

4.3. Conclusion

4.3.1. Positivist Epistemology of Social Physics

Overall then, such positivist, empirical approaches to the social sciences, generally, and to business, management and accounting studies, specifically, often and exclusively claim the label of 'scientific'. The assumption is that things can be studied as hard facts, and the relationship between these facts established as solid, empirically based, scientific laws. For such positivists, these laws have the status of truth, as social or financial objects, or indeed 'market forces', and can be studied in much the same way as natural objects. Not surprisingly, classical and neo-classical economics, with its belief in 'market mechanisms' is heavily influenced by positivism. Arguably, neoliberalism has taken this one step further, by incorporating the political values of conservative populist ideology into the economics and, equally, claiming these as positivist facts and 'iron laws' of globalised markets.

Indeed, the most influential early positivist in the social sciences was the French 19th century sociologist Auguste Comte. To replace 'divine truths', Comte looked to the natural sciences, calling his approach 'social physics'. Comte sought to identify the laws of social statics and social dynamics with a view to social engineering. The English utilitarian Jeremy Bentham, following in Comte's footsteps, characterised human beings as either pleasure-seeking or pain-avoiding, based on their making rational choices. This approach treated aggregate bodies as the total of individual actors, with a view to gaining 'the greatest good for the greatest number'. Thus, utilitarianism was born. The economy became an aggregate of individuals, firms and households; the political process an aggregate of voters in elections, which could be counted, together with parties and pressure groups; and the business enterprise became an aggregate of debits and credits, assets and liabilities, profits and losses, supply and demand.

But, as is argued in Bradley's Semiotic Economics, and by each of us in this volume, all of these positivist and empiricist assumptions placed together, are merely one meaning-making system amongst many. As we have sought to show, there are other models of accounting practice that can be based on phenomenology, hermeneutics and semiotics. We do not wish to deny *any* place to positivist accounting practices. Rather, we wish to indicate that the latter is only one, Western approach. But, problematically, it is not a West that builds on the rest.

4.3.2. Integral Accounting Revisited

Integral Accounts

In an empirically based accounting system, and the Western, positivist ontology that underlies it, whether we are thereby focused on a single or on a quadruple 'bottom line', the end result is almost, if not quite, the same. In Table 4.3.2., on the other hand, we have articulated, at least in outline, a set of integral accounts, whereby the easily recognisable Western empirical accounts, whether in the form of national or business accounts, are constituted of facts and data, while being supposedly free, and contained within a closed, monetary and financial system. To the extent, moreover, that such accounts are 'open' to environmental or social *data*, such as performance in relation to SDG ecological footprints, or 'well-being surveys', we maintain that they retain their positivistic, empirical character. As such, they remain an important part of an integral whole—25% of such, at the most, so to speak—whilst the other 75%, we would argue, is left out of the completed accounts.

In other words, the data collected, the value-free measures, and the supposedly positive facts, remain part of a 'Westernised' closed economic and enterprise system, that is closed to the natural and communal phenomena of the South, the cultural and spiritual interpretations of the East, and the semiotic science and technology of the North. No wonder, then, that 'social reporting' has remained stuck in a rut for four decades, if three quarters of the world, ontologically speaking, are left out in the cold.

Impact Investment's Failure to Integrate

In relation to 'the theory of the firm', the concept of a business enterprise, and of entrepreneurship, if not also leadership, so rules the roost that the organisation as an 'information-space', a 'management of flows', and one that lends itself to 'profit beyond measure' does not even get a look in. Ultimately then, 'accounting', as conventionally derived, is like a four-legged animal with only one leg able to function. To that extent, for us, the quadruple bottom lines may serve to strengthen that one empirical leg, but, overall, we remain, ontologically and organisationally, fundamentally dysfunctional.

Indeed, this is borne out today most vividly in the proliferating field of *Impact Investing*, introduced by Robert Dellner in our opening chapter and to which Tony Bradley will be further alluding in Chapter 7. While this is a field, which in practical and financial terms is growing like topsy, with ever more companies and individuals wanting to realise a social and environmental as well as an economic, return, the methods of 'accounting' for such still come out of the 'Stone Age', so to speak.

In fact, and interestingly enough, the founding fathers in the field, such as Jed Emerson (33) in *The Purpose of Capital: Elements of Impact, Financial Flows, and Natural Being,* who has authored seven books on social entrepreneurship and impact investing, is a wise man indeed, with wide-ranging insights into the world at large. Even so, even an Emerson fails to systematically map out such a field, into which trillions of dollars are being invested. The same could be said for his American colleague Benjamin Bingham (34) in his *Making Money Matter: Impact Investing to Change the World.* It is much as if the 'impact investment' emperor has only rags, whereby the social and the environmental, and even more so the cultural, are altogether left out of account. This is something we will seek to purposefully remedy (see Chapter 10) in the concluding sections of this volume. But next, we now turn to the *Islamic* financial world, from an all-round, integral perspective, starting in the South.

ACCOUNTING ONTOLOGY	ONTOLOGICAL TRAJECTORY	SUBJECT REALM	THEORY OF THE FIRM	ACCOUNTING ATTRIBUTES
Southern Phenomeno-logical Accounting	Grounding & Origination	Nature And Community	Community Building/Profit BeyondMeasure	Unique; Natural; Moral; Authentic.
Eastern Interpretive Accounting	Emergent Foundation	Culture and Spirituality	Conscious Evolution/ Managing Flow	Originate; Empathize; Co-construct; Regenerate.
Northern Semiotic Accounting	Emancipatory Navigation	Science, Systems and Technology	Knowledge Creation/ Organisational Objects, Concepts and Meanings	Object; Archetype; Sign; Innovations.
Western Empirical Accounting	Transformative Effect	Economy and Enterprise	Sustainable Development/ Business Enterprise	Positive Facts; Value-Free Measures; Data Collection; Closed System.

Table 4.3.2. Integral Accounts

4.4. Bibliography

1 **Chapra** U (1992) *Islam and the Economic Challenge.* Leicester. Islamic Foundation

2 **Akomolafe** B (2017) *These Worlds Beyond our Fences: Letters to My Daughter on Humanity's Search for Home.* Berkeley. California, North Atlantic Books

3 **Lessem** R (1974) Accounting for an Enterprise's Well-being. *Omega Journal of International Management Science,* 2, 1, 77–95

4 **Campbell**, D E (2004) Using financial accounting methods to further develop and communicate environmental accounting using Emergy. *Paper presented at University of Florida 3rd Biennial Emergy Conference*, Gainesville, FL, January 29–31, 2004.

5 **Lessem** R (1977) *Corporate Social, Reporting in Action.* Journal of General Management, March 1, 1977

6 **Lessem** R (2001) *Managing in Four Worlds: Culture, Strategy and Transformation.* Long Range Planning, 34. Pages 9–32

7 **Lessem** R and **Schieffer** A (2009) *Transformation Management: Toward the Integral Enterprise.* Abingdon. Routledge

8 **Lessem** R and **Schieffer** A (2010) *Integral Economics: Releasing the Economic Genius of your Society.* Abingdon. Routledge

9 **Lawson** T (1997) *Economics and Reality.* Abingdon. Routledge

10 **Lessem** R and **Schieffer** A (2010) *Integral Research and Innovation: Transforming Enterprise and Society.* Abingdon. Routledge

11 **Lessem** R and **Schieffer** A (2010) *op cit*

12 **Husserl** E (1970) *The Crisis of the European Sciences.* Chicago. North-Western University Press

13 **Johnson** T and **Kaplan** R (1987) *Relevance Lost: The Rise and Fall of Management Accounting.* Boston. Harvard Business Review Press

14 **Kaplan** R and **Norton** D (1996) *The Balanced Scorecard.* Boston. Harvard Business Review Press

15 **Johnson** H.T and **Broms** A (2000) *Profit Beyond Measure. Extraordinary Results through Attention to Work and People.* New York. Free Press

16 **Johnson** H.T and **Broms** A (2000) *op cit*

17 **Daly**, H E (1991) *Steady-State Economics* (2nd Edn.). New York. Island Press

18 **Abram** D (1997) *The Spell of the Sensuous.* New York. Vintage Books

19 **Ndudzo** C (2019) PHC Becoming an Integral Enterprise – Unpublished PhD Thesis (forthcoming). Johannesburg. Da Vinci Institute

20 **Biko** S (1987) *I Write What I Like.* London. Heinemann

21 **Husserl** E (1970) *op cit*

22 **Nonaka** I and **Takeuchi** H (1995) *The Knowledge Creating Company: How Japanese Companies Create the Dynamics of Innovation.* Oxford. Oxford University Press.

23 **Nonaka** I, **Toyama** R and **Hirata** T (2008) *Managing Flow: A Process Theory of the Knowledge Based Firm.* New York. Palmgrave Macmillan

24 **Gadamer** H G (2004) *Truth and Method.* London. Continuum

25 **Saqib,** A and **Malik,** A *Integral Finance – Akhuwat: A Case Study of the Solidarity economy.* Abingdon. Routledge, 2019

26 **Al Zeera** Z (2001) *Wholeness and Holiness in Education: An Islamic Perspective.* Leicester. International Institute of Islamic Thought
27 **Abouleish** I and **Kirchgessner** M (2005) *Sekem: A Sustainable Community in the Egyptian Desert.* Edinburgh. Floris
28 **Bradley** T (2019) Introducing the Semiotic Economics of Alternative Economic Systems. *Liverpool Hope Business School, Working Papers,* 2. May
29 **Corrington** R (1993) *An Introduction to C.S. Peirce: Philosopher, Semiotician and Ecstatic Naturalist.* New York. Rowman and Littlefield
30 **Bigg**, A E, **Wilson** H and **Langton** A (1961) *Practical Book-Keeping and Commercial Knowledge.* HFL, London.
31 **Lessem** R (1974) *op cit*
32 **Lessem** R and **Schieffer** A (2010) *op cit*
33 **Emerson** J (2018) *The Purpose of Capital: Elements of Impact, Financial Flows, and Natural Being.* San Francisco. Blended Value Group Press
34 **Bingham** B (2015) *Making Money Matter: Impact Investing to Change the World.* San Francisco. Prospects Press

PART THREE

Integral, Semiotic and Islamic Finance in Practice

CHAPTER 5

Africa's Triple Heritage:
Indigenous, Christian, Islamic: South

Anselm Adodo, Paxherbals, Director

Jubril Adeojo, SMEFUNDS Capital Ltd, Co-Founder

Ntu... life, force, to live strongly, vital force. In calling upon God, the spirits, or the ancestral spirits, the Bantu asks above all 'give me force'. What we brand as magic is in their eyes nothing but setting to work natural forces placed at the disposal of man by God to strengthen man's vital energy.

Placide Tempels, Bantu Philosophy

Ask and it will be given to you; seek and you will find; knock and the door will be opened to you. For everyone who asks receives; the one who seeks finds; and to the one who knocks, the door will be opened.

Matthew 7:7–8, Gospel of Matthew,
New International Version of The Bible, *Biblica Inc.*

Ibn Khaldun's word for social organization was *itjima*. In going beyond this primordial account of the origin of the human community, he accounted for a particular society's relative cohesion or integrity by measuring its degree of *asabiyah*. In his dialectical model such depicted communal solidarity. In fact Ibn Khaldun reckoned that the presence or relative lack of *asabiyah* constituted the single most important trait that distinguished the nature of one society from another.

Stephen Dale, *The Orange Trees of Marrakesh:
Ibn Khaldun and the Science of Man*

5.1. Introduction

5.1.1. The Triple African Heritage: Semitic Impact: Judaism, Christianity, Islam

The most successful Semitic religion in the world, for the late, great Islamic philosopher of Africa, Ali Mazrui, is Christianity; the most successful Semitic language is Arabic; the most successful people globally are the Jews. Contemporary Africa's triple heritage of indigenous, Islamic and Western legacies is just the modern culmination of a much older triple heritage of indigenous, Semitic and Greco-Roman influences on Africa. The ancient Semitic strand has now narrowed and focused more firmly on Arab and Islamic influences, whilst the ancient Greco-Roman strand has now expanded to encompass wider European and American intrusions.

Every society tends to have two paramount myths: the myth of ancestry (how the society started and developed), and the myth of mission or purpose (what is special about the society in terms of human values). For example, in Africa, Ethiopia's myth of origin is heavily Hebraic, their Royal House tracing its origins back to King Solomon and the Queen of Sheba, with Emperor's title having been the 'Lion of Judah'. Ethiopian Christianity, moreover, is Judaeo-Christian.

Even so, the Jewish influence in Africa, as such, is indirect; that is, via Christianity and Islam. The Jewish myth of origin, for example, the Genesis creation accounts, including that of humanity, with Adam and Eve in the Garden, has been replacing Africa's own tribal myths of origin. Monotheism has been conquering Africa under the banner of either the cross or the crescent, but behind both banners is the shadow of Moses and the Commandments he conveyed. Then, the third Jewish impact on Africa is through the Jewish experience as a metaphor for the African predicament. The Jewish release from slavery in Egypt, under Moses' leadership, has captured the imagination of many an African nationalist, throwing off the yoke of colonialism. Chief Albert Luthuli entitled his book *Let My People Go*, echoing Moses' demand to the Pharaoh.

But, even more weighty than the Jewish factor, in Africa's historical experience, has been the Arab factor. First, there is language. There is no doubt, for example, that Kiswahili in East Africa is the product of interaction between Arab culture and African linguistic structures. The Arab conquest of North Africa in the seventh and eighth centuries, moreover, initiated two processes: Arabization through language, and Islamization through religion. Africa in fact, for Mazrui, is a cultural bazaar. A wide variety of ideas and values, for Mazrui, drawn from different civilisations, competes for the attention of potential African buyers. This marketing of cultures in Africa has been going on for centuries. But a particularly important impact has come from the Semites (especially Arabs and Jews) and the Caucasians (especially Western Europeans). This is the background for understanding African ontology in every aspect, including finance, which is both indigenous and Semitic.

5.2. Indigenous Heritage: Re-GENE-rating African Ontology

5.2.1. Going to the Roots

The African world, for me (Anselm Adodo) indigenously and exogenously (herein most specifically in relation to Islam) is inherently religious. Granted, the word 'religious' has, today, come to conjure negative images of fanaticism, religiosity, mental and psychological bondage. Many people do not want to be described as 'religious', as such a label could be a complete turn-off for others. Yet, in African ontology, being religious has a very different meaning and connotation. The African 'religious' worldview is fundamentally radical, in the sense of *radix*, going to the roots.

Many development workers, international development and aid agencies, corporations and global economic analysts, have wondered for so long why the African political, economic and social system seems to defy all known paths of progress. It appears to defy, and cannot be captured within, the Euro-American framework of analysis. Euro-American economists are still inventing ways of interpreting the African economic landscape. What could be the problem? Why is Africa different from other continents—which it is?

In the first place, as Nigerian writer and Nobel Laureate, Wole Soyinka observed, Africa is the only continent that was not discovered by anyone. We know that Columbus 'discovered' America. However, no one has ever claimed to have discovered Africa. Africa has always been there. Africa, then, is the original first world, not the third. Secondly, while many other races can claim to have been colonised, no colonisation can be compared in scale, scope, brutality and shape to what Africa has experienced (1).

5.2.2. The Threat of Epistemicide

For over 400 years, Africa was completely and comprehensively taken over: politically, socially, economically, culturally, psychologically, mentally, militarily and religiously. It was a subjugation the like of which the world has never seen. Africa's artificially created nation-states are, latterly, practising an imported form of democracy, the principles of which they neither understand nor believe in. They are operating economic models which they do not understand,

and which are not built on their worldview. Nevertheless, Africa must pretend to adhere to these, in order to have any recognition on the global space. They are running a system of education they inherited from their colonial rulers which they often criticise, yet are not able to change. This means that even the process of knowledge creation and how knowledge is applied is grounded in Western epistemology; an epistemicide, as De Souza Santos (2) describes it.

5.2.3. Donor Funds Won't Solve the Problem of Underdevelopment

In this chapter we argue that a review of African ontology and epistemology in light of modern realities is crucial to a new understanding of Africa, not least in respect of finance and financial institutions. The future and fortunes of our world will depend on how we all manage the issue of an increasingly poor Africa (representing the world's poor) and an increasingly wealthy North/West (representing the wealthiest 10% of the world population). Who is leading the discussion about Africa and the world's so-called bottom billion today?

The discussions about Africa and African realities are being led mainly by Euro-American politicians and financial institutions, together with China and the new form of African sinoisation. African leaders, including her scholars, intellectuals and thinkers, are standing by the roadside, waiting, with bowls in hand for donor funds and interventions for running their government, feeding their population or conducting research. However, history has shown that donor funds have not and never will help to solve the problem of underdevelopment in Africa (3, 4, 5).

Many Western-trained Africans passionately argue that implementing Western-formulated economic policies, and the application of Western financial models will help to catapult Africa into the so-called 'first world' (6). However, this is only a pipe dream. As the world becomes ever more digitalised and commercialised, the need for Africa to reconnect with her origin, and re-GENE-rate her sources and resources is more urgent and critical than ever before, lest she loses her soul. How, then, can Africa reconnect with her inner resources? The first step is to revisit the African epistemology.

5.2.4. Indigenous African Rhythm

Sound as a Mode of Gaining Knowledge: An African Epistemology

For the Traditional African, the Drum is the carrier of the Word, the primordial sacred Sound by which the world came into being. The Drum is to the Traditional African what the Bible is to the Christian, and the Qur'an is to the Muslim. The Drum is the supreme symbol of God's incarnation, of God among us, which is depicted in the Greek word, Logos. The African Logos is the sacrament of the Divine in the human, of spirit in matter, Sacred in the profane. Sound, for the African, is an emotive and creative force. Through the medium of Sound, the African can evoke and manipulate potent psychic forces (7).

In the beginning was Thought. Thought became Desire, and life came into being, for where Desire is, there is life. Where there is no Desire, there is no life. Desire became Allurement, and Love came into being, for where there is Allurement, there is Love. Where there is no Allurement, there is no Love. Love became Word. From Word came the primordial Sound, the I Am or the Other, which has been described in different ways in many religious traditions. For the Yoruba of western Nigeria, the great Other is Olodumare, the Supreme Being, while the Igbo of Eastern Nigeria calls this Other 'Chukwu'. Whatever name is given to this Supreme Being, Sound is the medium through which human beings interact with the Supreme Other.

Where there is Sound there is a Response, for Response is a sign of life. Where there is no Response there is death, for to die means to cease to respond. The physical sign of Response is movement. Movement is the most noticeable thing about the cosmos. When movement is organised, rhythmic and calculated, it is called Dance. Dance is the response of the cosmos and its inhabitants to the silent echoes of the primordial creative Word, Dahbar, Logos, Sound, through which the world was created and is maintained. Dance is not just a body movement, but also a way of life. Dance is a mission, a vocation, and a responsibility. When Dance leads to greater harmony of the cosmic elements, or the increase of the vital force of creation, or promotes a clearer vision of the bond between human beings, spirits and animals, or rebinds humanity to Olodumare, Chukwu, the Supreme Other, or heals the wounds of alienation or helps to sustain the rhythms of creation, it is called Work. To work, then, is to take part in the Cosmic Dance of creation (8).[1]

There is Not One But Many Modes of Knowing

George Worgul (9) argues that from the Renaissance up until today, the epistemological attitude of Western Euro-America is that man/woman is a

1 **Editor's footnote**: This wonderful exposition of African roots could, equally, be applied to the Celtic lands of the Northern world. Recent historical and DNA analysis indicates that the Celts came out of Africa, with a very strong genetic link to the Berber and Tuareg peoples of North Africa. Perhaps the semiotic importance of rhythm, music, dance to the peoples of Ireland, Scotland, Wales and the North-Western fringes of Europe is not so strange, in an out-of-African context. In this respect we can understand that there is a South of the North, as much as a distinctive North (episteme) of the South. The question remains: how have the Celts created a rhythmic dance in the world of Finance, given that so much financial and economic thought and practice has its origins in Scotland, particularly?

'being for himself'. The institutions and patterns of behaviour in Western/ Northern culture during this period aimed at human fulfilment from within. Culture no longer relies on God or on the supernatural. Rather, it depends solely on reason and science. This attitude lends itself to individualistic tendencies. The individual, because he/she is a 'being for himself', works to make him/herself as comfortable as possible. What matters most is 'me', not 'us'. The African/Southern epistemological attitude is essentially holistic. Unlike his/her Western/Northern counterpart, the African/Southerner does not have to separate himself or herself from the object in order to know it. Objective knowledge is not a function of the rational faculties alone. There are two ways of knowing an object.

One can know the object by its physical features and appearances. On the other hand, one can go beyond the physical qualities and know the object in its essence. To know the object in this latter way is to allow oneself to be affected by the object. One knows the object as part of oneself and not as something separated from oneself. Contrary to the classical Euro-American epistemological stance, the traditional African makes no distinction between himself and the object. He does not hold it away from himself to be examined or analysed; rather, after having examined it, he takes it in his hands, alive as it is, careful not to kill it. He touches it, he feels it, he is conscious of it. It is with his subjectivity that he discovers the Other (10).

Knowledge by reasoning can only give a partial knowledge. One also knows by feeling, sensing, reacting and responding. For the Yoruba of western Nigeria, as indeed for most other African nationalities, the traditional religion allows the Yoruba to feel the Other, sense the Other, respond to the Other. In knowing the object, one also knows something about oneself. The subject cannot detach himself or herself from the object, the Other, in order to know him/her/it, because they are a part of the reality to be known. The subject is part of the object, and both exist together in the real world. It is, therefore, quite unrealistic to analyse the unified experience, by breaking it down into 'subjective' and 'objective' (11).

5.2.5. From Epistemology to Ontology

The Yoruba word for dance is *Ijo*. Ijo derives from the verb *jo* which means to burn. Ijo, then, means burning in dance. The notion of burning brings up the image of fire, for when we say that a king is burning, we are saying that it is being consumed by fire. The Yoruba word for fire is *ina*. The noun ina (fire) and *jo* (burn) often go together in Yoruba usage. *Ina n jo:* ('Fire is burning') and *O n jo ninu ina*: ('It is burning in the fire'). Ijo can also be used figuratively to refer to a person's qualities or manners. A child who constantly scratches his/ her body in an unusual way is asked, *Ki lo n jo e?* ('What is burning you?'). If a person appears restless and not composed, it is remarked that *Kini kan n jo o lara* ('Something is burning him/her'). When we say that somebody is being burnt by fire, the image that comes to mind is not that of someone calm and relaxed. Rather, we have the image of someone crying, running helter-skelter, wriggling in pain. These gestures of pain are a response to the heat of the fire (12).

The Yoruba notion of *ijo* (dance) seems to be derived from these gestures which are the responses to the heat of the fire. This gesture or response is dance, ijo. Dance, then, is a *response*. This is a crucial point to keep in mind. The person who dances is burning (*o n jo*), is on fire. For us to fully appreciate the notion of dance as a response, we have to understand the words 'response' and 'fire', in the general context of life. Desire is a form of fire. Fire, *ina*, embraces whatever motivates, moves and calls for a response. The responses could be fear, hatred, love, awe, adoration, fascination, dread. To dance is to react, to respond. To cease to dance is to die, *ku, bec*ome passive, no longer having any fire (13). As Ajayi points out, the Yoruba dance is a means of semiosis, a meaning-system of itself, in movement. As such, it expresses a different economy, not calculated in terms of money, but expressed in the living gestures of human bodies, pointing a response to the things of life.

The Yoruba word for death is *Iku*, which means to be immobile, to quench, and to be unresponsive. Iku is a negation of dance (Ijo), which, as we have said, is a response, a movement. There are many stories about the origin of Iku, but the general belief of the Yoruba is that Iku is a messenger of Olodumare. Iku recalls anyone whose time is ripe back to Olodumare. Iku is believed to be meant for those in ripe old age, and so the Yoruba rejoices when such an elderly person is taken away. Such a person is said to have gone home to the ancestors. When a young person dies there is great mourning, for it is believed that something has gone wrong somewhere.

Iku is so powerful that he cannot be controlled. Not even the most powerful of the Orisa can control him, for Iku is subject only to Olodumare. Iku is not an Orisa (deity) and so is not an object of cult (14). For the Bantu, the concept of sound and Iku is expressed in their notion of the life-force (*ntu*). The people are the *Ba*, who live by the 'ntu'. In calling upon God, the spirits, or the ancestral spirits, the Bantu man or woman asks above all give an increase of 'life force'. Each being is believed to be endowed by God with a certain force. Whereas Western epistemology can conceive of the transcendental notion of 'being' by separating it from 'force', the Bantu does not (15). This is because their conception of being is dynamic, not static. They hold that there is the divine force, celestial or terrestrial, human or animal, vegetable or even material. What is conceived as 'being' in Western epistemology is conceived of as 'force' in Bantu epistemology. The Bantu speak of God as 'the strong one', who is the source of every force of every creature. Not to have life force is to 'ku', die.

5.2.6. The Village Square: A Hermeneutical Metaphysics

The Village Town Crier as a Cosmic Messenger

As stated earlier, the African epistemological stance is essentially religious, and it is necessary to understand this if one is to understand African society. In African societies, the physical place is at once both natural and supernatural, sacred and secular, profane and holy. This paradox is exemplified in the village square. The village square is the meeting point between human beings and the spirits, between the deities and their worshippers, between the natural and the supernatural. When important announcements are to be made, they are made from the village square.

The town crier is a very strategic office in African societies. This office is directly under the ruler, king or the village head. The town crier is the only one empowered to make official announcements on behalf of the king and the elders. Moreover, the 'laboratory' where he performs this duty is the village square. When a person dies, the announcement is made at the village square. When there is to be a war or an imminent attack from nearby villages, the king sends the town crier to make announcements. When community rules have been violated, the town crier is sent to make the announcement. He rings a traditional gong, and people then gather in the square, to listen to the message. The village square is a school where men and women gather to discuss issues. It is the people's parliament. The chiefs, elders and different age groups gather there to discuss issues. The discussion could last all day and then continues at the next gathering (16).

People and places are inextricably linked. One's environment conditions one's knowledge about life and how one moves through the world. This relationship between people and place creates a great sense of values and attachment. Our world is composed of places with meaning and experiences that are connected or attached to particular people. A village square is a place for learning, for spiritual practices, for events that bring people together. The village square is a 'universitas' (a gathering of wise men and women), where young people are introduced to fundamentals of their local history, and where they interact with themselves, others and their ancestors. The village square is also the equivalent of a parliament, where issues are openly discussed and concluded, laws and policies are made and judgments are passed by community elders to resolve crises, such as land cases, family and inter-family conflicts, marriage problems and minor crimes.

By studying the village square, we get a glimpse into how ancient people organised their societies, their politics, economy, religion, culture and social lives. Young people from the village learn about their history and tradition from the village square. It is a place where communal cultural properties such as figurines, pottery, gongs (wooden and metal), textile materials, shrines, musical instruments and many other treasures are kept. The village square is also a festive space. Feasts, performances, ceremonies, games and sporting activities are held there. All of this brings people together and means that ancient practices and an ancient space remain entirely relevant today (17).

In Chinua Achebe's *Things Fall Apart*, the village square is also the main centre of business, play, dance, music and war. In one of the scenes in Achebe's story, the people of Umuofia, an Igbo community, gathered at the village square to discuss the killing of their daughter by a neighbouring community. Ten thousand men gathered to discuss the issue and the prospect of war unless the offending village made proper amendments. The same venue is also a place for celebrations. In *Things Fall Apart*, at the beginning of the harvest season every year, the New Yam festival is celebrated at the village square to mark the harvest season.

The highlight of the festival was the wrestling match between Okonkwo's (the main character in the story) village, Umuofia, and its neighbours. All these show the constantly shifting mode between permanency and temporality, being and nothingness, bravery and villainy, sacredness and profanity, professionalism and ordinariness, joy and sorrow, success and failure, all of which are played out in the village square, not as opposites but as different modes of being. The market then, in the African worldview, is not just a place of business, but a place of celebration, creativity, innovation and community.

Market, Community, Beauty and the Moral Core of Society

Good character and integrity are the very heart of business and enterprise, and this is the lesson that young people must imbibe at the village square. The village square is a school for the formation of character and the place one learns to conform to established norms for the promotion of harmony in the community. In African aesthetics and management, goodness and beauty are moral issues (18). For the Yoruba of western Nigeria, to be good is to have *iwa*. The word 'iwa' is a summary of Yoruba ethics, meaning character or virtue. The person of good iwa is a human being in the full sense of the term. Such a person has attained a certain disposition to act following his/her *eri-okon*, (conscience) and act as the ancestors acted. The constant advice to every Yoruba child is '*Maaa se rere, se rere ko ba Ie ye o*' (Learn to do good, be good so that it may be well with you).

115

A person without character is seen as acting more like a beast. Such a person is described as *'alai-ni-Iwa'*, a person of no character. Thus, in Yoruba, character and being are spelt and pronounced in the same way: *'Iwa'* (19). The person of character is honest, kind, obedient, considerate, tolerant and hospitable. All business management and economic transaction must be based on these principles. According to Kosemanii (20), the key characteristic virtues of the typical African personality are a wholesome relationship with others, respect for elders, community solidarity and generosity of heart. In Yoruba culture and in African culture generally, the good is the beautiful (21). Unlike in the English language where there is a clear dichotomy between 'good', which describes moral or religious qualities, and 'beautiful', which describes physical attractiveness, most African languages equate the good with the beautiful. In African usage, 'goodness' is absolute quality. The good, ultimately is the beautiful. A beautiful thing can be so only on the outside. For this reason, the African place emphasis on the good, not the beautiful (22).

The Yoruba word for 'good' is *dara,* which is a combination of *da* (to create) and *ra* (well, in good state, attractive). The notion of creation necessarily implies beauty. When we say that something is created, we are also saying *'O dara'* that is, it is good. The word *buruku* is a negation of Iwa. *'Buru'* means 'bad', 'unattractive', 'not charming', thus, *Iwa Buruku* is 'bad existence', 'bad spiritual life', 'evil character'. A person who has Iwa Buruku is *Aburewa (buruku ewa)* i.e. ugly, not charming, has a bad 'physical existence'. This is expressed in various African proverbs such as, 'Ugliness with a good character is better than beauty.' Another proverb says, 'If there is character, ugliness becomes beauty; if there is none, beauty becomes ugliness.' Finally, another adage says, 'Judge not your beauty by the number of people who look at you, but rather by the number of people who smile at you.'

5.2.7. Work as Cosmic Dance: Rethinking Work and Profit

There is a tendency in our time to draw a sharp line between the 'developed' and 'underdeveloped' peoples of the earth. The 'developed' people are the workers, the revolutionaries, the world-changers (23). The 'underdeveloped' people are the life-celebrators, known for their dances, folklore, music and 'archaic' mentality. The life-celebrators are backward and lack inventiveness and intellectual rigour. They are passive receivers of Western technology and civilisation, with no capacity for originality of thought. Is that not what often comes to mind when we use the word 'indigenous'?

Behind this division lies a false conception of work, indeed of all reality and an arrogant conception of Western civilisation as the ideal model of civilisation (is that not what we call the exogenous?). Work has come to be seen solely in terms of material utility or being useful. The ideology is that human beings live to work. Besides, to be a worker means to be engaged in the production of consumer goods. The worker does not smile or play. His/her chief characteristics, according to Pieper (24), are:

1. An extreme tension of the powers of action.
2. A readiness to suffer just for the sake of suffering, in vain.
3. Complete, total absorption in the social organism which is geared towards utility. The worker is expected to be busy or at least to appear to be busy. Not to be busy is to cease to *be*.

For Immanuel Kant (25), the 18th century German philosopher, noted for his magisterial depiction of deontological (duty-based) ethics, knowledge is work as opposed to intuition. Intuition, for the fact that it is effortless, is base, and cannot lead to knowledge. However, knowing, because it is discursive, and therefore demanding, is superior. Knowing requires comparing, examining, relating, distinguishing, demonstrating. It is work. Kant concluded that knowing, especially philosophising, is and must be regarded as hard work. Any form of philosophy that does not involve toil and sweat is no philosophy. The philosophy of the romantics, or that of Plato, which is based on both intuition and enthusiasm, is not real philosophy. They are too easy, and nothing easy is worthwhile. However, the philosophy of Aristotle is real, because it is work.

The tendency to overvalue work according to Pieper (26) and the effort of doing something difficult is so deep-rooted it affects even our notion of love. We want to earn and acquire love as we acquire other properties. From the African (indigenous) point of view, the human person is not just a working being, nor a thinking being. The human person is *homo festivus* (one who celebrates) and *homo fantasia* (one who intuits) and *homo ludens* (one who plays).

To regard the human person as merely a trained functionary in a consumer society is an insult to human dignity. In societies where human beings have lost the capacity to celebrate and fantasise, and have jettisoned play in favour of work, cases of disillusionment, suicide, violence, depression and meaninglessness are common. The word 'school' originally means leisure and is known as *skole* in Greek, and *scola* in Latin. School means a place of leisure, where one relaxes and lets go. Work in ancient time and, indeed up until the Middle Ages in the exogenous North, was closely linked with play, with leisure. The lazy man or woman was one who occupied him/herself with so many activities that he/she had no time to play, to be still, to be. It is precisely the fear of facing the truth about him/herself, of facing the reality that drives the so-called 'hard-worker' to fanatical and restless activity. This is what laziness means: refusal to be oneself. For Danish existential philosopher and theologian, Soren Kierkegaard (27), it is the 'sickness unto death'. The compulsive worker is lazy. He/she cannot bear the pain of silence, and gaze and let go.

Dialogue and understanding will help to bridge the gap between so-called 'world-changers' (Northern exogenous mindset) and 'world-celebrators' (Southern indigenous mindset). This research work argues that a dichotomy is hugely artificial and unreal, and sets about to propose an alternative viewpoint. There is no reason why those who celebrate life cannot also be committed to fundamental social change, and world-changers need not be joyless and ascetic. Africans need to embrace and further develop their indigenous intellectual tradition and cultural heritage in order to be genuine contributors to modern civilisation. African dance, music, vivacity and *Joie de Vivre*, are relevant to a balanced and creative world.

A Research Academy for Real Transformation

To develop this research work, beating to the rhythm of the African drum, which connects the world-changers, in a joyous celebration, and the world-celebrators, as they commit to social change, we have conceived a model of research academy that operates alongside a co-laboratory for economic and financial transformation. Each of the two authors of this chapter work within the context of Nigerian universities. But, even in an African context we have recognised that they fail, by and large, to function as centres for societal renewal. Yet, that is their vital role, in our context.

In focusing on individual education, both students and staff become disconnected from the social realities in a particular society. This is particularly damaging in 'developing' societies. Being separated from local culture and need is, for us, a main factor in economic and financial education becoming increasingly irrelevant, whether that is in Nigeria, Nicaragua or the Netherlands. Consequently, we are working towards a model of financial education that embeds the transformative GEN*E*-ius amongst economists and business administrators, who are open to enrol in a research and educational process that supports them in releasing the real economy of their particular community. Such research-and-education would be offered by local integral economic laboratories, that explicitly serve the needs of a particular society—and thereby of a prospectively integral economy.

As a model of that, we now turn from indigenous and Christian perspectives, on the South, to a more Islamic one, through the sustainability finance perspective of Jubril Adeojo. Through his research academy, based in what he terms 'communipreneurship'—whereby the entire community is educated and skilled in joyful creativity yoked to economic levers for social change—we see a model whereby finance is removed from the abstract to the embedding of policies for tackling climate change in West Africa.

5.3.1. Unfolding African Journey to Combat Climate Change

Communipreneurship to Caring for Society

In 2017, I (Jubril Adeojo) completed my PhD research-to-innovation journey, which was grounded in the co-creation of sustainable livelihoods, referred to as 'communipreneurship', as the true and lasting means of financial inclusion in and for Africa. Such can only be achieved with the right inclusive forms and consciousness of financing and banking: integral banking and finance. After the transformative and life-changing journey, in the same spirit of CARE-ing for the society, I heard from Barack Obama, the then President of the United States of America, as well as at the United Nations, in 2015–16, that the greatest threat to humanity and societal survival is climate change.

I sought to understand how far the ravages of climate change had spread, particularly in Africa. Whilst I understood that the major cause of climate change, via global warming, was the emission of greenhouse gases, including carbon dioxide, from the heavy global exploitation of coal and fossil fuels, it was obvious that the major polluters were from developed nations in America, Asia, and Europe.

Unfortunately, the most vulnerable nations are in Africa, in particular those that are economically disadvantaged, dominated by poor rural communities. These communities were most vulnerable to climate change effects, because their major livelihoods are from seasonal agriculture, both crop farming and livestock husbandry. Furthermore, their lack of basic economic amenities makes them particularly vulnerable and unable to adapt to climate change. Arable lands in Africa are increasingly susceptible to flooding, from sporadic and unpredictable rainfall, together with drought from rapid desert encroachment (desertification). Therefore, the standard of living of surviving rural and economically disadvantaged populaces is falling rapidly, due to the increasing fragility of their livelihoods, exposing women and children to infectious disease and increased malnutrition. In turn, these severe environmental changes have led to societal tensions and conflicts, resulting from climate-induced mass migrations. These effects further exacerbate the problems of those peoples who are closest to the affected communities and countries, by the influx of affected groups, who seek refuge and need to create a subsistence living for themselves and their households, in their chosen new homelands.

Climate Action Consciousness: Activating the Global Community

Within the United Nations Sustainable Development Goals (SDGs), SDG 13 refers to Actions to Combat Climate Change, focusing on the co-creation of solutions that can sustainably mitigate the causes of, and adapt to the effects of, climate change. What is needed, urgently, is a change of consciousness by everybody, every company, institution, state, and country. SDG 13 also talks about the fact that severe and unusual weather conditions and rising sea levels are affecting people and their properties in developed and developing countries. From a small farmer in rural Nigeria to a businessman in the city of London, climate change is affecting everyone, but its most severe effects are on the poor and vulnerable, as well as marginalised groups like women, children, and the elderly in vulnerable, rural, economy-based countries. As such, climate action is urgently needed because of the irreversible consequences on fragile communities through such effects as desertification and the movement of the Sahel region further South, in central Africa. Failure to act will increase the likelihood of global temperature exceeding 3 degrees Celsius, above pre-industrial levels, and adversely affect every ecosystem on the planet.

It is well-known that the 2015 Paris Agreement to combat climate change captured every country's ambitious Nationally Determined Contributions (NDCs) targets. The primary objective of the Paris Agreement and the NDCs was to avoid presenting the quest to combat climate change as a charitable and humanitarian affair. Rather, it was to be seen as offering commercially viable investment opportunities to transform the world economically, while still combating climate change, in order to protect our planet.

New financial and economic models were proposed to mitigate the causes of climate change, transitioning from mass logging and cutting down tropical rainforests, together with substituting the use of coal and fossil fuels, with cleaner, ambient energy sources, as well as leveraging technologies and new financial partnerships to adapt to the new situation. As a way to strategically activate and awaken the climate action consciousness of the private sector and public sector, the Paris Agreement unveiled that over $23 trillion would be required by 2030, in climate-resilient investments, globally, in order to win the fight against climate change, and sustain the victory. The question was, how could this be achieved? Instinctively, I employed my integral banking and finance consciousness to explore and co-create innovative and sustainable climate financing methods that would help crystallise the flow of the required funds for Africa to achieve its NDCs and combat climate change.

5.3.2. Awakening Climate Finance Consciousness Through Experiences of Suffering

The driving motive for climate finance, to mobilise private sector funds, is in response to the dire sufferings of people and ecosystems. In pursuit of a phenomenological approach, I sought to engage in a process of radical inquiry, as well as becoming immersed in the life-world of chaotic experiences facing large numbers of people who are affected by ecosystem destruction, across central Africa. It was important to me to be able to adopt their perspective.

Africa is the most vulnerable continent to the dire effects of climate change, as negligible investment has been made in climate change adaptation, in order to sustain healthy and peaceful living economies. In 2012, President Ali Bongo Ondimba of Gabon asserted that climate change in Africa will cause armed conflicts in 23 countries and political unrest in another 13 countries in the coming years. In addition, the United Nations claims that there are currently 350,000 climate-related deaths per year worldwide. This may rise to 1 million per year by 2030 if no action is taken by the private sector and government institutions, in the areas of infrastructure investments and formulation of climate-resilient governing laws.

In Nigeria, its vast land space of 923,768 sq. km, spanning across different climatic regions is now understood to be highly vulnerable to climate change. It is a country where 90 percent of food production comes from small rain-fed farms of a few hectares. The main effects of climate change—crippling the livelihoods of Nigerian rural economies as well as increasing food insecurity—are gross desert encroachment and drought in the arable lands, particularly in the northern regions of the country.

Due to widespread practice of seasonal farming and food production, investments from the private sector are grossly affected by the drought that now extends from April to June, particularly in the northern regions. Incessant flooding and erosion affects the southern regions, limiting expected food production yields and driving investment failures. Equally, in the case of Ghana, only 1 percent of arable land is under irrigation. As a result, the vast majority of farmers rely on rainfall for food production, therefore making them highly susceptible to the looming effects of climate change.

Another story of climate change pertains to the current state of Lake Chad. Before the drought and desert encroachment, the lake, its banks and its islands were a source of livelihood for nearly two million people. It is a food-exporting hub, playing a key role for food security, in respect of a hinterland with nearly 13 million inhabitants and two metropolitan centres, N'Djamena, the capital of Chad, and Maiduguri, the capital of the State of Borno in Nigeria. The entire basin was home to about 50 million people as of 2015. The rich biodiversity of the Lake enabled small communities to develop productive activities based on fishing, agriculture, and livestock farming. The dynamism of the area was mainly based on a complex system, adapted to the variability of the environment and characterised by the articulation of mobility, multi-activity, and multi-functionality (28).

Now, the Lake has dried up by more than 95%, forcing migration and conflicts in the region and neighbouring countries. Between 2017–18, in Nigeria, there were sporadic killings of people in the northern states and a few western states. These were, allegedly, perpetrated by the herdsmen, as they migrated cattle from the drought-affected zones to fertile regions, for the sole purpose of establishing new colonies for feeding their cattle. In the course of unpredicted migrations, forced by climate change, conflict ensued, as the herdsmen migrated to the fertile arable lands of indigenes and, forcefully, took over their primary livelihood, for the sustenance of their own primary livelihood. These are realities across the countries of sub-Saharan Africa.

The emigrants are termed 'climate or environmental refugees'. They are defined as persons who can no longer gain a secure livelihood in their traditional homelands because of environmental disruption factors, notably drought, desertification, deforestation, soil erosion, water shortages and climate change. Equally, they are, increasingly, susceptible to natural disasters, such as cyclones, storm surges and floods. In the face of these environmental threats, people feel they have no alternative but to seek sustenance elsewhere, whether within their own countries or beyond and whether on a semi-permanent or permanent basis. (29). Therefore, between 1995–2015, the issue of climate change had escalated from an environmental matter to a developmental matter, as an existential threat to humanity in these regions (30).

Forming Climate Finance with a Conscious Pan-African Outlook

In response to the climatic pandemic in Africa, I co-founded a firm, SME-FUNDS Capital Limited, with a conscious Pan-African outlook. The burning desire of the firm was to leverage strategic partnerships in every ecosystem, to facilitate mobilisation of the required funds from both public and private sector institutions, in order to fund commercially viable and socially responsible climate-resilient infrastructure projects and enterprises, in the areas of climate mitigation and adaptation.

We utilise integral finance ideology to co-create innovative and inclusive climate finance methodologies, grounded in the particularities of each ecosystem. According to the United Nations Framework Convention on Climate Change (UNFCCC), climate finance is defined as financial flows supporting the mitigation of climate change, i.e. targeting the reduction of net greenhouse gas emissions. It, also, includes supporting adaptation to climate change, i.e. enhancing resilience to the impacts of climate change and variability. In the next section I comment on our specific innovative climate finance solutions and the climate projects that Climate Finance Advisory Limited is focused on, for the common good of Nigeria and the rest of Africa.

Climate Finance Towards Enterprise and Community Survival and Resilience

As I alluded, my consciousness transformed from combating poverty via innovative finance, to combating climate change, to save our existence as communities and societies, via innovative finance. SMEFUNDS Capital Limited (SFC) is charged with the burning desire to co-create innovative finance methodologies that will not only GEN*E*rate sustainable livelihoods, but climate resilient communities, technologies, and societies. To demonstrate our commitment to the cause, I led a strategic consortium in co-operation with a leading investment bank in Nigeria, Vetiva Capital Management Limited, to co-create the Green Energy Fund Programme (GEF programme). It is, currently, being co-implemented on our tripartite partnership with a Pan-African development finance institution (DFI), and the African Guarantee Fund (AGF) based in Nairobi, Kenya.

AGF is willing to commit its Partial Risk Guarantee (PRG) to the tune of $50 milllion, to enable local commercial banks in Nigeria to invest in climate resilient projects and enterprises, contributing to the achievement of the country's NDC targets for combating climate change. On the back of the PRG of $50 million, our strategic consortium is charged to mobilise up to $100million, in two to three years of the GEF programme, in investments from the private sector and public sector institutions.

Figure 5.1. shows the financing model developed for the GEF programme. From the model, it is can be seen that the required concessional loans are from the public sector financial institutions, but managed by the local private sector commercial banks, under an on-lending mechanism. I define concessional loans as credit facilities (intervention funds in a Nigerian context) granted by financial institutions (both public and private sector), with concessional and uncommon features compared to the typical features of 'vanilla' commercial credit facilities.

It is our contention that concessional loans must address the criteria that accompanies every credit facility, such as: long-term payback period; below the prime lending rate in the market, i.e. single digit lending interest rate; flexible and more liquid forms of collateral, i.e. insurance, credit guarantee, risk sharing, and project cash-flow-based security; target emerging economic sector(s) with high socio-economic potentials in the best interest of the country and its populace; and encourages blended finance, i.e. grants, equity, suppliers' credit, projects aggregation, and other available forms of finance.

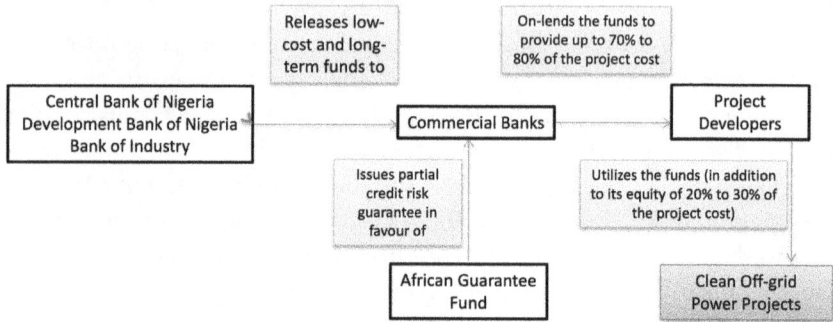

Figure 5.1. Financing Model of Green Energy Fund Programme

Many development finance institutions around the world, from multi-lateral, to bi-lateral, and local, consciously engage in innovative concessional finance to mobilise financial and non-financial resources needed for the combat against climate change. GEF programmes aim to enable climate funding for green and clean energy projects in Nigeria. Green energy technologies are such renewable energies as solar, wind, hydro, biomass, and 'clean', i.e. gas.[2] These technologies are climate-friendly. Investment in renewable energy and clean energy technologies mitigates the causes of climate change, i.e. reduction of greenhouse gas emissions. The programme also supports the blending of climate mitigation and climate adaptation, such as projects focused on solar-powered irrigation enterprise, in order to adapt to the drought and desert encroachment in the arable lands.

In respect of climate mitigation projects, the GEF programme aims to replace the fossil fuel-powered generating sets—owned by end-users i.e. households, businesses and industries—to generate up to 95,000 megawatts of the 100,000 megawatts of the national energy demand and consumption in the next few years. The cumulative capacity of off-grid energy generated by the end-users continues to exceed the entire national grid generation i.e. national energy demand/consumption is over 100,000 megawatts; grid provides less than 5,000 megawatts (five percent). As a result, over 80% of the energy used by domestic users and industry is self-generated fossil fuel power, which contributes significantly to the causes of climate change i.e. greenhouse gas emissions.

2 **Editor's footnote**: It is notable that 'gas-based' energy production is described as 'clean' in this context. This reflects the substantial reliance on 'dirty' fuel sources, such as coal, oil, lignite and other carbon-rich fossil fuels, hitherto.

In the area of addressing development issues via the GEF programme, we found that 80% of businesses and industries, representing the major employers of labour in the country, failed due to the exorbitant costs of doing business. From further inquiry, we realised that fifty percent of the operating overheads goes to self-generating energy to power their businesses. One of the pivotal propositions of the GEF programme is provision of power or energy to businesses and industries as a service. In return, they receive a significant reduction in the cost of doing business, by more than 30%, so as to prevent early business mortality and job losses, as well as augmenting the working capital of the businesses. All this, while still combating climate change, via the use of renewable or clean energy technologies to generate power and energy instead of the conventional use of fossil fuels.

5.4. Conclusion

5.4.1. Communita Technologia Integrazione

Communal well-being entails communities living in peace, socio-economic prosperity and harmony, through a formidable force of participatory orientation and co-creation among the people. In the wake of the catastrophic damages of climate change threatening the existence of communities, the emerging paradigm is centred on ecosystem-oriented participation and co-creation, towards achieving communal resilience and adaptation to climate change, via innovative climate finance and contemporary technologies.

Contemporary technologies have been mobilising financial and non-financial resources from the West and North into the South and even East. These include seedless and soilless (e.g. hydroponic) farming practices for food production, artificial intelligence for predicting behaviour of the weather, innovative insurance products, and monitoring and remote drones for detecting and removing pesticides, and for applying fertilisers, as well as solar-powered irrigations. Each of these technologies are being implemented with the participation of the climate-vulnerable communities, in order to make their communities and livelihoods climate-resilient, mitigating the dangerous effects of droughts, flood, and desert encroachment. For communities, globally, particularly in Africa, to survive the climatic pandemic, there must be communal consciousness to continue to integrate with, and embrace, the technologies that stimulate their well-being.

The participatory action of *communita technologia integrazione*, which is an Italian concept, and in English, means 'community technological integration', reflects another alternative economic semiosis: a meaning-system pointing to alternative ways of doing economics and finance. This semiosis promotes the integration of the several worlds, the urban and the rural voices and technologies, the north-western technologies and the south-eastern suffering communities. There is now a shared paradigm that for societal well-being to be achieved and sustained, both worlds must consciously co-create and collaborate via innovative financing models and solutions, ever-evolving technologies and artificial intelligence capabilities, to combat climate change and protect the existence and prosperity of our humanity. This represents a different meaning of economy and finance for the two-thirds world, especially focused in sub-Saharan Africa.

5.4.2. Promoting Community Well-being

From such an overall perspective, community well-being can be adapted to define societal well-being in a wider context, that is:

1. Place to live (satisfaction with local conditions)
2. Social community (community networks and involvement)
3. Economic community (income, employment, investment, and spending patterns)
4. Political community (levels of participation of the people in decision-making)
5. Personal space (feelings about, and meaning of their locality)

Throughout this chapter—both in respect of Anselm Adodo's understanding of economics in respect of the semiotics of the 'dance-of-life' and Jubril Adeojo's alternatives for financing community resilience, in the face of potential climate catastrophe—we have followed a course of overall *relational accounting* (see previous Chapter 4), which the following Table reminds us of:

Uncover **Uniqueness**
Reveal **Natural** and Communal Essences
Go Beyond Surface 'Facts' **to** Underlying **Moral** Values
Locate what is Particular to the Place that makes you **Authentic**ally Who You Are?

Table 5.4.2. Relational Accounting

At this point we turn East, towards cultural and spiritual renewal, once again to Akhuwat in Pakistan and the remarkable work of Mohammed Saqib, Aneeqa Malik and their community.

5.5. Bibliography

1 **Ake** C (1995) *Democracy and Development in Africa*. Washington DC. Brookings Institute

2 **Santos** B (2014) *Epistemologies of the South: Justice Against Epistemicide*. London. Routledge

3 **Deaton**, A (2015) *The Great Escape: Health, Wealth, and the Origins of Inequality*. Princeton. University Press

4 **Collier**, P (2008) *The Bottom Billion. Why the Poorest Countries are Failing and What Can Be Done About it*. London. Oxford University Press

5 **Akhaine**, S (2015) *Patrons of Poverty: IMF/World Bank and Africa's Problems*. London. Lambert Academic Publishing

6 **De Soto,** H (2003) *The Mystery of Capital: Why Capitalism Triumphs in the West and Fails Everywhere Else*. Basic Books

7 **Anyanwu**, K Chukwulozie (1987) Sound as Ultimate Reality and Meaning. The Mode of Knowing Reality in African Thought. _Ultimate Reality and Meaning_ 10 (1):29–38

8 **Abimbola**, W (1977) Ifa Divination system, in *Nigeria Magazine*, Nos. 122–123, 35

9 **Worgul,** G (1980) *From Magic to Metaphor*. New York University Press

10 **Fadipe**, N A (1979) *The Sociology of the Yoruba*. Ibadan. University Press

11 **Abram**, D (2011) *Becoming Animal: An Earthly Cosmology*. London. Vintage

12 **Adodo,** A (2017) *Integral Community Enterprise in Africa: Communitalism as an Alternative to Capitalism*. London. Routledge

13 **Ajayi**, O (1998) *Yoruba Dance: The Semiotics of Movement and Yoruba Body Attitude*. New Jersey. Africa World Press

14 **Abimbola**, W (1977) *op cit*

15 **Tempels**, P (2014) *Bantu Philosophy*. Orlando. HBC Publishing

16 **Ugwuanyi,** J K & **Schofield,** J (2018) Permanence, temporality and the rhythms of life: exploring the significance of the village arena in Igbo culture. *World Archaeology*, 50, 1, 7–22

17 **Douny** L (2014) *Living in a Landscape of Scarcity: Materiality and Cosmology in West Africa*. London. Routledge

18 **Nwoko,** D (1979) Basic Elements of Aesthetic Experience, *New Culture*. Feb

19 **Ladele**, T A, **Mustapha**, O, **Aworinde** I A, **Oyerinde**, Oyedemi & **Oladapo**, O (1986) Akojopo *Iwadi Ijinle Asa Yoruba*. Ibadan. Macmillan Publishers

20 **Kosemanii,** S (1987) *Owe ati Asa oro Yoruba*. Ibadan. Vantage Publishers

21 **Nwoko,** D *op cit*

22 **Euba**, T (1986) The Human Image: Some aspects of Yoruba Canons of Art and beauty, *Nigeria Magazine*, 54, 4, 9ff. Oct–Dec

23 **Cox**, H (1970) *The Feast of Fools*. New York. Harper and Row Publishers

24 **Pierper**, J (2014) *Leisure: The Basis of Culture*. California. Ignatius Press

25 **Kant**, I (2005) *Critique of Pure Reason*. London. Penguin

26 **Pierper**, J (2014) *Op cit*

27 **Kierkegaard**, S (1980) *The Sickness unto Death*. Connecticut. Princeton University Press

28 **Deressa**, T T and **Hassan**, T (2010) Economic Impact of Climate Change on Crop Production in Ethiopia: Evidence from Cross-section Measures. *Journal of African Economies,* 18, 4, 529–554

29 **Magrin** G, **Pourtier** R, **Lemoalle** J (2015) *Atlas du lac Tchad.* Paris. Passages, République du Tchad, AFD-IRD

30 **Myers** N (1995) *Environmental Exodus: An Emergent Crisis in the Global Arena.* Washington, DC. The Climate Institute

CHAPTER 6

Integral So(u)lidarity Economy: Mawakhat Finance: East

Aneeqa Malik, Senior Strategist & Research Facilitator, Akhuwat Foundation

We (God the creator) shall show them (human beings) Our signs upon the horizon (universe) and within themselves (the self) until it is clear to them (human beings) that He (God) is the Real (haqq).

The Holy Qur'an (41:53)

There are no solutions; there is only the ongoing practice of being open and alive to each meeting, each intra-action, so that we might be able to use our ability to respond, our responsibility to help awaken, to breathe life into ever new possibilities for living justly.

Karen Barad, Meeting the Universe Halfway

6.1. Introduction

6.1.1. From Semiotics (Meaning-making) to Signification (Ayahs)

A Book of Signs

Throughout the Holy Qur'an, God emphasises that one of the most crucial purposes of the Qur'anic revelation is to invite people to ponder. By thinking while isolating his conscience from all social, ideological and psychological obligations, the person should eventually perceive that the entire universe, including himself, is created by a superior power.

Furthermore, in the Qur'an, God invites men of understanding to think about the issues which other people overlook or just dismiss, using such barren terms as 'evolution', 'coincidence', or 'a miracle of nature'. The book of revelation and guidance, Al-Furqan (Qur'an) has constant such reminders:

> In the creation of the heavens and the earth, and the alternation of night and day, there are Signs for people of intelligence: those who remember God standing, sitting and lying on their sides, and reflect on the creation of the heavens and the earth. (3:190)

Thus, people of understanding see the signs of God and try to comprehend His eternal knowledge, power and art by remembering and reflecting on them, for God's knowledge is limitless, and His act of creating is flawless.

The symbiosis of semiotics/*signi*fication, philosophical mediation and intuitive knowledge, is how the Qur'an and God/Allah invites *insan* (the individual) to take guidance from the book that codifies a way of life for the whole of humanity and Muslims, in particular. Admittedly, this human agency comes with a heavy responsibility of acknowledging and accounting for one's place in the universe. Therefore, the concept of *al-Insan al-Kamil* (perfect man), is an honorific title to describe Prophet Muhammad (may Allah's peace be upon him). With his creation the prototype of the perfect human being was perfected as the perfect microcosm of a metacosm, the God-reality.

6.1.2. Science of Ethics, Economics (includes Home Economics), Science of Politics

Laleh Bakhtiar (1), the first American female Qur'an translator and the President of the Institute of Traditional Psychology, in Chicago, writes:

> When the human being becomes conscious of self and then freely chooses to learn to read and to live by the Signs within and without, God's will is done. Such a person will have completed the perfection of nature in its mode of operation within the self, will be centred, having gained experiential knowledge of the oneness of God (monotheism, Tawhid) reflected in nature and within themselves.

She further explains that understanding the signs *within* develops through the natural sciences (the branch known as medicine) and philosophy (the branch known as practical philosophy). From the 13th century to the present, in the Muslim world, the latter science has included three branches: the Science of Ethics, the Science of Economics (including Home Economics) and the Science of Politics. Traditional psychology is found in the Science of Ethics and can, therefore, most clearly be referred to as psycho-ethics. In order to develop a fair evaluation of psycho-ethics, in general, and its personality paradigm, in particular, it is necessary to understand its perspective on the human being's place in the universe, perspective which is both holistic and integrative.

Subsequently, the (human) self is guided by the signs of nature/nurture guidance. The self is capable of reflecting the oneness of God's self-disclosure in nature, in its mode of operation in the universe (macrocosm) and within the self (microcosm).

The Islamic doctrine, thus, is contained, as a whole, in the *tawhidic* view, the 'affirmation of the Divine unity'. For the ordinary believer, this affirmation is the clear and simple access of the religion. For the contemplative, it is the door which opens on to the essential reality (*haqq*). Further, the more the mind of the contemplative penetrates into the apparent rational simplicity of the Divine unity, the more complex that simplicity will become, until a point is reached where its different aspects can no longer be reconciled by discursive thought alone. *Meditation* on these contrasts will, in fact, take the faculty of thought to its very furthest limits. Intelligence will, in this way, be opened to a synthesis lying beyond all formal conception. In other words, it is only in intuition, beyond form, that one has, for Burckhardt (2) access to Unity.

The above forms, for me, the prelude to this chapter which establishes the intuitive de-codification of a set of rules/guidance bestowed onto human *nature*/self. These enable us to run the affairs of this world—be they social, political, economic, or financial—with Divine guidance (Al-Qur'an), emulation of Prophetic tradition (*sunnah*), using inner wisdom/intuitive knowledge (*hikmah*) and Divine grace/spiritual aspiration (*himmah*). This, latter, is the praxis, as we shall see, of our Soul-idarity (*Mawakhat*) organisational and societal paradigm. Furthermore, these (submerged) patterns were observed, by me, through a Sufistic/mystical lens, to acknowledge their manifestation in matters of finance and a solidarity economy of which one such model is presented in this chapter.

6.2. From Primal to Paradigmatic – GENE-a-logical Emergence

6.2.1. Socio-Economic Eastern Culture Relies on Prophecy More Than Empiricism

Thereof, this chapter is fashioned in a GEN*E*-a-logical order (see Chapter 3), being inspired by the 'Transformational GEN*E*' rhythm as contemplated by Ronnie Lessem and Alexander Schieffer (3), albeit here in an *integral Islamic* perspective. Herewith, the task assigned for me is to provide an Eastern perspective, as per our integral GEN*E* rhythm, i.e. of spiritually-laden **Emer**-gence of an economic model, imbued in Eastern cultural and philosophical submergence, in spirituality/perennial philosophy of Eastern mystical wisdom (hikmah), lodged in the region of the Indian subcontinent.

Without delving deeper into the argument on Islamic spirituality or 'philosophical' thought—which is often believed to have been inspired by the Greek *philosophia* (*falsafa*)—I intend to draw on the perennial wisdom and experiential/intuitive knowledge which forms the basis of the Qur'anic esoteric interpretation. This interpretation states that the Qur'an has an inner meaning, and that this inner meaning conceals a yet deeper inner meaning, and so on (up to seven successive levels of deeper meaning). The task, here, is to indicate how it is manifested in the socio-economic Eastern culture that relies on prophecy more than empiricism.

Primordially, (wo)man (the microcosm) is connected to the universe (the macrocosm) and God (the metacosmic). This constitutes the origin of all things. His/her inner being is a laboratory, where man controls experiments (spiritual) which forms man's worldview. The transcendental nature of universal reality/truth characteristics manifest themselves in all the religions, on both the ethical and metaphysical level.

Indeed, my inspiration comes from many past and present Muslim philosophers and Sufi masters, most recently from Seyyed Hossein Nasr (4), an Iranian professor emeritus of Islamic studies at George Washington University, a renowned Islamic philosopher and a major advocate of the perennialist perspective. As Nasr attests in his seminal work on *Islamic Philosophy from its Origin to the Present*, within this tradition, philosophising is done in a world in which *prophecy* is the central reality of life; a reality related not only to the realms of *action* and *ethics* but also to the realm of *knowledge*. Nasr stresses that the Islamic tradition is a living tradition with significance for the contemporary Islamic world and its relationship with the West. Thereby, this chapter aims to draw out on that implicit subtle impulse that manifests itself, in matters of human 'subsistence' (*falah*), when the human will/*nafs* is fully submerged in the Divine Will, also referred to as *Shariah* (divine law).

6.2.2. An Integral Paradigm Shift in the Way We Perceive Finance and Economics

The Soul-idarity paradigm is thus an attempt to bridge the contrasting divide between the realm of inner knowledge (sacred) and the matters of finance and economics (material), which remains my quest on a personal level and my contribution to this collective endeavour. Therein, we see the emergence of an integral paradigm shift in the way we perceive finance and economics, which is ever more compelling for our human (collective) ecology. Realistically, it is not even a matter of finding 'alternatives' to our local and global financial woes, as mentioned in the opening chapter of this book. Rather, it is a matter of reviving the natural flow/system which has been ever-present since time immemorial—the 'subsistence' of the human race being its primary driver.

From an Islamic perspective, acquiring knowledge is an *ibadah* (act of worship). Here knowledge means to know about God and creation, the purpose of creation, and their relation. In several verses, the Qur'an clearly explains the primordiality of Divine Law as the foundation of knowledge. To explore knowledge, in Islam, we need to know what that Divine Law is, how it existed from the very beginning of the world and its physical manifestation in such matters, for example, economic (subsistence), social solidarity (*ikhuwah*), knowledge (*ilm*) and so on and so forth.

As stated by Umer Chapra (5), the crucial Islamic goal of overall human well-being (falah) is to be attained through material as well as spiritual uplift. This includes socio-economic justice, spread of moral and material education, technological advance, good governance, and family and social solidarity. For Chapra, moreover:

> ...while a great deal of effort has been, and continues to be, made to increase the strength, efficiency and stability of the financial system, not enough attention seems to have been given to the need to make it more equitable.

He further emphasises that human/socio-economic development cannot be attained except through justice (*al-adl*). Indeed, Chapra is alluding to economic justness and equitable acquisition and distribution of wealth within human societies, in the case presented here, of Islamic societies.

The North African, 14th century Arabic philosopher Ibn Khaldun (6), proposes a hierarchy of 'civilisation sciences' according to the 'attributes of man' (*insan*), which distinguish him from other 'living beings' (*hayawanât*). At the pinnacle, he places the 'sciences and arts that are the product of thought (*fikr*)', then political science which reflects 'the need for a brake and a solid authority, indispensable to human survival'. Third, is the economy, which concerns 'man's efforts to earn a living, the result of the need to feed himself in order to live and survive'. Sociology and ethnology, if we can afford this modern qualification, are finally mentioned as the study of the 'civilisation', inherent in the fact that 'cooperation' (*ta'âwun*) is in the nature of men.

It is in this guise that we can turn, briefly, to inquire into the ontological basis of the objectives (*maqasid*); of human well-being, as adduced by Chapra, and human 'subsistence', which is the most common ground for Qur'anic ordination. Whereas the maqasid are heavily emphasised by the Islamic finance scholars and jurists, the real 'essence' (spirit) is often lost due to limited understanding of the relationship between economics (of household) and human

133

subsistence (*rizq*). For whereas Islamic finance is seemingly a new, 20th century economic phenomenon, many Muslim thinkers and philosophers in the past have reflected upon such—that is, upon man's economical needs for survival/subsistence.

6.2.3. The Ontology and Epistemology of Shariah-compliance

In his seminal work on *Maqasid al-Shariah as Philosophy of Islamic Law*, Dr. Jasser Auda (7), a scholar and distinguished professor of the Shariah, quotes the words of an important medieval Islamic jurisconsult Ibn al-Qayyim (d. 748 AH/1347 CE):

> Shari'ah is based on wisdom and achieving people's welfare in this life and the afterlife. Shariah is all about justice, mercy, wisdom, and good. Thus, any ruling that replaces justice with injustice, mercy with its opposite, common good with mischief, or wisdom with nonsense, is a ruling that does not belong to the Shari'ah, even if it is claimed to be so according to some interpretation.

Maqasid al-Shariah (the objectives), thus, explain the 'wisdoms behind rulings', such as 'enhancing social cohesion', which is one of the wisdoms behind charity, being good to one's neighbours, and greeting people with peace. Wisdoms behind rulings also include 'developing consciousness of God', which is one of the rationales for regular prayers, fasting, and supplications.

In Islamic economics, according to Auda, productive human activity is mandatory. Islam does not endorse every human wish, with many prohibited on moral grounds. Moral reasoning, within the golden rule, under the guidance of one's conscience, does not exist in a vacuum. It requires complementary principles or values, consideration of context, and a maturity of thought to operate in a workable manner. In Islamic finance then, the term 'loan' refers only to a benevolent loan (*Qard al-Hasan*), a form of financial assistance to the needy to be repaid free of charge. However, for Muslims living in the West, little attention is paid to the propagation of such, which would provide a solution to debt slavery (see our opening chapters), which is widespread in the financial cultures around the world, be they Islamic or non-Islamic societies.

It is with the above in mind, in this chapter, that I present one of the world's largest Qard-al-Hasan financial institutions—Akhuwat, already introduced in Chapter 3—meaning 'brotherhood', in Pakistan. It is a financial model inspired by the Prophetic wisdom of *Mawakhat-e-Medina*—a paradigmatic tale of 'spiritual brotherhood' between two communities, namely, the *Muhajirun* from Mecca and the *Ansar* of Medina, the two most holiest cities for Muslims.

6.3. The Mawakhat/Solidarity Paradigm

6.3.1. Building on the Spirit of Solidarity

With a view to taking the ontological interpretation of Maqasid al-Shariah (the objectives) further on—thereby, epistemologically, expounding upon the spirit of Solidarity—Akhuwat, as a financial institution, revives the *sunnah* of Mawakhat (solidarity), a Prophetic tradition. It seeks to re-evaluate how Islamic finance, in direct comparison to a capitalist-based, global financial model, works its way through an upward integral-spiritual trajectory, providing a viable alternative/parallel to the world of debt-slavery/*riba*.

By building on the spirit of solidarity/Mawakhat, social justice and communal brotherhood, Akhuwat, from Pakistan, turns a new leaf in the history of Islamic finance, by presenting a living example of the world's largest Qard-al-Hasan (benevolence loan/interest-free) model. We—that is Akhuwat's founder Amjad Saqib and I (8)—have explicitly termed such an *integral finance* model, going beyond the boundaries of the 'micro-ness' of what the world knows as microfinance: a (perceived) remedy for poverty alleviation.

6.3.2. Grounding and Origination: Mawakhat – Asabiyah - Reciprocity/Akhuwat

The incident of the Prophetic *hijrah* (migration) from Mecca to Medina, by Prophet Muhammad in the year 622, along with his companions, holds a special significance in Islamic history for many reasons. One of these is that of initiating the tradition of Mawakhat (solidarity amongst brothers). Upon the advice of the Prophet of Islam, the Ansar (helpers) of Medina, adopted one Muhajir (emigrant) from Mecca, as their brother, thereafter, sharing their wealth and property with them. In doing so they set a historic precedent of 'unity amongst believers', what is also declared as 'spiritual brotherhood'.

After emigrating to Medina, the Prophet (peace be upon him) also drafted the constitution, which established an alliance/federation of eight Medinan tribes and Muslim emigrants from Mecca, specifying the rights and duties of all citizens, including that of the Muslim community to other communities: the Jews and other People of the Book (*ahl al-kitab*). Following this, the term *asabiyah* (9) was used by the Prophet. This clearly sets the precedent for a communal caring and sharing without any distinction of faith, caste or creed, by warning people not to fall into the trap of kinship and tribalism or, even, nationalism. In other words, when a man supports his kinsmen and friends, purely for the sake of upholding justice and defeating injustice, this kind of asabiyah is commendable and praiseworthy.

135

The term 'asabiyah' has been variously translated as 'solidarity', 'group feeling', social cohesion', and even 'clannishness'. Ibn Khaldun did not invent the term, but he did retool it for his own purposes, thereby articulating principles that remain relevant today despite their antiquity. The first and most important of these is that social cohesion should be understood as a vital element of national power. A nation need not be engaged in existential conflict to benefit from strong asabiyah. Absent solidarity and internal controversies absorb the attention of statesmen, and internal divisions derail all attempts to craft coherent policy. Strategic malaise is one byproduct of a community deficient in asabiyah (solidarity).

In other words, Ibn Khaldun sought nothing less than to discover and explain the basic laws and principles upon which all human societies operated. For his efforts, he has been acclaimed as the first economist, the first sociologist, and the first true social scientist in human history.[3] Moreover, in Khaldun's view, asabiyah is not permanent. Almost inevitably, it dwindles away. The process can take generations, but the reason is always the same: 'They have lost the sweetness of fame and asabiyah, because they are dominated by force.'

For Khaldun, asabiyah, as a cyclical process, will rise and fall as communities grow and then splinter, bureaucracies expand and then calcify, and laws are established but then too quickly multiply. What was constructed for the glory of a people in past ages only hampers their progress and hastens their decline in the present. All the good man can do, in such a time of decline, is wait for the old order to fall apart and join the asabiyah-driven group of men and women ready to rebuild upon the ashes. But who are these wise/good men and women who are willing to take on this burden?

In what follows, we note the emergence of the spirit of Mawakhat being revived in its essence to balance the negative aspects of asabiyah; that is, of 'tribal' or 'caste-laden' prejudice against the poor and downtrodden by the powerful and resourceful. By invoking the spirit of solidarity, Akhuwat, in Pakistan, is turning a new leaf in Islamic economics, drawing also on Chapra's connotation of realising the common goal of falah (human well-being) in any particular society.

For us, the impulse of solidarity (10) has always appeared in different cycles, in different regions/generations and at different times in history as per the

3 **Editor's footnote**: This may be overstating Ibn Khaldun's role, given the work of Aristotle and his Greek school and Ma Tuan-Lin, in 13th century China. But, even so, Khaldun's contribution to sociology is enormous and, frequently, overlooked in the West. Certainly, the US scholar Abdemajid Hammoun (2003) regards Khaldun as the world's first social economist. See: *Translation and the Colonial Imaginary: Ibn Khaldun Orientalist*. Middletown, CT: Wesleyan University.

spirit of Soul-i-darity: the soul (essence) of solidarity. This is able to sustain human civilisations as the invisible/divine intervention, to guide communities on the path of falah (human well-being) and *adl* (justice). What does this more specifically mean?

6.3.3. Ihsan Emergent Foundation: In the Beginning was Consciousness

The concept of Islam, for me, broken down to its bare elements, is comprised of *aqidah* (a set of beliefs), Shariah (a set of laws) and *akhlaq* (a code of morality). The concept of the Shariah is not only to govern man in the conduct of his life in order to realise Divine Will, but covers all behaviour: spiritual, mental and physical. Thus, the Shariah principles are more than law, covering the total way of life that includes faith (*iman*) and practices (*amal*), personal behaviour, legal and social transactions. As such, Islam is also known as *Shariah al-kubra* in that it encompasses the way of life as ordained by Allah.

In the words of my spiritual guide Pir Zia, a contemporary mystic: 'The human soul comes to gather experiences on this earth and to leave a mark, which we often call the legacy. We are constantly inscribing our signature on the tablet of nature. What is that signature?' He then goes on by reminding us of the knowledge and wisdom humans have created together:

> There have been times in human history when these questions have been asked, and human beings have come together to step out of the narrow conditioning of one's own immediate experience, and to seek, and to embrace, and gather together the fullest extent one can encompass of the whole gamut of life's experience on earth. Moments when humans have gathered together to sum up, the epitome of human knowledge and human experience. This has taken, at times, at the form of House of Wisdom in Baghdad; the Baitul Hikmah which gathered together the insights of Mathematics and produced Algebra, through the insights of ancient Sages of Mesopotamia that inside of, as far as, Hindustan (India). Now, today we are here, with all the resourcefulness and creativity that exists, and lies in wait to be galvanized; to be put to the service of coming together of human beings, concerned with our collective future. Human beings that are pondering over; what are our spiritual and cultural traditions of the planet, that are our true heritage.

Meanwhile, in the world around us, it is reassuring to be working with people who believe in this 'togetherness', as mentioned by Pir Zia, and drawing from their inner wisdom, spirituality and cultural traditions. They are persistently working towards finding new solutions to our world's ever-lingering problems; in effect, doing 'God's work' on the earth.

One such example of a sagely person, who has been relentlessly working towards that goal, along with his allies, is Dr. Amjad Saqib, the founder of Akhuwat Foundation, in Pakistan. The 'solidarity impulse' started transmutating in him whilst working with the poor rural people, on a Rural Support Program in Punjab, Pakistan, activating the spirit of 'asabiyah' (group spirit) in him. For Amjad, then, the cure of society's ills—that is, abject poverty as a result of social injustice and manmade caustic divide and greed—should come by following the Qur'anic ordination: to offer interest-free loans/Qard-al-Hasan, and, most importantly, by following the Prophetic tradition of Mawakhat—sharing one's abundance with the brothers and sisters of one's community. For Saqib: 'In the accounting of passion and of *ishq* (love); two and two do not equal four. The result is contingent only on *intention*. When the intention is noble, an extra zero can easily be added.'

Thereby, Amjad, in reviving this tradition of Mawakhat, initiated a new cycle of 'Soulidarity': soulful solidarity, combining the physical (solidarity) with the spiritual (soul-idarity) mobilising/activating the communal spirit, and, thereby, awakening the collective consciousness of his community of Akhuwateers and Pakistani society. As maintained by Nasr (10):

> When we turn to the sacred scriptures of various religions, we discover that in every case the origin of the cosmos and of man is identified as a Reality which is conscious and in fact constitutes consciousness understood on the highest level as absolute Consciousness, which is transcendent and yet the source of all consciousness in the cosmic realm including our own. Furthermore the 'in the beginning' is understood, not only, as belonging to the past, but, also, to the present moment, which is the eternal now. That is why 'in the beginning' must also be understood as 'in principle' as the Latin translation of the opening verse of the Gospel of John asserts, *'in principia erat verbum.'* Whether we speak of Allah who commands things to be and they are, or the Tao, or the Word by which all things were made, or Brahman, we are speaking of Consciousness of an ever-living and present. This truth is made explicit in Hinduism, where the principal Reality, which is the source of all things, is described as at once Being, Consciousness and Ecstasy. Nor is this unanimity of vision of the Origin of all things, as identified with consciousness, confined to sacred scriptures.

For the 'practical mystics' amongst us, including people such as Pir Zia Inayat Khan (spiritual leader) and Amjad Saqib (social integrator), here in the 21st century, we find the spirit/rhythm of Mawakhat. It is embodying oneness with the divine through social mobilisation and economic upliftment, for the well-being of the downtrodden and neglected ones in our societies, this being the highest state of *taqwa*; an Islamic term for being conscious and cognizant of God, of truth, of the rational Reality.

Shah Wali-Allah was an 18th century leading Islamic scholar, reformer, historiographer, theologian, and philosopher from India, hailing from the region Amjad Saqib was born in. He saw a natural process of development—what he terms *al-irtifaqat*—as the four stages of socio-economic development within an Islamic society.

The first stage is primitive society. The second stage is when the society organises itself, adopts divisions of labour, develops trade, hiring, credit, modes of fair dealings and mutual cooperation. At the third stage, a city-state comes into being with proper governance. At the fourth stage, a super authority, that controls and wields power over all the city states, comes into being. Shah Wali-Allah combines the concept of socio-economic development with the concept of securing the pleasure of Allah (*ridwan Allah*) and termed it as *iqtirabat*, that is, ways and stages of purifying and spiritually developing oneself.

In Pakistan, Amjad takes on the path of iqtirabat, combined with Pakistani contemporary philosopher-poet Muhammad Iqbal's concept of 'passion' (ishq)/love for Allah and His Messenger, by bringing the ihsan (excellence/beauty) a vertical dimension, to his community of ikhuwah (brotherhood), a horizontal dimension. For Saqib:

> Akhuwat was a struggle to create such a society, where there is no deprivation and exploitation of the poor and where, in place of rapacity and temptation, the ethos of benevolence and sacrifice rule.

This reflects the principle prescribed in the Qur'an, reinforced by the Prophet of Islam and expounded by many scholars, such as Seyyed Hossein Nasr, Shah Wali-Allah, Muhammad Iqbal and economists like Umer Chapra.

We now *navigate*, in the integral rhythm laid out in Chapter 3, towards the Northern realm of emancipation, the knowledge (ilm) realm of our Soulidarity hikma (wisdom) postulation, recounting Akhuwat's Mawakhat manipulation bringing the spiritual and physical (financial) together.

6.3.4. Emancipatory Navigation: Akhuwat/Brotherhood Model of Solidarity

Akhuwat's message of Mawakhat and its approach to alleviate poverty is described as 'The Akhuwat Model'. Through various economic interactions and educational interventions, the organisation speaks about the Akhuwat Model, with all the relevant and interested stakeholders, in order to promote its replication and for better understanding of the Islamic principles in general.

The Mawakhat (solidarity) community is ever-growing in Pakistan, due to Akhuwat's distinctive methodology of community-building, by raising a higher consciousness of the local communities. This is done through holding circles where Akhuwat staff members and Dr. Amjad Saqib, share the story of Mawakhat and Akhuwat's practical model of Qard-al-Hasan (interest-free loans) to support local/microbusiness/enterprises.

Thereafter, it also engages with other organisations by teaching this model to interested stakeholders, in order to either facilitate their transition, or to enable them to take the first step into this field. This includes educating the affiliate staff in interest-free, non-profit microfinance (Qard-al-Hasan). Their support for replications is purely based on Amjad Saqib's dream of building an interest-free Mawakhat community, throughout Pakistan and the world, without any interest in capitalising on market shares. They, thereby, invest their energy and resources into helping develop other organisations, without detracting from their objective. It contributes to Amjad's ultimate vision of a poverty-free society. In a period of over a decade several organisations have implemented 'The Akhuwat Model' and added Qard-al-Hasan as one of the tools for their community services.

Before we expand on the principles of Akhuwat's philosophical model of integral solidarity, let us briefly review the effects (in statistical terms) of Akhuwat's Qard-al-Hasan (benevolent loan) in practical terms.

6.3.5. The Transformative Mawakhat Effect

Having worked initially as the GM at the Punjab Rural Support Program (PRSP), in 2001, some 18 years ago, Dr. Amjad Saqib strongly condemned the 20% interest charged on loan distribution. One reason was that the policy was in direct conflict with the teachings of Islam. The other was that in the formal banking sector, the interest was much lower and available to 'creditworthy' affluent individuals only.

Inspired by the Prophetic philosophy of Mawakhat and the Iqbalian concept of ishq (divine love) as well as by *akhuwat ki jahangeri* (supremacy of brotherhood), to make a change, Dr. Saqib wanted to start a microfinance program where the loans were in the form of Qard-al-Hasan: benevolent loans. He took his altruistic big idea to a small gathering of friends and won over their support. With an initial donation of a humble 10,000 Rupees ($100) from Mr. Saleem Ranjha and the undying support of his allies, namely, Dr. Kamran Shams, Dr. Izhar Ul-Haq and Mr. Humayon Ehsan, Akhuwat was formed. The first loan was given out to a woman.

In its early years, Akhuwat was simply a philanthropic venture to see how interest-free microfinance would operate. However, by 2003, the donations had increased to a massive 1.5 million rupees, with a loan recovery rate of 100 percent, unheard of in either conventional banking or microfinance. Consequently, it was decided to initiate Akhuwat as a proper and registered organisation. At the same time, while drawing on the tradition of Qard-al-Hasan,

Akhuwat has grown to incorporate many of the lessons learnt from conventional microfinance movements from across the globe.

Akhuwat, thus, originally founded in 2001 with US $100 has disbursed loans of up to US $600 million, to date (in 2019), to over 3.2 million families in Pakistan. And, today, it has expanded to include over 800 branches in 350 cities of Pakistan, a UK branch, a microloan portfolio of over US $110m active loans, and a recovery rate of 99.94%. We now turn to what we term Akhuwat's '5 I Genealogy'.

6.4. Akhuwat's 5 I Genealogy

Akhuwat's 5 I genealogy (fourfold + centre) is a categorical postulation of Akhuwat's fourfold principles.

The 4 I's are *Iman* (faith), *Ikhlas* (sincerity), *Ihsan* (excellence) and *Ikhuwah* (solidarity), with *Infaq* (spending to please Allah) in the centre as the moral economic core, as postulated by Lessem and Schieffer (11) in *Integral Economics*. This proposition emanates from an absolute contemplation of three main Islamic principles: Islam, Iman and Ihsan as shown in the figure below.

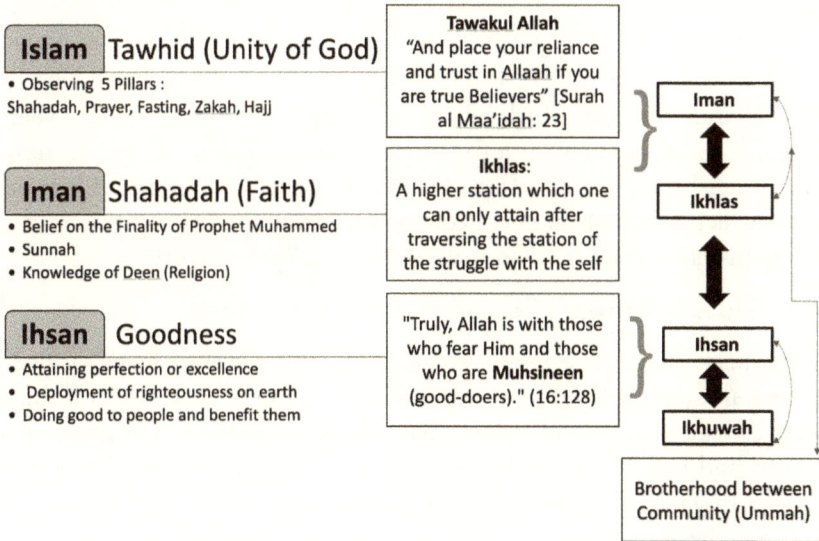

Figure 6.1. Akhuwat's Soulidarity Genealogy

6.4.1. The First I – Iman (Faith)

Primarily, in Islam, there are three levels of faith, that a person can attain: Islam, Iman and Ihsan.

The first level is Islam: Prophet Muhammad (pbuh) explained it as observing the five major ways of worship or duties (the adhering to which creates an Islamic structure, as these duties constitute the pillars of Islam's structure).

The second level is Iman: By properly practising the five ways of worshipping, Muslims as individuals and as communities benefit from the rewards Allah has promised to them. Yet, there are some who are more ambitious to be closer to God, to gain a higher level of his rewards, and to enjoy more intellectual happiness. They need to reach a higher level of faith than Islam, which is Iman, as we are told by Verse 14 of Surat Al-Hujurat (Chapter 49) of the Holy Qur'an:

> The Arab said, 'We have believed.' Say: 'You have not believed,' but say
> 'We have submitted,' for faith has not yet entered your hearts
>
> Al-Hujurat, 49:14.

For unless faith enters the deeper recesses of one's heart, it is not completed or sanctioned by God. Incidentally, this is the stage of Ikhlas: Akhuwat's second I.

The third level of Ihsan: This is the highest level of faith, and the closest to God. It is to worship Allah as if you are seeing Him. While you do not see Him, He truly sees you which relates to feeling God's presence everywhere. The word 'Ihsan' in Arabic is a derivative of the verb 'ahsana', which means doing things better. Thus, the literal linguistic meaning is doing the best one can do, which is doing what God commanded us to do. Ihsan petitions us to feel responsible for others as God's vicegerent (Caliph) on earth.

6.4.2. Ikhlas (Akhuwat's Second I) Stems out of Iman

The person whose heart reaches an ideal degree/level of Iman—called a *mu'min*—not only believes in divine destiny but also practises Iman through his/her own good deeds and action. That belief is borne out of Ikhlas/purity of the heart and Iman/*Shahada*. For Shahada is bearing witness by placing one's full faith in Tawhid (Oneness of God) and finality of Prophet Muhammad (may peace be upon him).

Consequently, Akhuwat's fourth I; *Ikhuwah* (Mawakhat/Brotherhood), flows through all of the aforementioned three I's, that is: Belief in God's Unity/Iman, with the purity and sincerity (Ikhlas) of heart/intention and doing good/spreading beauty around (Ihsan) for the well-being of community/society.

142

6.4.3. The Fifth I – Infaq: Spending in the Way of Allah

At the time of writing this book chapter, Akhuwat have now added a fifth principle to their previously articulated 4I genealogy. The fifth I is the I or Alif of *Infaq* which means 'spending in the way of Allah'. As often prescribed by the scholars, Infaq is referred to as a trait of *muttaqin* (those who have Taqwa/God-consciousness), that they spend (in Allah's cause) out of what Allah has provided for them. This is a physical trait, affecting the relationship between an individual and his community.

This concept is ordained in the Qur'an as '*Infaq fi Sabilallah*', as Allah stated, 'from what We (God) provided'. Islam encourages wealth to be circulated. Assets which are left idle are liable for *zakat*, i.e. compulsory alms giving, because the assets are supposed to be used for the benefit of all e.g. idle lands, minimum cash balance in the bank. Islam prohibits the accumulation of wealth by certain groups as this causes injustice in society and makes the economy susceptible to major downturn caused by a small group of people or one industry.

Akhuwat is commonly known and perceived as the largest (interest-free) microfinance organisation, inside or outside of Pakistan. As such, we view Akhuwat as much more than a microfinance organisation, in comparison to other such organisations in Pakistan or in its neighbouring countries. While Akhuwat aims to rid Pakistan of poverty, just as Muhammed Yunus wished to do with Grameen Bank originally in Bangladesh, Akhuwat parts ways with the Grameen model in its absolute immersion in the Islamic model of Qard-al-Hasan (benevolent loan); that is, of ridding the society of an imposed scarcity of resources, amongst the abundance of wealth possessed by the privileged class of the society. Moreover, Akhuwat (brotherhood or *bhai-chara* in Urdu), much more broadly, sets in motion its collective impulse of societal reciprocity by emphasising its four stages of self and societal development, through its 4 I orientation.

Ajaz Ahmed Khan (12) is a senior microfinance advisor with CARE International, Akhuwat's lending partner in the UK. According to him, Akhuwat of Pakistan is probably the purest Islamic microfinance institution and one of the largest anywhere but is at the same time one of the simplest. Akhuwat, however, is something of a hybrid. In fact, Akhuwat turns the concept of economic man (or woman) on its head. Such is the phenomenal nature of Akhuwat's paradigm: outwardly simple yet inwardly a whole philosophy of reciprocity, benevolence and compassion. It is thus important to draw on Akhuwat's implicit inner wisdom of hybridity.

6.4.4. The 4 I's of Akhuwat Paradigm

We have thus contemplated the 4 I's, plus centre, rooted in Akhuwat's 4 principles, transpiring from the three levels of faith as above.

As such Akhuwat's 4 principles are:

- Role of Religious Spaces: <u>Iman – Faith</u> being a higher degree of Islam, Iman covers all faiths on non-discriminatory basis as per Akhuwat's policy of non-discrimination to religion, race, class and gender.
- Interest-Free Loans (Qard-al-Hasan): <u>Ikhlas – Sincerity</u> is a derivative of Tawhid (Unity/Oneness of God).
- Transforming Borrowers to Donors: <u>Ihsan – (Spreading) Excellence</u> is the multiplier effect of virtue/Barakah – further forming a Solidarity Bond amongst the community of Akhuwateers.
- Volunteerism: <u>Ikhuwah – Brotherhood</u> is the eventual effect of the Solidarity GEN*E* rhythm, transforming the soul/spirit of Solidarity to Soul-idarity.

These principles came to me as I was delving deeper into the heart and soul of Akhuwat, after many interactions with Dr. Amjad Saqib. These are reflected in Akhuwat's philosophy and conceptualised by Amjad, who, along with being a true devotee of the Prophet of Islam (peace be upon him), is also an ardent disciple of Iqbal's philosophy of *ummah* (community) and Brotherhood.

Muhammad Iqbal (13) was a firm believer in religion without which, for him, in Pakistan at least, the social system cannot work properly. This was the reason he focused his efforts on the revival of Islam and the protection of Islamic society. He believed Islam, in his region, to be the most valuable contribution to world thought. For him, Islamic society has a permanent element in its structure of thought, involving the unity of God, the finality of Prophethood, the Shariah (scripture/text), the Islamic code of law and Ikhuwah (Brotherhood).

For Iqbal, the stable character of a society directly depends upon the essential regard for the ultimate realities that govern life. Iqbal defined Tawhid (Oneness), Risalah (Prophethood), and Akhuwah (Brotherhood) as the foundational and basic principles of the ummah (Muslim community). For him, if a community deviates from any of these principles, it will deviate from the actual goals of religion. In a manner of speaking, Iqbal's characterisation of a perfect *millat*/ummah reinforces our 4 I's positioning as per Akhuwat's Mawakhat (Solidarity) philosophy, love and sacrifice of the Ansars of Medina for the Muhajirun from Mecca, as are the proverbial instances of brotherhood (Ikhuwah) in Islamic history, to encourage genuine brotherhood.

As emphasised in the Qur'an and underlined by Iqbal in his poetic expositions, one cannot be a Muslim unless he/she has love for their brother as much as he/she loves himself. The integrity/Solidarity of the ummah has been compared with a human body: the entire Muslim society is considered as one body and if any one part becomes diseased the other parts shall feel the agony.

We now turn to our own postulation of an Integral GEN*E*-a-logical order of Solidarity. In doing so, it is important to recall the 'Transdisciplinary Realms' from Schieffer and Lessem's (14) seminal work on integral development, which is our reason for asserting the 'Akhuwat Model' as an Eastern integral finance model.

6.4.5. Transdisciplinary Realms

Each reality viewpoint has a different emphasis, which leads to four different knowledge fields or *realms*, each providing a particular perspective. Any given development calling and challenge requires the transdisciplinary engagement with all realms:

• *Southern Realm of Relationship*: **Nature & Community**	(Ikhuwah)
• *Eastern Realm of Inspiration*: **Culture & Spirituality**	(Iman)
• *Northern Realm of Knowledge*: **Science, Systems & Technology**	(Ikhlas)
• *Western Realm of Action*: **Enterprise & Economics**	(Ihsan)

Table 6.1. The Four Realms in Akhuwat philosophy

6.5. Solidarity Capital

6.5.1. Reciprocity of Ikhuwah (Bhai-chara)

To introduce this section, we address what may be interpreted as a new field, of *solidarity capital*, at least in Pakistan.[4] Akhuwat's philosophy is based on the premise that poverty can only be eliminated if the society is willing to share its resources with the poor/needy and less fortunate. For Akhuwat,

4 **Editor's footnote**: There are many capital provision expressions for the Solidarity Economy across the World, such as in the Iberian peninsula, in Barcelona, Catalunya, through Co-operativo Mondragon, in the Basque Country (see Chapter 3) and elsewhere. But, Akhuwat provides a unique model in Pakistan and the Indian subcontinent.

Qard-al-Hasan is a means to an end and not an end in itself. The end is a vibrant, economically strong society, based on sharing resources which is an idealist approach in itself. Their aim is to develop and sustain a social system based on compassion, solidarity and mutual support.

Indeed, Amjad's articulation of establishing one such society is what sets Akhuwat apart, particularly from other microfinance organisations operating in Pakistan and around the world. As microfinance organisations are considered one the most effective tools to reducing poverty, Akhuwat and Amjad Saqib, following Ibn Khaldun, appears to be more concerned about the decline in societal bonds of solidarity. Other microfinance-based organisations certainly lack that passion for community development, through awakening the collective conscious of their subscribing communities, to thereby form a Solidarity Bond, something which has been Akhuwat's core principal philosophy and practice.

That Solidarity Bond, as per Amjad's contemplation, following then a faith-based prescription, that which has been ordained by Allah and not dictated by the all too often 'Westernised' and individually oriented rules of microfinance. The term for that divine remedy, as per Amjad, is Qard-al-Hasan: a loan given with the intent of benefiting the needy and not to make business out of someone's needs.

6.5.2. Qard-al-Hasan: Zakat and Sadaqah: Akhuwat's Interest-free Loans

Akhuwat, in the public domain, is known as a Microfinance Institute (MFI). Its primary objective was to relieve people of the destitution and despondency of poverty. To accomplish such, for Amjad, it was necessary to draw on the rich customs of Islamic faith and beliefs, something, for example, that is significantly absent from the Grameen Bank, through it is based in a predominantly Muslim part of the world. Inherently, for Islamic societies, the main philanthropic acts are done as a religious obligation of giving zakat and *sadaqah*.

Sadaqah is the charity money given to people in need. For Amjad, giving charitable money (occasionally) was not the solution he had in mind. He does not believe in creating permanent dependence, but, rather, believes in sustainable growth in partnership with the poor and needy.

For this purpose, Akhuwat adopted the interest-free loan model as prescribed in the Qur'an as its operational strategy. Interest-free small loans are given to the economically active poor of society for establishing a new business or expanding an existing one. Such loans offer pragmatic solutions to the many hurdles that are now emerging in the field of microfinance. These loans aim at poverty alleviation, not as a business enterprise for the organisation, but to enable the lowest income classes and those who previously do not have a source of income to become economically independent and contributing citizens. Most importantly, they serve a purpose on humanitarian grounds without any discrimination. Amjad firmly believes, and speaks about, poverty arising not simply from being materially poor; rather, poverty is when a person loses their self-pride and dignity by being dependent on others financially.

We, now, explore the nature of a 'virtuous loan', as per Amjad's translation of Qard-al-Hasana, an Arabic term which if broken down epistemologically, means a beautiful (Hasana) loan (Qard). For as per his apotheosis of a quintessentially virtuous society, loans given should also be none other than virtuous and benevolent.

6.5.3. A Virtuous Loan

Akhuwat's interest-free loan model is inspired by the philosophy of Qard-al-Hasan, a Qur'anic ordination. According to the Institute of Islamic Banking and Insurance's definition, it is a virtuous loan that is interest-free and extended on a goodwill basis, mainly for welfare purposes. The borrower is only required to pay back the borrowed amount. The loan is payable on demand and repayment is obligatory. But if a debtor is in difficulty, the lender/creditor is expected to extend time or even to, voluntarily, waive repayment of the whole or a part of the loan amount. Islam allows loans as a form of social service among the rich to help the poor and those who are in need of financial assistance. Qard-al-Hasan may be viewed as something between giving charity or pure gift and giving a loan (Qard).

A debtor may, then, voluntarily choose to pay an extra amount to the lender/creditor over the principal amount borrowed (without promising it) as a token of appreciation. This principle forms Akhuwat's theory of 'borrowers becoming donors'. This type of loan does not violate the prohibition on riba (interest), since it is the only type of loan that does not compensate the creditor for the time value of money. Such loans have not been uncommon in human history among peers, friends, family and relatives but no other organisation, as far as we know, has been able to come up to Akhuwat's scale of channelising philanthropic funds so effectively, with a recovery rate of 99.9%.

At this point, we exemplify two of Akhuwat's main funds that continuously spiral out of each other; that is, its interest-free loans and its reciprocal endowment (Members Donation Program).

6.5.4. Two Principles: Interest-Free Loans and Reciprocal Endowment

Why Interest-free?

According to the *Financial Encyclopaedia*, the Arabic term *Riba al-qard* is associated with lending and borrowing (i.e. received in lending or paid in borrowing). It is a type of riba that constitutes an excess amount, pecuniary or non-pecuniary, over and above the principle (*asl al-qard*) in a loan (*qard*) that a borrower pays to the lender along with the principle, based on a precondition in the contract (*aqd*) or customary practices (*urf*). Riba al-qard also constitutes any excess amount paid for extension of a loan's maturity date. The majority of religious scholars are of consensus that riba, in this sense, holds the same meaning and import as the conventional notion of interest.

Borrowers Becoming Donors

However, any excess amount or consideration (*iwadh*) given by a debtor out of his own accord, and without the compulsion of a contractual stipulation or custom is not tantamount to riba, but is rather attributed to *Husnul-qadhaa* i.e. willingly offered by the borrower. *Riba al-qard* is also known as *Riba al-Qur'an* as it is mentioned in the Qur'an. In conventional finance, it is interest on loans.

The Mawakhat Model

The seed philosophy for both above principles originates from the Prophetic tradition of Mawakhat, right after the migration (*hijrah*) of the Prophet of Islam to Medina from Mecca, as indicated above. Allah's Messenger forged ties of brotherhood between the Muhajirun (followers) and Ansar (helpers). In doing so, the Prophet demonstrated the practical example of real management, as real wealth is yielded through real management of people.

For Agha Hasan Abedi (15), another Pakistani, a banking genius of his time, and president and founder of Bank of Credit and Commerce International (BCCI), so-called 'Real Management' models itself on the laws of nature: a management ecosystem. For Abedi, the concept of *giving* permeates all aspects of real management. More than a banker, Abedi was a visionary with a clear perception of the future—a divine gift. He believed that mankind could achieve far more if only it understood the divine scheme: that we all have a purpose in life, and we must feel honoured to be chosen for the task of building the future using our abilities and capacities.

Abedi, with an unconventional approach to banking, was amongst those who have taken it upon themselves to institutionalise a 'spirit of giving' and sharing amongst their employees. In 1980, Abedi addressed a letter to all BCCI employees emphasising their obligation to share the benefits accruing to them with the less unfortunate. In his letter, he also emphasised the fact that, while extending financial help is one way of sharing, the ultimate form thereof is giving of yourself, i.e. offering your time, energies and abilities with humility for the salvation of the less fortunate. For a start, employees were offered a sum along with their monthly salaries for this purpose.

This was the same concept of giving that Amjad has been persistently exerting to instil into his society's psyche for years. Similarly, for Amjad, as Abedi professed, *giving* instils a sense of acquisition in people which eventually creates a tradition of purposeful living and co-existence. Akhuwat has been successful in cultivating the same culture of giving amongst its borrowers by becoming its donors in the event. As per Amjad's presumption, learning from the historic example of Medina/Mawakhat, he religiously believes in the above categorisation of Ansars and Muhajirun, that in any given society, there will always be Ansars (helpers), those who are always willing to give of themselves and from their abundance. They act as anchors for every society. Then, there are Muhajrin (emigrants), those who are always in need of helpers.

Such wisdom of cooperation (*Al-Hikmat al-Ta'awuniyah*), and solidarity existent in Akhuwat's case, is a reflection of Shah Wali-Allah's fifth wisdom, in the second stage of socio-economic development, which relates to cooperation among the members of the society on economic issues. Qutb ad-Din Ahmad Wali-Allah Dihlawi, an 18th century prominent Sufi philosopher and scholar of Delhi, was known as Shah Walli-Allah because of his piety. For Shah Wali-Allah (16):

> This cooperation necessitates itself as people in the society are not equally good for all things. Some of them have good intelligence while some others are imbecile. Some of them have capital, while some others are empty-handed but can work hard. Some people hate to do petty works, while some other do not, and so on. Thus, their mundane life would have become very difficult, had they not sought the cooperation of each other. Take the example of Mudarabah (profit-sharing), a person might have capital, but he cannot persuade himself for trade and travelling or any other such kind of job. Thus, they need cooperation and help of each other. Some people cannot do that directly, so they resort to power of attorney, sponsorship and middleman ship.

He maintains that the idea of *waqf* was unknown to people before Islam. This institution was established by Prophet Muhammad (peace be upon him) for different welfare considerations. The merit of waqf is that the needy people benefit from this source of income generation while its ownership remains with the endowment maker. This is the Mawakhat paradigm of Soulidarity between communities. And what lies in the nature of Solidarity, for too much decadence eludes the spirit of solidarity and Iqbal's exigency of *faqr* (spiritual poverty).

6.6. Conclusion

6.6.1. 'Spiritual Brotherhood' Revived in an Eastern Muslim Society

I have attempted to convey a unique 'solidarity impulse', as an Eastern orientation to Islamic finance and economics, which I term as Soulidarity, as the vital energy for human as well as ecological 'subsistence'. Thereby, from the case study presented above, we can see its archetypal resonance with the Mawakhat philosophy of 'spiritual brotherhood', revived in an Eastern Muslim society for the subsistence of 'poor' and needy people and its explicit effects in communal upliftment and well-being.

Yet, the challenge for one such organisation, like Akhuwat, remains, to explicitly maintain their position in the Islamic economics or finance field—an area which is primarily regulated by either the Shariah scholars or economists/financiers/bankers. Meanwhile, the common man and woman still struggles for their 'subsistence' in an unjust neoliberal economic system, which remains problematic for scholars, champions and intellectuals of alternative finance. Every effort, therefore, needs to be made to convey the distinction and hybridity of Akhuwat's model of soulful solidarity i.e. Mawakhat (soulidarity) by authenticating the micro-ness of its benevolent (interest-free) loan: Qard-al-Hasan as Islamic microfinance.

6.6.2. Four Streams of Money Allocated for Charitable Purposes

Inherently, most Islamic societies have four streams of money allocated for charitable purposes, whereby zakat is obligatory for every Muslim to pay. The table below illustrates the structural definition and semiosis of charity/alms distribution within a Muslim society:

Akhuwat banks on the spirit of fraternity and brotherhood that inhabits the very core of an Islamic society—in this case, Pakistan—rather than relying on institutional loans and grants. Amjad had his heart set on channelling through the, above mentioned, four streams of philanthropy installed within Pakistan's Islamic society. Therefore, for Akhuwat, it was a case of channelling these voluntary streams (Zakat, Sadaqah, Qard-al-Hasan), as illustrated above, into a more effective way, so that the most vulnerable of the society, could take benefit of a pool of funds. These were readily available and flowing out of the benevolence of a society that believes in sharing their abundance as a religious and moral duty, just as decreed by Allah and Maqasid-e-Shariah (objectives).

ZAKAT	SADAQAH	SAQAQAH JARIYAH	QARD-AL-HASAN
Purification	Charity	Perpetual (ongoing) Charity	Goodly Loan
Obligatory	Voluntary	Alms	Interest-free Loan
One of the five pillars of Islam 2.5% paid annually on wealth/assets	Voluntary offering at the will of the benefactor	Remains active even after one's death	Given with sincerity and not asked back if the borrower fails to pay

Table 6.2. The Semiosis of Islamic Charity

But what happens when the free-flow of these benevolent streams are disrupted by our (man's) selfish desires to accumulate wealth for himself? It is at times like these the natural/divine *impulse of solidarity* is activated to salvage the *human subsistence* (falah)—the primary instinct of the maqasid (objectives). Similarly the archetypal Mawakhat (see Chapter 7) instinct (Soulidarity) starts pulsating through social integrators like Amjad Saqib from Pakistan. It is at that particular juncture in time that the world finds an 'alternative' to our contemporary financial miseries, debt-slavery, being one example. Yet, we choose to look away because the 'state of affairs' should be maintained in their current (unnatural) flow with the odd precept: TINA, but 'there is no alternative'.

6.6.3. From Debt Slavery to Soulidarity Economics: Metempsychosis

Metempsychosis is a concept in Greek philosophy related to reincarnation and the transmigration of the soul. It's a rebirthing of a new form. In retrospection and in relation to our call, we need to collectively investigate: what does it mean to transmigrate our financial (greed-driven) soul to a liberated or soul-disciplining of Soul-idarity? And how could that be implied to finance or economics?

151

For after residing in a debt-based society (UK) for several years, and by intuitively studying and discovering Akhuwat's phenomenal 'Mawakhat/Solidarity' paradigm, I am proposing a universally Trans-Formed Integral paradigm of Trans-migration (moving away) from the misery of 'microfinance'—of 'granting' microloans to the 'poor and needy'—to a self-generated autonomy of virtuosity. Why am I suggesting this?

We have all witnessed the devastation of debt-servitude which has enslaved modern societies. When more than $100 billion of national debts were cancelled in the 2000s, many people thought the issue of debt was done and dusted. Instead, the debt payments of impoverished countries are increasing rapidly and are at the highest level for more than a decade. Closer to home, the numbers of households in persistent and dangerous debt continues to rise and students leaving UK universities now face higher average debts than American students, with the average student graduating with more than £44,000 of debt.

These figures tell us that serious and systemic action is needed to make debt justice a reality. But, lenders—the banks and richer governments—currently set the narrative (see Chapter 2), making it difficult for those suffering from unjust debts to be heard. Whilst disadvantaged communities are suffering in silence, few are providing them with a solution to be self-sufficient through a balanced-reciprocity. Marshall Sahlins described such original affluent societies, in *Stone Age Economics* (17). But, self-enterprise—based in social soulidarity—is postulated through Akhuwat's facilitation of Qard-al-Hasan (benevolent loans), as per Qur'anic ordination and the Prophetic tradition of Mawakhat: sharing abundance (excess) with community (ikhuwah).

Whereas the diseases of the soul, such as greed and wealth accumulation, could be cured by disciplining the Self, organisations are rethinking 'personal development' of their staff—little or no attention is paid to healing or liberating *the Self from the false Self* and its greed to accumulate and own more. Therefore, it remains my personal calling to integrate and heal the 'spirit' of solidarity by (re)thinking it through the wisdom (hikma) of the soul; the SOUL of solidarity. Akhuwat's 'Mawakhat' paradigm, as such, coming from an Eastern philosophy, is a primal example of such a discipline based on its fourfold 5 I's (Iman, Infaq, Ikhlas, Ihsan and Ikhuwah) genealogy, which has been generating a plausible financial uplift for their micro-communities.

6.6.4. Towards Integral Renewal

In the final analysis, then, such soulidarity economics can be set within the overall context of what we have termed *Accounting for Renewal.*

| Reconnect with your **Origins** |
| Empathise with 'the Other' |
| Understand how your World is 'Co-constructed' |
| Regenerate Tradition in the Light of Modernity |

Table 6.3. Accounting for Renewal

We now turn from the South and East to the North and as such will move away from a singular focus on Islamic finance and economics, to a more broadly based Semiotic Economics.

6.7. Bibliography

1 **Bakhtiar,** L (1993) *God's Will be Done – Traditional Psychoethics and Personality Paradigm.* Chicago. The Institute of Traditional Psychoethics and Guidance

2 **Burckhardt,** T (2008) *Introduction to Sufi Doctrine.* Indiana. World Wisdom Inc

3 **Lessem,** R, **Schieffer,** A and **Rima,** S (2013) *Integral Dynamics: Cultural Dynamics, Political Economy and the Future of the University.* Abingdon. Routledge

4 **Nasr,** S H (2006) *Islamic Philosophy from its Origin to the Present: Philosophy in the Land of Prophecy.* New York. State University of New York Press

5 **Chapra,** U (2014) *Morality and Justice in Islamic Economics and Finance.* Cheltenham. Edward Elgar

6 **Marouani,** A (2017) *Ibn Khaldûn's Contribution to Economic Thinking: An Essay on Critical Reassessment.* s.l.: Université Nice-Sophia Antipolis/Université de la Côte d'Azur/GREDEG.

7 **Auda,** J (2007) *Maqasid Al-Shariah As Philosophy Of Islamic Law – A Systems Approach.* London – Washington. the international institute of Islamic Thought

8 **Saqib,** A and **Malik,** A (2019) *Integral Finance – Akhuwat: A Case Study of the Solidarity Economy.* Abingdon. Routledge

9 **Eighth Hadith** (1995-2018) Prejudice ('Asabiyyah). *Al-Islam.org.* [Online] Ahlul Bayt Digital Islamic Library Project. [Available at: https://www.al-islam.org/forty-hadith-an-exposition-second-edition-imam-khomeini/eighth-hadith-prejudice-asabiyyah#f_01b9e511_1]

10 **Nasr,** S H (2006) In the Beginning was Conciousness. *The Essential Sophia (Library of Perennial Philosophy).* The Essential Sophia. Bloomington, Indiana. World Wisdom Books

11 **Lessem,** R and **Schieffer,** A (2010) *Integral Economics: Releasing the Economic Genius of your Society.* Farnham. Gower Publishing

12 **Harper,** M and **Khan,** A (2017) *Islamic Microfinance: Shariah Compliant and Sustainable?* Rugby. Practical Action Publishing Ltd

13 **Iqbal** M (2000) *The Reconstruction of Religious Thought in Islam*, New Delhi. Kitab Bhavan

14 **Schieffer** A and **Lessem** R (2014) *Integral Development: Transforming the Potential of Individual, Organisation and Society.* Abingdon. Routledge

15 **Shahid,** A B. (2016) Remembering Agha Hassan Abedi. *Business Recorder.* [Online] http://fp.brecorder.com/2015/05/201505161186840/ 16th May

16 **Al-Ghazali** M (2008) *The Socio-Political Thought of Shah Wali Allah.* New Delhi. Adam Publishers

17 **Sahlins,** M. (2017, reissued) *Stone Age Economics.* Abingdon. Routledge

CHAPTER 7

Semiotic Economics: The Fourth Way Beyond Neoliberalism: North

Tony Bradley, Lecturer in Social Economy,
Liverpool Hope Business School, UK

7.1. Introduction

> When markets do not include the costs of negative externalities, then firms do not receive price *signals* telling them that their products are causing harm, either to those whom they affect directly, or to the whole society, or to the ecosystem on which the economy ultimately depends. This is a situation that economists call market failure. Our system is full of market failures.
>
> Neva Goodwin, *What Can We Hope for the World in 2075?*

7.1.1. Trans4ming Finance

In many respects Islamic finance has been taking the world of conventional, neoliberal capitalism, by storm. Of course, for those outside the Islamic community it may be seen as rather more controversial. But, the reason for this maelstrom is that, at least in principle, applying a religious epithet to the operation of financial institutions seems, to contemporary ears, to be mixing oil with water. Moreover, in for example the Akhuwat case, outlined in the previous chapter, it spiritually runs so deep that in the secular 'North-West' it is a non-starter, so that Saqib is obliged to put his pre-emphasis on 'microfinance'.

As for Ibn Khaldun, and the backdrop of '*asabiyah*', that is relegated to sociological, and North African history. Finance, proverbially speaking, is the liquidity which makes the economy flow. Surely as such, the 'oil of Allah's

155

light' (see Holy Qur'an 24:5) cannot be mixed with the secular activities of finance, banking and investment? So, as we turn to the European North, it is my turn to draw on a broader based approach, which some will regard as relating to the three Religions of the Book, specifically, but which addresses the general question of: 'What are the meaning-systems of alternative economic models, and, how may we analyse them, in order to understand what they signify?'

This is what we term 'Semiotic Economics'. Whilst this is an 'alternative' approach to much conventional economics, it is not very far from the economic core, as our opening quote indicates. As Neva Goodwin (1) points out, prices are *signs*. Semiotics is the study of signs. As such, Semiotic Economics is very much part of the signs of the economic times, as we see the world trans-4ming, requiring new value pointers, in the economy, to address 21st century challenges.

Within the three Religions of the Book (*Ahl al-Kitab*, namely, Judaism, Christianity and Islam) a shared core value is that faith is to be practised in every aspect of life. That is true worship of God and respect for human beings. As such, whilst the faiths may be experiencing a secular challenge of hitherto unimagined proportions—particularly in the Northern and Western realms—the moral values which they enshrine are becoming increasingly significant in the 21st century world.

Hence, the reason for this book. It comes from a team of scholars who have been connected for many years through the work of Trans4m, a committed association of projects, programmes and personal journeys, with the aim of developing economic transformation, through social and enterprise innovation in each of the Four Worlds (South, East, North and West). At the heart of the Trans4m methodology is an understanding of the integral connectedness of these worlds, so far as global-to-local transformation is concerned (see Preface and Chapter 3, inter alia). Equally, the Trans4m process identifies that economic and social change is Grounded in local communities and Emerges when their cultural, spiritual and core values shift from an inner latency to an outer, manifest energy.

Furthermore, innovation requires method, technique, technologies and the operation of knowledge-systems, which, usually, arise from patterns of research, which connect the academic and the personal, the spheres of intellect and culture. For that reason a major theme of this book has been to consider the ways in which meaning-systems influence the application of 'ethical' economics to finance and investment. These systems serve to Navigate emergent communities of innovation, through research, towards Effecting enterprise transformation. This is the Trans4m GEN*E*. Moreover, and in the context of this chapter, I am positioning Islamic finance and especially economics, alongside other 'alternative'-to-the-mainstream (neoliberal), economic systems, in a transformational light.

7.1.2. Interpreting Meaning-Systems

In so doing, we have taken a further bold step, within this book, duly emphasised in this Northern chapter, which is to identify ways of interpreting these meaning-systems, using the theories and techniques of semiotics. As such, as will become apparent in this chapter, as was also intimated in the preceding one, related to the Soulidarity of Akhuwat, the Four Worlds and the GEN*E* are connected, integrally to the four stages of a semiotics method (see Chapter 3, where this was introduced), by which the signification of alternative approaches to finance can be made explicit.

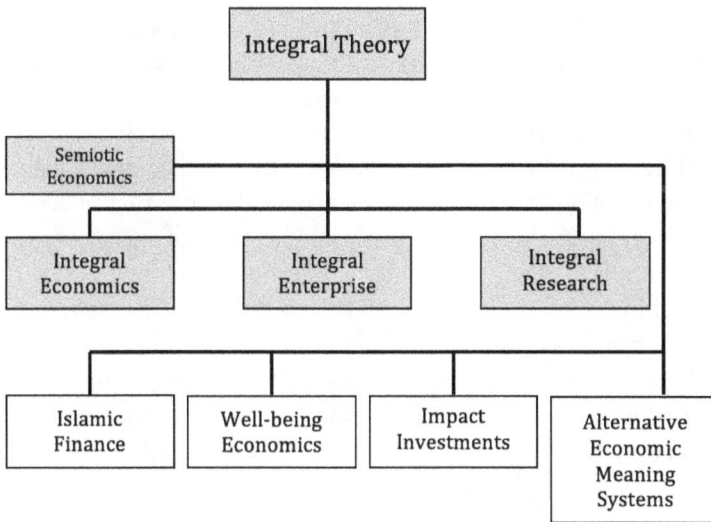

Fig 7.1. Connecting the fields of economics-related knowledge-creation

The thematic flow that I follow in this chapter (see above, Fig 7.1.), then, is to take the super-ordinate perspective of Integral Epistemology and Knowledge—which has been worked out theoretically and applied practically, by Lessem and Schieffer (2, 3), in a considerable range of texts over nearly two decades—and to develop it using the Semiotic Economics model presented here. Using this meta-theoretical basis, the various authors in this volume apply the integral and the semiotic to the specific problematics posed by Islamic, Well-being and Impact economics, finance, and investment, inter alia, as they relate to the semiotic realm of what is, frequently, termed 'ethical finance'. In this respect, the hierarchy of knowledge-creation connections developed here can be depicted as in Fig 7.1. above.

7.1.3. Integral, Semiotic, Islamic

What we term as 'rational' is not always sensible or meaningful. There are worlds of economic meaning that fall outside the narrow equations, econometrics and graphs of neoliberal economics. Semiotics is the study of how meanings are made, interpreted, communicated and utilised, for example, in marketing or media production. But, so far as we can tell, at least in the way laid out here, this is not a discipline that has often been applied to alternative economic models. This is the approach we are terming 'Semiotic Economics', of which *Islamic* economics-and-finance forms a substantive part, albeit for us with an *Integral* orientation, whereby we, purposefully, draw from the South (Africa), the East (Asia), the North (Europe) and the West (America).

Consequently, by way of introduction, we will first remind ourselves why alternative economics is undergoing something of a resurgence. From there, we will turn to the writings of Karl Polanyi, one of the 20th century's most influential heterodox economists, to look at what he said and what he, crucially, missed. Following that, we will consider the core role of semiotics in analysing meaning-making, particularly in the light of recent work by the late Latin American semiotician Juan Magariños de Morentin (4), through the over-arching perspective of the integral model. We will, then, in Chapter 9, consider some brief examples of how Semiotic Economics may be developed, connected to the main thematic flow of this volume, from the spheres of Christian 'Kingdom' Economics, Islamic finance and Impact Investing, before concluding on possibilities for future research and innovation.

7.2. The Resurgence of Alternative Economics

7.2.1. The Limits to Growth and Beyond

During the mid-1970s a series of textbooks were produced which challenged the economic orthodoxy of what was, then, called 'neo-classical economics'. The surge in books on topics such as environmental economics, followed both the first *Limits to Growth* (5) report and Fritz Schumacher's iconoclastic *Small is Beautiful* (6). They reflected deep concerns, within a narrowly prescribed but informed population, about a looming environmental crisis. Journals such as *Resurgence* and *The Ecologist*, equally, propagated challenges to neo-classicism, albeit from a populist and non-technical standpoint.

These academic concerns—to contest the perceived hegemony of marginalist, optimising strategies, based in the methodological individualism of 'homo economicus'—reflected a wider political debate. The left counter-cultural surge of the late 1960s, represented by student protests at Berkeley, California, as well as in Paris, London and other Western capitals, in the summer of 1968, gave rise, following the Oil Crisis of 1972–73, to left-leaning groups suggesting rethinks of the post-War consensus. In the UK, led by the socialist politician Tony Benn, a faction of the British Labour Party produced an *Alternative Economic Strategy* (AES, 1974, when Benn was Trades & Industry Secretary, in the second Wilson Government).

According to John Medhurst (7) the political economy arguments that led to the AES and its subsequent policy projections, from within the UK government, represented a pivotal moment in UK and Western thinking. By 1976 the AES was buried and the seeds of 'neoliberalism' had been planted. Chancellor of the Exchequer, Dennis Healey, famously ate humble pie when he met bureaucrats from the IMF at Heathrow Airport, to address Britain's 'Balance of Payments Crisis'.

Clearly, cracks had begun to appear in the carefully polished surface of neoliberal economics several decades before the Great Crash. But, fascinatingly, 40 years after 1968 that was what occurred, in 2007–09. Ten years after the Crash there is a renewal of interest in alternative economics, just as there was in the 1970s. Again, the current ferment has been stimulated by students who are mistrustful of an economics establishment which, they perceived, was unwilling to address real world or alternative theoretical issues.

Post-Crash Economics began in Manchester, in 2012, (http://www.post-crasheconomics.com/), after that university's students, in economics and business, challenged their professors about why neoliberal economics hadn't seen the Crash coming. The establishment response was, essentially, 'Believe our textbooks, not the world'. The story of the ensuing battle is written-up in the best-selling *The Econocracy – the Perils of Leaving Economics to the Experts*, by Earle, Moran & Ward-Perkins (8). And they weren't alone. Students across the world were raising similar issues. This led to Oxford economics students, together with many others, founding *Re-Thinking Economics* (http://www.re-thinkeconomics.org/about/). In America, *Alternative Economics* (https://alternativeeconomics.co/) was launched, led by eminent scholars such as Professor Neva Goodwin (9).

The essential point is that a range of models are being dusted off, fashioned and re-emphasised, many of which are centuries old, to challenge the dominance of neoliberal market-based capitalist economics. Not that there is consensus. We are dealing with economists after all. Some, sympathetic economists, such as Cambridge Professor Diane Coyle (10), share many of the sentiments exhibited by these rebellious students (sic) but, nevertheless, revert to type in claiming a spurious econometric scientism for economics. As she put it, in a blogpost on January 4th, 2017:

> I am not interested in an economics of competing theories and world views; we do better work as economists when we listen to these, confront them with evidence and careful statistical or logical reasoning, and try to establish a bit of knowledge – context-dependent and historically contingent as it might be.

This does, rather, give the game away. The point of Semiotic Economics is that it acknowledges that the meaning-systems on which economic arguments are based are, precisely, cultural, dependent on local context and contingent on historical formations. Far from there being anything wrong with this, the task of Semiotic Economics is to understand these specific cultural particularities, in terms of the meaning-systems that undergird them.

Alongside the *integral* model to economics (see Chapter 3), we need to consider the community grounding, the cultural values, the technical systems and market enterprises which are based on different economic theories. But, additionally, we need to study the meaning-systems that prioritise alternative explanations. This can be accomplished from both expert and indigenous perspectives. We do so in order to understand how to reshape the economic world in response to real human concerns.

Such analysis, when yoked to practical policy-making and enterprise action, offers the best prospects for an economics that is based in public discussion and open to cultural critique and alternative interpretations. Karl Polanyi offered a clear historical perspective, which cut through the somewhat sterile economic polarity of the mid-20th century. His analysis was both brilliant and, yet, missed one key element, which Semiotic Economics seeks to redress.

7.2.2. Polanyi's Great Transformation and Its Critics

After Polanyi

We may consider all the economic activity that we undertake in society, which we don't monetise or work at through the market. What *is* their value and meaning in the economics of the real world? Part of my reason for raising this arises from a recent resurgence of interest in the work of Karl Polanyi, whose magnum opus, *The Great Transformation* (11), was published towards the end of WW2.

Embedded and Dis-embedded

Polanyi pointed to two economic systems which he considered to embed social relations and one which was dis-embedded from them. The first two were those of 'reciprocity', or gift and sharing economics, characterised by the non-monetary activities of households and communities. These can be associated with the Southern Realm (see Anselm Adodo and Jubril Adeojo's Chapter 5). Reciprocity focuses social relations through the patterns of family and wider, usually local, social systems and 'communities'.

The reciprocity mode, in the North and West is seen as a, largely, historic economic system, that had been displaced. Most indigenous cultures operate patterns of reciprocity, the study of which has been the basis for much economic anthropology. This dates as far back as Marcel Mauss (12), Howard Becker (13), Alvin Gouldner (14), Marshall Sahlins (15, see previous chapter) and F.G. Bailey (16), to the more contemporary writings of Daniel Miller (17), Charles Eisenstein (18, see Chapters 2 and 3) and David Graeber (19).

The second of Polanyi's modes was that of 'redistribution', which has become one of the most significant aspects of state apparatuses, since Polanyi's era. Although we may associate this with the modern state, it has ancient antecedents and was, in Britain, enacted through the Elizabethan Poor Laws and Speenhamland of the 16th century. In its contemporary guise, this is increasingly under pressure, in an age of low economic growth and so-called 'austerity'—as standardly measured—particularly in respect of fiscal policies for welfare transfers.

The current debate in Britain over the introduction of 'Universal Credit' and similar schemes (see Mark Anielski's discussion in Chapter 2)—itself, a particularly obscuring use of language—highlights the way in which the linguistic categories of equity are being requisitioned to reinforce patterns of poverty and inequality (20). There is nothing 'universal' about this scheme. Nor do its recipients consider it to be credit, more often recognising it as debt-based. Such are the ways in which politicians and their policy-making apparatchiks twist and mangle meanings.

All liberal democracies operate some form of redistributive fiscal policy. But, ever since James O'Connor's (21) seminal work, left economists have been questioning the capacity of the state to avoid permanent fiscal crisis (22, 23, 24, 25, 26). In the current 'age of austerity' it is highly debatable how long such redistributive policies will last. Indeed, in the Merseyside area where I was a director of the local social regeneration trust, central government funding for local government had reduced by 50% since 2010. Of the 2018 year's budget of £240M, 78% needed to be pre-allocated to care of the elderly, children's services and other statutory duties (27), leaving very little for other redistributive policies.

We may associate redistributive economics with the Northern Realm, in integral terms, as different economic theories, policies, systems and models pertain. Throughout the 20th and into the 21st centuries such policies have oscillated between Hayekian free-market neoliberalism, from the political right, and Keynesian, state-interventionist demand management, from the left. But, state redistribution has a much longer lineage, pre-dating the emergence of capitalism.

Even so, Polanyi considered both reciprocity and redistribution as embedding social relations in economic models. The former model of reciprocity acts at the family, household, inter-personal and inter-organisational levels, to deliver micro-economic social relations. The latter mode of redistribution embeds the whole of society, in using the fiscal power of the state, and its capacity to determine levels of national income allocations—to different sectors and class fractions—using borrowing, taxation, investment and expenditure policy calculations and practices. In each case, then, as Polanyi saw it, the economic was embedded within social formations, at both micro- and macro-economic levels.

Nevertheless, a great transformation had taken place towards the end of the 18th and throughout the 19th centuries, led by the Industrial Revolution in Britain, which *dis-embedded* economy from society, so he argued. This was the rise of market-based, monetised capitalism, focusing on profit-maximisation, for the benefit of owners and shareholders in joint-stock companies. The market, of course, represents a substantial part of the economic genius of the Western realm. As such, the state's increasing powers of redistribution resulted from the need to ameliorate the worst excesses of market-monopoly capitalism.

Critiques of Polanyi

Many critiques have been made of Polanyi's overarching thesis. From the Marxist left, Polanyi is criticised for insufficiently understanding the exploitation of subordinated class fractions; for not having an overall theory of capitalism; and equivocating on the role of markets within socialist societies (28). His emphasis on the *commodification* of people, rather than their *alienation* from the means of production, is seen as a case of left revisionism.

Furthermore, his inherently structural-functionalist view of society, as organic, wherein there is an inevitable counter-movement between markets and the state, can be seen as overly optimistic, especially in an era of ecological crisis. Block and Somers (29), additionally, accuse Polanyi of inconsistency in respect of arguing that market-based economies are, necessarily, dis-embedded, whilst pointing to their lack of pure dis-embeddedness creating crises in capitalism. Sandbrook (30) defends Polanyi, for indicating that the double movement—of a left, redistributive, counter-movement to neoliberal extensions of free-market mechanisms—leads to capitalist shocks, such as experienced in the Global Financial Crisis (2007–09). Even so, he regards Polanyi as shifting from 'hard left' (neo-Marxist socialism) to 'soft left' (democratic social market) positions during his lifetime.

Equally, Polanyi has been challenged from those more sympathetic to the neoliberal right, for being a left idealist (31). Economic liberals challenge him for blaming capitalism for being dis-embedded, whilst arguing that it is founded on the legal and political social codes of the ruling class. Polanyi wants it both ways, they argue. In this respect both left and right round on his theory of the double-movement.

Moreover, neoliberals challenge him on empirical grounds, in terms of his approach to economic history, particularly in respect of his elision of pre-capitalist modes with reciprocity and the lack of market penetration into economics prior to the late 17th century. For example, a range of economic history articles have been produced, which challenge Polanyi's theory about the dominance of reciprocity and the absence of markets prior to the rise of mercantilist pre-capitalist modes in the 16th century (32, 33, 34, 35, 36).

There is ample justification for the view that Polanyi adopted a form of left idealism. He had been heavily influenced by Fabian socialists, such as G.H.D. Cole, R.H. Tawney and the WEA, in wartime and immediate post-War England. They reflected a less strident form of socialism, deeply influenced by religious values. In many respects, then, Polanyi was searching for a form of romantic, communitarian and spiritual socialism (with a small 's') that was antithetic to the increasingly globalising world of finance-based capitalism. As an Austrian émigré he lamented the economic wreckage of his beloved Vienna, which had occurred at the time of the Great Depression.

This idealism, equally, sprang from his position as a Jewish-Christian apologist, for which he has been heavily criticised. More recently, however, he has received a more sympathetic reading, in terms of the period in which he was writing, given the horrors of *The Shoah* and *The Jewish Question* (37). In this respect, his own religious and spiritual moral economics remained unresolved in him. It may be that he was so close to his own times—his Jewish upbringing and Christian conversion—that he failed to see the deep spiritual contours of his own economic philosophy, which was profoundly anti-capitalist, at least in terms of the meaning-system of neoliberalism.

7.2.3. Beyond Polanyi — The Fourth Economic Realm

The irony, then, in respect of Polanyi's economic analysis was that, whilst he eloquently paved the way towards an understanding of the diverse economics of three of the four worlds, the one that he was personally closest to was neglected. As so often, the sphere we know best is the one that we can least see. It is, simply, the environment in which we live, as fish swim in water.

We can recognise a contrast in the perspectives of Polanyi and his immediate theoretical predecessor, Max Weber, whose theory that Protestant puritanism provided the ideological soil in which industrial capitalism could flourish (38). Weber had become distanced from his religious upbringing. As such, he was able to identify the association of post-Reformation Protestantism with the rise of capitalist thriftiness. As he put it, 'the spirit of capitalism' enabled investment in factories, machinery and, most crucially, mass migrations from land to urban spaces.

In similar vein to Weber, Karl Polanyi saw, in reciprocal and redistributive systems, embedded modes of economic activity, contrasted with the dis-embedded nature of market-based capitalism. But, he failed to see a fourth economic way, based in spirituality—derived from reciprocity—which pointed towards a variety of alternative economic systems, with their diverse innovations in social enterprise and societal entrepreneurship.[5] That is hardly surprising since very few recognised the capacity of a social and solidarity economy in the 1940s, when Beveridge was formulating plans for what became known as 'the welfare state'. Even so, where Weber had seen new religious values as accommodating a 'capitalist spirit', Polanyi missed the significance of cultural meaning-systems to generate alternative economic forces.

In respect of the integral Four Worlds/GEN*E*alogical theory presented earlier in this volume (Chapter 3), Polanyi's three modes reflect the Southern (reciprocity), Northern (redistribution) and Western (capitalism) realms, respectively. But, what of the Eastern world, both metaphorically and in terms of literal geography? This is where we introduce the concept of *Semiotic Economics*, which can be applied, inter alia, to the faith traditions emergent from the Middle East, of Judaism, Christianity (see Chapter 2 and 5) and Islam (see Chapters 5, 6, 8 and 10), as we do so later in Chapter 9.

Our argument is that, the task of Semiotic Economics is to uncover the meaning-systems and, most particularly, the economic forces and forms that emerge in the fourth way of the Eastern integral realm, alongside those that pertain in the other three. As Lessem and Schieffer (39) indicate, the Eastern world can be depicted as the source of pathways to 'Renewal', as indeed

5 **Editor's footnote:** In fact, Polanyi did identify a fourth economic mode, that of household or peasant production. But, in his later work he identified this as, simply, one type of the redistributive mode, in this case operating processes of redistribution through households, families and local communities. In this respect, it represented a mid-point between reciprocity and redistribution. But, the more substantive point holds, that Polanyi failed to identify a mode of the economic that was based in spiritual culture, albeit, what he saw as the entirely historic nature of, reciprocity-based economics does shade into this.

reflected in the previous chapter on Akhuwat, wherein the roles of culture and spirituality are taken seriously, as discourse, in respect of economic society. Furthermore, there is a need, we argue, to understand the ways in which economic meaning is fashioned in each realm.

This is important, to recognise the significance of the burgeoning range of alternative models that are seeking to displace neoliberalism from its dominant position in economic discourse. But, perhaps, more significantly (sic) Semiotic Economics can help us to identify and recognise the capacity of new enterprise innovations, in what has previously been termed 'the social economy'. Most of these are underpinned by meaning-systems which are antithetic to neoliberalism. Semiotic Economics shines a different light on both economic theory and contemporary shifts in the economy itself.

It owes a debt to the work of Karl Polanyi, in elucidating alternative economic modes—as, equally, to Marx, Weber and other students of political economy—not least in his elaboration of three of the four ways. But, it needs to break out, beyond that work, to focus on the fourth way. This means understanding the contribution that semiotics can play in assisting with interpreting economic modes and the enterprise forms that they effect. It is to a brief depiction of the fourth way that is emerging in semiotics theory and methodology that we, now, turn.

7.3. Introducing Semiotics

7.3.1. Historical Development

It is, of course, wholly beyond the scope of this orienting chapter to introduce the entire discipline of semiotics.[6] But, there have been recent developments in this field which align with both the integral worlds model and the missing fourth in the Polanyian depiction of economic modes. As such, it is helpful to identify these as a way into outlining the scope of Semiotic Economics.

Semiotics developed during the late 19th and early 20th centuries as the study of meanings and how these are communicated through signs and symbolic processes, especially by Peirce (40) in America, and Saussure, (41) in France. This discipline overlaps with socio-linguistics, the philosophy of language and hermeneutics. The specific focus of semiotics is on the ways in which understanding is shaped through the relationships of language, image

---

6 **Editor's footnote**: That is the purpose of the fourth volume in this series on Insights in Semiotic Economics, from Beacon Academic: *Introducing Semiotic Economics: Understanding the Meanings in Alternative Economic Systems* (forthcoming, Bradley, 2021).

and media to the objects, concepts and forms that they seek to represent. Oddly, however, for a discipline in which the objective is to uncover meaning, the language of semiotics, itself, can appear impenetrable (42).

As with many humanities fields, the task of creating a 'science of signification' has generated a complex, indeed baroque, terminology, which can be daunting to the uninitiated. It is, however, possible to simplify, albeit recognising that the following will, undoubtedly, appear lacking in rigour to experts in the field. That said, it is important to do so, to propose a way of applying semiotics to the vast corpus of economics.

7.3.2. Saussurean Dyadics, Peircean Triadics and the Missing Fourth

The two originators of the discipline then—although semioticians argue over whether they were both following the same scientific inquiry—were Ferdinand de Saussure (1857–1913) and Charles Sanders Peirce (1839–1914). Interestingly, whilst their writings received attention throughout the 20th century, it is in the 21st that the discipline they generated has come to increasing prominence.

Saussure had been the dominant figure in the science of semiology, largely because of his influence on French structural anthropologists, such as Lucien Levy-Bruhl (43) and Claude Levi-Strauss (44), inter alia. Peirce was, however, regarded as one of America's greatest 19th century philosophers, so that his theory of semiotic logic was less influential than his work in mathematical philosophy, learning theory and pragmatics, at least in his own lifetime and immediately following.

Saussure's theory of 'semiology' was dyadic, posing an understanding of the relationship between an object and its signifier, or sign. This was an enormous insight for all social science, as it required scholars to identify the relational nature of language, particularly, to the concepts, social facts (cf. Emile Durkheim) and societal objects that they were involved in interpreting. He was instrumental in coining the search for meaning. Even so, as Peirce was able to indicate, the simple object-sign relationship—important as it is—missed the *outcome of the process* of identifying the dyadic relationship.

As such, Peircean semiotics is triadic. One of Peirce's greatest accomplishments was to recognise the way in which a 'representamum' (sign) generates a range of interpretations, which he termed 'interpretants'. Peirce was seeking to explain thought processes. Given that all thought happens in time, there must be a relational gap between one thought and another. As such, each thought, as a representation of a correspondence between a sign and an object, issues in a further interpretant thought, as a logical process of signification. All thought is, therefore, in signs, that do not only act as pointers to the world but generate effects, which, in turn, further describe and interpret the world. A sign is a pointer towards meaningful thought processes.

Take, as an example, the word 'elephant'. This indicates an object as a particular member of a group of species of large, tusked and trunked mammals, that are indigenous to Africa and South Asia, classified as paciderms. As you had been reading the preceding sentence your thoughts will have gone in a variety of directions, as soon as you reached the word 'elephant'. Thoughts spin in all sorts of lines, indicating the range of interpretants that are generated by the word-sign 'elephant', in a process of thought.

The *sign relation* is, thus, the key to Peircean semiotics. It is the relation between the sign (representamum), its subject matter (object) and its meaning/interpretation/thought process (interpretant). The object is the sign's grounding. In itself, it acts as a pointer, which navigates thought. As a representamum it generates a range of interpretant effects. These effects can be understood as having extension (expanding the range of meanings) or intension (restricting the range of meanings). When grouped together (or multiplied), the extension and intension denote the full *informational* range of interpretants that are generated by a sign. As we will see below, this is a vitally important point in respect of *economics*.

Peircean semiotics is, also, triadic in a third way, in addition to describing the semiotic relation and the ways in which meanings are generated. Peirce (45), equally, identified three types of sign and, additionally, three ways in which each sign-type can be phenomenologically classified. His typology classifies the nature of the sign itself, the type of relation it has to its object and the relation it has to its interpretant (in respect of its object). In addition, each relational type of sign can be identified as having a quality, a capacity for re-action/resistance and a capacity for mediation/further representation. Because Peirce saw that every actual sign featured each of the sign types and related to each of the phenomenological classes, there could, logically, be 27 patterns of sign. But, empirically, he identified that not all signs held capacities for resistance and further representation, so he concluded that there were, in reality, nine or ten sign classes.

	SIGN QUALITY (GROUNDING)	SIGN-REACTION/ RESISTANCE (POINTING/ NAVIGATION)	SIGN-MEDIATION/ FURTHER REPRESENTATION (EFFECT)
SIGN-RELATION TYPE (BASE)	Qual-sign Word: 'elephant'	Sin-sign A particular elephant e.g. 'Dumbo'	Legi-sign The scientific classification of elephants as 'paciderms'
SIGN-OBJECT RELATION (PRIMARY RELATION)	Icon Picture of: 'elephant'	Index The class of elephants	Symbol E.g. 'Samanyanga', when, in Shona, considering who to give the totem-name 'elephant'
SIGN-INTERPRETANT RELATION (SECONDARY RELATION)	Rheme 'Elephantness' e.g. 'never forgets'	Dici-sign Situated elephants e.g. elephants in the DRC are threatened by ivory poachers	Argument e.g. in Hinduism, 'Ganesha', the elephant-god, symbolizes success/ victory over problems and points towards a consideration of wisdom and education

Table 7.1. Peircean classification of sign-relations (using the 'elephant' example)

Table 7.1. depicts a simplified Peircean sign-relation classification, without its third dimension. From this, it becomes clear that the simple dyadic Saussurean relation—between sign and object—is insufficient to depict the complexity of thought-processes (interpretants) of signification that can be generated by something as, relatively, simple, as the object that is called 'elephant'. Even so, it may have been noticed that there is a homologous relationship between Polanyi's scheme of economic modes and the Peircean model of semiotics.

Furthermore, those who have followed the logic of the integral GENEalogy (see Chapter 3) will, already, have recognised a gap. Whilst the Peircean schema aligns perfectly with the GN*E* of the integral GEN*E*, there is a missing element, which reflects the emergence of awakening cultural consciousness. Once again, as we saw with Polanyi, the missing element (Eastern depth below consciousness) is the very one that we might have expected to be uppermost in the development of semiotics. The environment of semiotics can be invisible to semioticians.

In both Polanyian and Peircean systems there is a missing fourth. For Polanyi, this reflected a lacuna of understanding economic systems in respect of cultural consciousness and spirituality. Within Peirce's, albeit highly complex, classification of sign relations, there is a similar missing element, which, strikingly, also relates to the Eastern aspect, connected to a renewed awakening of integral consciousness, as per Lessem's, 2017, caRe model (46).

The specific feature that is missing is a depiction of the *subconscious structural bases for meaning-systems*—from which conscious ideations emerge—to direct thought-processes from the object to its developed reaction/resistance or, equally, from its base sign-type to its sign-object relation. This can be understood, following the analytical psychology of Carl Gustav Jung (47), as missing the *archetypes of the collective unconscious*, that are invoked as structuring principles for thought. Although controversial, similar concepts, as organising psychic phenomena for the ways in which signs and language are directed— have been indicated in many 'structuralist' disciplines, as in Wittgenstein (48), philosophy; Chomsky (49), linguistics; and Jung (50), analytic psychology.

Nevertheless, this isn't simply (sic) a question of meaning. It is an issue of the structures through which meanings become signs for signification, which are intensely important in defining, for example, what we mean by 'economics'. These, frequently, lie beneath the surface of consciousness, outside the observation of institutional processes and are, usually, invisible in respect of how signs come into being. They are the slick subterranean surfaces across which objects glide, to generate signs, so that we, habitually, fail to notice these meaning-systems.

For example, in the cases of Kingdom Economics, Islamic finance and Impact Investing (outlined below, in Chapter 9), these slippery meaning-systems can be stated as 'grace', '*ihsan*' and 'value', respectively. Nevertheless, they require some effort to be identified and, even when this has happened, their linguistic expression can be regarded as deeply unsatisfactory, as we shall see. That is a main reason why structuralist analysis is so hard to engage in and requires so much explanation.

The point is that the Peircean triadic semiotic system—albeit a development of Saussurean dyadics—exhibits a critical missing linkage between the signs that provide the grounding for objects in language, images and media and the ways in which such signs become represented in diverse reactions and mediations. The missing fourth aspect—between object-signs and their signification-reactive force—are the subterranean meaning-systems, often unconsciously held, which condition the ways in which objects become signified. These function, akin to the Jungian archetypes (and their cognates, as above), as innate releasing mechanisms for the transmission of meaning. Fascinatingly, this gap in the Peircean system has, recently, been closed through the work of the late, great Latin American semiotician Juan Magarinos de Morentin.

7.3.3. The Fourth Edge of Juan Magarinos de Morentin

De Morentin (51) takes a lead from C.S. Peirce's classic explanation of the triadic semiotic process. But, importantly, he identifies that the process by which meaning is transformed depends on the fact that we have a *prior understanding* of the basis on which such transformation can take place. There is a previous moment of semiosis, even before the present moment, in which we believe we are establishing relationships between objects, signs and their interpreted transformations. He describes this as being 'on the edge of semiotics' as if looking in at the transformative instance. This is the missing fourth moment of semiosis, albeit the second step in the process of the movement from object to a multitude of its interpretations.

Interestingly, given the point that in this volume we are considering the shift from faith-based (see Chapter 6) to value-based finance (Chapters 8–10), he uses two analogies from the Bible (ibid p.256ff), which he sees as foundational for Western history, in terms of semiotics. It should be noted that whilst these are not Qur'anic, they are from texts which are revered within Islam (as from Musa-Moses and the Injil-Gospels, respectively).

The first concerns the Adamic task of naming the animals (Genesis 2:19–20), an exemplar for semiosis, par excellence. Adam (the man) can name the different animals, once the Lord has presented them to him. But, this is only possible because he has a prior, intuitive or pre-conscious, understanding of what the act of naming constitutes, what the animals are (compared to all the other objects in the Garden) and what is the meaning of 'naming'. The act and meaning of naming, together with the concept of the category 'animal', are each examples of being 'on the edge of semiotics'.

The text indicates that, as the Lord God accepts the names that Adam gives, that naming is more than ascribing a label. It is about a meaningful sign-relationship between God, the Man and the created order. Yet, there is, in the act of naming, a prior awakening of consciousness, which is implicit, but which becomes clarified once the names are given.

To return to our 'elephant' example, naming something as 'elephant' depends on the prior signification of what giving that name means. This is, essentially, to create an ordered index (Peirce's 'reaction' in the sign-object relation, see Table 7.1.). Equally, within the worldview of ancient Semitic (and many other indigenous) peoples, naming is to take power over the living object, as an act of epistemic creation, following God's ontological creation. Human knowledge results from understanding the hidden structures in the being of creation. In this respect we can interpret the act of Adamic naming as a structure of pre-scientific epistemology, where the 'pre-' does not mean subordinate or inferior to but, rather, an alternative epistemic process, based in spiritual discernment instead of empirical observation (see Adodo's discussion of African Southern epistemology and epistemicide, in Chapter 5).

Tellingly, de Morentin, further, reflects on the post-resurrection narrative from John's Gospel (20:24–29), in which the disciple Thomas refuses to believe that Christ is, indeed, risen, unless he sees the marks of the nails, following Jesus' crucifixion. As he points out, John's Risen Christ expresses: 'Because you have seen me you have believed; blessed are those who have not seen and yet have believed' (v29). But, it is clear that the Evangelist is making the point, to his contemporary followers, that belief is not based on sight but, rather, Thomas' sight is based on a prior belief, that such faith is a possibility.

As such, and contrary to the way this passage is usually explained in sermons, there is, inherently, no distinction between Thomas and generations of later believers. Both understand the resurrection 'Christ-event' because of a prior meaning-system of faith. It may even be that, because there are no question-marks in Koine Greek, that the first part of John 20:29 is better rendered: 'Then Jesus said to him, "Is it because you have seen me that you have come to belief?"' (the Greek is πεπιστευκειϛ, pluperfect). In an earlier section de Morentin indicates the basis for a semiotics methodology that takes account of this fourth feature of post-Peircean analysis. He points to the way in which we might specify the methodology for investigating the semiosis of a text, concept or way of interpretation, within particular social science disciplines. Given that he is not, immediately, easy to understand, especially in translation, the following section (ibid, p.47) may need some further explanation, important as it is.

> Each researcher should take into account the quality of the phenomena that are objects of the study (may be law, psychology or psychoanalysis, sociology, history, philosophy, literature, politics, anthropology, etc.) and should try to establish which are the texts (or, in a broader sense, the semiosis) that confer to such phenomena the specific signification or the conflict of significations that constitute the problem under study…the phenomena constituting the world are not given by themselves, but instead we identify them by adapting them to our possibilities of designation; nor [do] they contain in themselves their rationale, but instead *we project it according to categories available in our conceptual structure; nor are they seen (or understood) as they are, but as our modality of enunciation*

makes us to see them (or understand them), in the corresponding per-
ceptual environment. (My emphasis)

Revealingly, *economics* is missing from his list of objects of study. Whilst
we cannot be sure why, one suspicion is that economics is regarded as of lesser
breadth, in terms of signification. Economics is seen as a more singular discipline, less subject to the inherent contradictions ensuing from alternative semiotic processes, or sub-structures of meaning, than, say, sociology. That said, it is
unlikely that a Latin American scholar would fail to see the 'conflicts of signification' involved in economics, given the problematic political economy of that
region, at least since European colonisation in the 16th century. Economics is,
surely, not an in-itself phenomenon, as TINA neoliberalism would give us to
understand, but is adapted 'to our possibilities of designation... according to
categories available in our conceptual structure'.

The point is, that only as the archetypal, pre-judgmental (52) 'innate releasing mechanisms' (53) of economics become 'unconcealed' (54), then, we
see that economics involves a far more complex semiotic process than might
first have been understood. Nor is this, simply, a matter of 'alternative' economics perspectives, as has surfaced post the 2007 Crash. Instead, economics
needs to be subject to an entire post-Peircean analytical methodology, such as
that indicated by de Morentin. It is to presenting an introductory sketch of
such, that we, now, turn and elaborate on in Chapter 9.

7.4. Towards A Semiotic Economics Methodology

7.4.1. Utilising the GENEalogical Cycle

Thus far we have indicated two missing fourths, in the classical works
of Karl Polanyi, in respect of understanding economic history and, in those
of Charles Sanders Peirce, regarding the methodology of semiotics. This latter concerns identifying the relations of signs, to objects and, additionally,
the thought-processes (interpretants) which signs (representamums) generate
amongst their interpreters. As we have argued, it is in the Eastern realm—
when viewed from the perspective of Lessem & Schieffer's integral economics
theory—that we identify these lacunae.

Consequently, the initial requirement for a semiotic economics is to complete the GENEalogical cycle, identifying how to conceptualise the emergence
of awakening consciousness to non-conventional, contra-neoliberal, alter-
native-to-capitalist economics. The completion of Polanyi's schema requires
the identification of economic systems that connect Southern reciprocity to
Northern redistribution and, thence, to Western capitalism, via uncovering
the Eastern *archetypes of economic signification*. We identified, above, that a

distinctive semiotic economics takes seriously the cultural and spiritual mean-ing-systems which serve to transmit patterns of reciprocity to systems of re-distribution. As such, this is meant as an evolution of the considerable work of integral economics, as produced hitherto, albeit that it is reconfigured in respect of the Polanyian tripartite understanding of embedded and dis-embed-ded economic systems.

Where we see a genuine technical innovation, in the semiotics of eco-nomics—viewed through the lens provided by de Morentin's theory—is in identification of the archetypal bases for such Eastern meaning-systems. Even so, that is hardly very practical or integral. Far more important is to be able to conceive the entire GENEalogical cycles of signification, which proceed from having identified the missing Eastern sub-structures of these economic meaning-systems.

7.4.2. Beyond Neoliberalism

To do so, is to show the coherent and integral ways in which entire eco-nomic to societal innovations have occurred, are being developed and may proceed, through a systematisation of signification. Furthermore, we regard it as critical to be able to identify actualised local models and examples of such systems in place. We do not see much value in theory for its own sake. The urgency comes from the social fact that economics is a discipline that seeks to change the world but is in a state of disarray, precisely at a point when it is most needed.

And, because such an endeavour is founded on the post-Crash pressing need to 'unconceal' such, to borrow Heidegger's term, it is vital to signify the processes of Semiotic Economics in their full dynamic cycle, from ground-ing in communities to effective innovations. But, in order to do so, we must emerge the sub-structural meanings, 'on the edge of semiotics', if we are to more fully understand their significance and interpretation, as alternative eco-nomic systems. In effect, that has been the purpose of the chapters in this vol-ume, particularly in respect of understanding unconventional and 'alternative' finance. More fully, it will be the purpose of each of the volumes in this series, on *Insights in Semiotic Economics*, to express this task.

Further, it is worth reminding ourselves why this project is so important at this time, as indicated by this volume as a whole. As Neva Goodwin (55), puts it:

> People are being shaken up. It's going to take a lot of doing to get econ-omists to question the goals of the economy. And… the goal of the economy should be to support and encourage human well-being in a sustainable manner for present generations and into the future. That's a very different goal from [neoliberal] growth!

A dominant facet of economic neoliberalism is that it is predicated on the ideology of growth in money systems, which fuels unsustainable patterns of production, consumption and investment, acting against, both, reciprocity and fairer distributive mechanisms (see, again, Chapters 1 and 2). This indicates something that is, often, neglected, which is that the emergence of economics arises out of meaning-systems, rather than algorithms based in iron laws. In other words, as we have sought to show, here, it is the missing *meaning giving* realm in economics and semiotics that requires further elaboration, not simply in theory but, vitally, in terms of actualised practice.

Such practice will bring us, in the next chapter, to the Western version of Islamic finance and in the subsequent chapter to a fuller articulation of the semiotic economics of faith-based models. But, prior to that it is important to conclude with a brief statement of a semiotic economics methodology, applied, for example, to ecological economics and the issues that Adeojo raised in Chapter 5.

7.4.3. A Statement of Methodology, Related to 'Ecological Economics'

The purpose of ecological economics is to demonstrate that the economy exists as a sub-system of Nature-Creation, not the other way around, and to generate valuations and models of transactions that recognise this. Hence, the interpretation of capital, in terms of planetary sustainability—rather than the sustainability of individual firms, the economies of nation states, or, even, the entire global economy—is to understand that it can only be accounted for in terms of the enhancement of ('interest'-payments to) Natural Capital. This upends the standard understanding of a debt-based economy. It requires discounting on the basis of payments to the planet, not as returns to conventional economic agents. Those agents owe a debt to the planet, which is required as credit to Nature-Creation (cf. Lessem's double-entry environmental accounting in Chapter 3).

That is what ecological economics does, in a nutshell, so to speak. So, what is the methodology of Semiotic Economics that will uncover the—alternative to neoliberalism—meaning-systems that are made within ecological economics? As indicated above there are four stages to the process of elaborating a semiotic economics, which follow the GEN*E*alogical dynamic cycle.

The four basic steps of the Semiotic Economics methodology are to:

- Identify the economics object e.g. Nature-Creation, Natural Capital.
- Uncover the cultural/spiritual/integral/*archetypes of signification* e.g. the (initial pre-conscious) emergent understanding that human beings and society are part of the Natural World.

- Specify the sign/signification question (*signifier/representamum*) to be addressed i.e. how do we conserve 'the Commons', to re-GEN*E*-rate sustainability effects, through e.g. by embedding circular economy production processes?
- Effect the co-creation of local material interpretations (*interpretants*) e.g. by firms that are implementing circular economy practices, such as *Blue Economy*, *WRAP* and *Provenance*, amongst many thousands, at least aspirationally.

But, this is insufficient as an integral and GEN*E*alogical methodology and process. To a considerable extent, the methodology outlined above is 'universalist' in conception. Rather, it needs to be grounded in local context, emerge through local-to-global culture, navigate through global science, technology and systems and effect in global-to-local innovations. That said, what should, immediately, become clear is that this semiotic economics is, precisely, a way of fulfilling that global navigation. It is a methodology that reflects its Northern-ness in integral worlds terms. Even so, although reflecting the North, in needs to demonstrate a re-GEN*E*-rative potential to help to recast economic analysis in integral cyclic terms. In Chapter 9 I will apply this methodology for uncovering economic semiosis, within three examples of 'faith-based' economic meaning-systems: Kingdom Economics, Islamic finance and Impact Investing, with which I am directly involved.

7.4.4. Semiotic Accounting

In the final analysis, moreover, whereas the Southern community and economy is underpinned by our Southern path to research and innovation, and Eastern soulidarity economics by our path of renewal, this Northern approach to Semiotic Economics is underscored by the path of reason, and hence Semiotic Accounting, as shown in Table 7.2. below.

Identify the **Economic Object**
Uncover **Signification Archetypes**
Specify the **Sign to be Addressed**
Effect **Local Material Innovations**

Table 7.2. Semiotics Accounting

Having, identified the Northern methodology of Semiotic Economics it is now time to turn West, to its application and effect.

7.5. Bibliography

1 **Goodwin**, N (2010) What can we hope for the world in 2075? *Thirtieth Annual E. F. Schumacher Lecture*. Schumacher Centre for a New Economics. [Available at: https://centerforneweconomics.org/publications/what-can-we-hope-for-the-world-in-2075/]
2 **Lessem,** R and **Schieffer**, A (2010) *Integral Economics – releasing the genius of your society*. Abingdon. Routledge
3 **Lessem,** R (2017) *Embodying Integral Development*. Abingdon. Routledge
4 **De Morentin**, J M (2011) *Semiotics of the Edges – notes on semiotic methodology*, (transl. Winchkler, G.). [Available in online archive: http://semioticmethodology.com/]
5 **Meadows**, D H, **Meadows,** D L, **Randers**, J and **Behrens** III, W W (1972) *The Limits to Growth*. Washington. Universe Books
6 **Schumacher**, E F (1973) *Small is Beautiful – a study of economics as if people mattered*. London. Blond & Briggs
7 **Medhurst**, J (2014) *That Option No Longer Exists*. London. Zero Books
8 **Earle**, J, **Moran**, C and **Ward-Perkins**, Z (2017) *The Econocracy – the perils of leaving economics to the experts*. Manchester. University Press
9 **Goodwin,** N et. al. (2014) *Microeconomics in Context*. Abingdon. Routledge
10 **Coyle**, D (2017) *What to do about the econocracy*. Blogpost, January 4th. [Available at: http://www.enlightenmenteconomics.com/blog/index.php/2017/01/what-to-do-about-the-econocracy/)
11 **Polanyi**, K (1944) *The Great Transformation – origins of our time*. New York. Farrar & Reinhart
12 **Mauss**, M (1925/1954) *The Gift – forms and functions of exchange in archaic societies*. New York. Martino Fine Books
13 **Becker**, H P (1956) *Man in Reciprocity: Introductory lectures on culture, society and personality*. New York. F. A. Praeger
14 **Gouldner,** A W (1960) The Norm of Reciprocity: A Preliminary Statement. *American Sociological Review*, 25, 1, 161-178
15 **Sahlins**, M (1972) *Stone Age Economics*. New York. de Gruyter

16 **Bailey**, F G (1973) (Ed.) *Gifts and Poison – the politics of reputation*. Pavilion Series in Social Anthropology. New York. Schocken Books.

17 **Miller**, D (1998) *A Theory of Shopping*. New York. Cornell University Press

18 **Eisenstein**, C (2011) *Sacred Economics – Money, Gift and Society in the Age of Transition*. Berkeley. CA. Evolver Publications

19 **Graeber,** D (2011) *Debt – The First 5000 years*. New York. Melville House Publishing

20 **Livingston**, E (2017) Universal credit doesn't reward hard work. It makes the most vulnerable pay. *The Guardian On-line*, May 1st. [Available at: https://www.theguardian.com/commentisfree/2017/may/01/conservatives-universal-credit-hard-work]

21 **O'Connor,** J O (1973/2017, New Edn.) *The Fiscal Crisis of the State*. Abingdon. Routledge

22 **Osborne**, D and **Hutchinson,** P (2006) *The Price of Government – getting the results we need in an age of permanent fiscal crisis*. New York. Basic Books

23 **Krugman,** P (2008) *The Return of Depression Economics and the crisis of 2008*. New York. W.W. Norton & Co

24 **Foster**, J B and **Magdoff,** F (2009) *The Great Financial Crisis – causes and consequences*. New York. Monthly Review Press

25 **Stiglitz**, J (2010) *FreeFall – America, free markets and the sinking of the world economy.* New York. W. W. Norton & Company

26 **Varoufakis**, Y (2017) A New Deal for the 21st century. *New York Times*, July 6th. [Available at: https://www.nytimes.com/2017/07/06/opinion/yanis-varoufakis-a-new-deal-for-the-21st-century.html]

27 **Goodman,** P S (2018) In Britain, Austerity is Changing Everything. *New York Times.* May 28th. [Available at: https://www.nytimes.com/2018/05/28/world/europe/uk-austerity-poverty.html]

28 **Selwyn**, B and **Miyamura,** S (2014) Class Struggle or Embedded Markets – Marx, Polanyi and the meanings and possibilities of social transformation. *New Political Economy*, 19, 5, 639-61. DOI: 10.1080/13563467.2013.844117

29 **Block**, F and **Somers,** M R (2014) *The Power of Market Fundamentalism – Karl Polanyi's critique*. Cambridge, Mass.: Harvard University Press

30 **Sandbrook**, R (2015) *Why Polanyi and not Marx*. Blogspot piece, May 2nd. [Available at: https://sandbroo.faculty.politics.utoronto.ca/why-polanyi-and-not-marx/]

31 **Adelman**, J (2017) Polanyi, the Failed Prophet of Moral Economics. *Boston Review – a political and literary forum*. May 30th. [Available at: http://bostonreview.net/class-inequality/jeremy-adelman-polanyi-failed-prophet-moral-economics]

32 **Silver,** M (1983) Karl Polanyi and Markets in the Ancient Near East – the challenge of the evidence. *The Journal of Economic History*, 43, 4, 795–829. December

33 **Law**, R (1992) Posthumous Questions for Karl Polanyi – price inflation in pre-colonial Dahomey. *The Journal of African History*, 33, 3, 387–420

34 **Aubet**, M E (1993) *The Phoenecians and the West – politics, colonies and trade*. Cambridge. University Press

35 **Hoffman**, P T, **Postel-Vinay**, G and **Rosenthal,** J-L (1999) Information and Economic History – how the credit market in old regime Paris forces us to rethink the transition to capitalism. *The American Historical Review*, 104, 1, 69–94. February

36 **Ogilvie**, S (2001) The Economic World of the Bohemian Serf – economic concepts, preferences, and constraints on the estate of Friedland, 1583–1692. *The Economic History Review*, 54, 3, 430–53

37 **Dale**, G (2016) *Karl Polanyi – a life on the Left*. New York: Columbia University Press

38 **Weber**, M (1930/ 2001) *The Protestant Ethic and Spirit of Capitalism*. Abingdon. Routledge Classics

39 **Lessem**, R and **Schieffer**, A (2010) *Integral Research and Innovation: Transforming Enterprise and Society*. Abingdon. Routledge

40 **Peirce**, C S (1904/1998, Vol 2, Eds.) *The Essential Peirce – Peirce edition project*. Bloomington I.N. Indiana University Press

41 **De Saussure**, F (1916/1983) *Course in General Linguistics* (transl. Roy Harris). London. Duckworth

42 **Lewis**, J (1991) *The Ideological Octopus: An Exploration of Television and its Audience*. New York. Routledge

43 **Levy-Bruhl** L (2015) *How Natives Think*. Eastford. CT. Martino Fine Books

44 **Levi-Strauss**, C (1963) *Structural Anthropology*, (transl. C. Jacobson, B.G. Schoepf). New York. Basic Books

45 **Peirce**, C S (1867/1977) *Semiotics and Significs*. (Ed. Charles Hardwick). Bloomington I.N. Indiana University Press

46 **Lessem**, R (2017) *op cit*

47 **Jung**, C (1969) *The Archetypes and the Collective Unconscious*. Princeton. University Press

48 **Wittgenstein**, L (1953) *Philosophical Investigations* (Ed. G.E.M. Anscombe). London. Blackwell Publishing

49 **Chomsky**, N (2011) *Current Issues in Linguistic Theory*. The Hague. Mouton & Co. N.V. Publishers

50 **Stevens**, A (2001) *Jung – a very short introduction*. Oxford. University Press

51 **De Morentin**, J M (2011) *op cit*

52 **Gadamer**, H-G (1989) *Truth and Method*. London. Bloomsbury Press

53 **Stevens**, A (2001) *op cit*

54 **Heidegger** G (2010) *Being and Time*. Albany. State University of New York Press

55 **Goodwin**, N et. al. (2014) *op cit*

CHAPTER 8

Islamic Finance:
A Globally Oriented Approach: West

*Basheer Oshodi, Head of Islamic Banking at Sterling Bank in
Nigeria and Founder of CISER*

Today we are subjects of a neoliberal hyper-capitalist sof 'nature' into
resources and profit. It has changed the way we live, educate ourselves,
the way we understand knowledge and produce it, the way we eat and
encounter food, the way we relate with the world outside and with the
world inside. Every world comes with its own shadows.

Bayo Akomolafe, *These Worlds Beyond our Fences*

It was common practice, overall then, to present Islam as a 'third way'
which strikes a perfect balance between the claims of the individual
and the community—moderating the extremes of capitalism and communism, respectively. It was then for Islam to remind people of the
spiritual aspect of existence, filling the void left by these two materialis-
tic philosophies.

Charles Tripp, *Islam and the Moral Economy:
The Challenges of Capitalism*

8.1. Introduction

8.1.1. Shariah-Compliance Alongside Profitability

The Western-type growth model, which I shall be depicting here, focuses
on *Shariah*-compliance, alongside profitability as the true, combined measure
of achievement. The strength of the West is heavily dependent on the provision

of financial services across the world. These services are supported by other consultants who ensure that transactions are sealed.

The financial services industry, in my view, unlike the case of Akhuwat in Chapter 6, has been virtually silent on the Maqasid al-Shariah, which is aimed at impacting communities. Such impactful activities were left to the international agencies to provide education to children; healthcare for the poorest in the society; clean energy for rural communities; and entrepreneurial opportunities for the bottom billion. I will explore the case of the Abraaj Group, in this context, compared with the expectation of the model integral financial institution. This case is, then, considered within the realm of Western and global realities.

8.1.2. Islamic Finance – Western and Global Realities

The moral economic core—as, initially, considered by Lessem and Schieffer (1), and, then, by Oshodi (2)—is an integral aspect of ethical finance and spreads its tentacles across the globe, in the development of economic theories emerging from the West. Philosophers in ancient Rome set the stage for ethical finance 500 years before Christ. The Jews were quick to implement learnings from the Old Testament around moral and ethical business ventures. Thereafter, great Christian writers in the field of classical and neo-classical moral economic theories emerged. While some tilted towards more people-oriented economic models, others sought a more market-driven economic system.

Suddenly, a hybrid moral economy was moulded in Europe. But, towards the last quarter of the 20th century, Muslim writers started to build on the works of 15th century Islamic scholars, while learning the moral aspects of Western writers, within the context of what the Qur'an permits. These new writings were initially theoretical, with much emphasis on morality wrapped around the prohibition of interest, avoidance of uncertainties, gambling and unethical concerns. Core academic writings in the 1960s and 70s culminated with practical Islamic finance towards the end of the 70s and into the 1980s.

The theoretical writings started to reinterpret existing economic thinking and practically mimic existing financial offerings, by simply making them Shariah-compliant. This meant that Islamic economics and finance experts were hugely influenced by the West. In fact, they mainly studied in the West, or used books from that world. This gave validity to the 'false-paradigm model', which is a less radical international-dependency approach to development (3). In the same vein, having the bulk of the Muslim population in developing economies, the neo-colonial dependency model also showed its face, insinuating that historical evolution of colonialism—Marxist or capitalist—influenced the practicality of Islamic finance.

While mimicking conventional banking products, Islamic finance also ensured Shariah-compliance, as an integral part of the proposition. This was coupled with ensuring consistent profitability for Islamic financial institutions. Apart from the experience which emerged in Malaysia, Islamic finance, in my view, bypassed the 'social impact' side of the business. This can be seen as resulting from the undue influence of neo-capitalism. Thus, there was an insistence on prioritising profitability, as the primary objective.

So, there were many questions. Are loans equity or debt? What is the expected return on equity in the first two years? How often is profit from debt expected? Has profit been bench-marked to conventional interest rates or LIBOR? How much has risk been priced? What has been done to truly share risk and reward? How much involvement do Islamic financial institutions, or their financiers, invest in the business? Are impact and innovation an integral objective for shareholders?

The 'capitalism of Islamic finance' has arisen in answer to these questions. Thus, without the welfare-based 'mixed economy' system of the West, developing economies suffer from predatory capitalist approaches. These, deliberately, forget that basic infrastructures are not in place, while their funders, also, insist on even higher margins than the West, arguing that greater risk needs to be effectively priced. So, the Islamic finance world, in my view, experienced fast global growth with minimal societal impact.

8.2. Finance Turns West

8.2.1. The Power of the Financial Services Industry in the West

Moving from an agrarian economy to the Industrial Revolution two centuries ago, the West has been able to build a viable economy around services. Services have become the highest earning sector for the West. More specifically, financial services are the bedrock of successful Western economies. More recently, however, the astronomical advancement in the digital business world has attracted even greater incomes than 'vanilla' financial products. Thus, there has been a strengthening collaboration in the financial and digital economies. Digital finance has 'become king'.

In today's financial realm, institutions offering financial services tend to keep their base in tax-free havens, while locating their operational offices in London, Brussels or New York. These strategic offices attract entrepreneurs from around the world, from Dubai to Mumbai and from Taiwan to Brasilia. A USD 100m debt or equity transaction between Lagos and Riyadh will pass through London, with a team of financial advisors—lawyers, accountants, notary public and a host of others—taking their fees for signing against their brands.

So, practically, a small impact investment or transaction of USD 10m is unattractive to fund managers. The only attraction is where a much bigger financial institution mobilises such funds, packaged in multiples of several USD 100m, and retailing it to impact investors. This allows the advisors to justify their fees, whilst the impact investors remain expected to give a high return on investment, even in the short term. As such, for example, a hospital building project in Kenya accepts the funds, takes two years to build the specialist hospital, imports used medical equipment from Europe and, still, is unable to break-even by the fifth year. In no time, the fund-arrangers identify the deal as non-performing.

The same trend happens when a Pakistani impact investor mobilises funds that are Shariah-compliant. The foreign funder transfers risk to the investors in the form of a *murabaha* (mark-up sale), at LIBOR plus 8%, on the argument that Pakistan is highly vulnerable. Again, the investor builds a school, combined with a *madrassa* (Islamic school), using an Islamic debt-finance contract, with predetermined returns. He struggles to pay back the facility and the funders, subsequently, avoid Pakistan, alongside many other struggling economies. So, at the beginning, the high street banks and financial advisors get paid, the funders take little or no risk, even though it is Shariah-compliant, and the investors struggle to pay back in time.

This trend shows how neoliberalism has crept into the Islamic finance space and, equally, distorts the drive for impact investments. How, then, do emerging and struggling economies attract the right type of impact investments? A renewable energy and school project in rural northern Nigeria, with more than 12 million children out of school, simply wants to affect people's lives and still pay back the facility provided, but not at LIBOR plus 8%. The project owner, almost, does not care if the facility is Shariah-compliant or not. He or she, simply, wants a convenient facility that allows easy payback. More so, equity-type funding makes more sense where the funders constitute an integral part of the project roll-out; where financial advisors not only wait eagerly for their returns but, also, consider the social returns on investment (SROI, cf. Chapters 1 and 2); where the local investors are sincere enough not to engage in rent-seeking behaviour from the impact funds; and where shareholders and stakeholders of impact funds prioritise their expected return on the environment, the people, the society, and the cause that the investment is for.

Shariah-compliant impact funds, for social investment, will become more amenable, where short-term returns are tied to performance or project achievements. This is enhanced where all the parties have one clear and precise social goal. As such, these become crucial considerations for attracting impact funds that are Shariah-compliant.

8.2.2. Attracting Impact Foreign Funds through Western Financial Structures

The ability of projects to attract their own cash-flow is an integral part of the foreign direct investment bargain. Regardless of whether the project is for impact investment or Shariah-compliant purposes, payback ability needs to be established and ascertained. Fund arrangers will, always, advise on a funding term-sheet that reflects the expectations of fund owners. Practically speaking, the World Bank, Bill and Melinda Gates Foundation, Norfund and similar institutions show little interest in impact investments, even for more advanced economies.

Some funding comes in the form of convertible loans, especially where there is counterpart funding. Others are loans with moratoriums of one to three years. The family of funds may become more flexible and the funders happy to take on larger projects that would support government welfare systems, thereby reducing poverty. In another guise, impact foreign funders prefer that the local obligor also puts a 10–20% stake into the business, to demonstrate capacity. While funders are cautious of greenfield projects, they are, however, quick to support expansion projects.

Petro-dollars from the Middle East wander the globe in search of investment destinations, finding comfort in Western Europe. London, pre-Brexit (as I write the deadline of 31 October 2019 looms large), housed such funds seeking Shariah-compliant modes. Islamic investment banks gained quick reputations and acceptance, while the big financial actors did not hesitate to offer Islamic finance propositions and services. As funds are lodged in the West, the arranger, then, channels funds for viable projects within its economy, while a more limited number are given to struggling economies.

In this way, the Islamic mode of finance in Western economies mimics conventional products and distributes attractive returns to depositors. With more ethical offers from even the conventional financial system, Islamic finance players, then, quickly flesh their offerings with green, humanitarian and impact-seeking schemes. The question is: are such drives motivated by the Maqasid (see Chapter 6), the primary purpose of the Shariah, or an attempt to gain market share? Is this just another way to mimic conventional financial products? In other instances, Islamic finance experts may simply have been energised by the quest for justice or desire to truly touch lives. However, while Islamic financial institutions are particularly interested in Shariah governance, are they equally concerned with fairness and sincerity?

It is this burning desire to develop more integral approaches to Islamic finance, drawing on nature and community, culture and spirituality, as well as technology and enterprise, that has created the motivation for developing a research academy, related to such, to be aligned with effective impact laboratories, through an all-round communiversity (4). More specifically, it has inspired the writing of this book and the establishment of a financial institution with a head office in the Middle East and operational base in London (see Chapter 10).

This sets the stage for a unique type of financial institution, with the purpose of offering Shariah-compliant services, as well as demonstrating socio-economic and ecological impact. This requires that the Shariah Board is augmented by activities of the impact officers. And, here, such impact is a true reflection of an institution concerned with a different form of *integral* returns, as intimated, integral accounting-wise, in Chapter 4. It, then, measures return on community activation, return on socio-economic impact and impact on people's happiness. This drive for profitability in people and community is, thence, transformed into a conflict with providing return on average equity that takes ethical concerns seriously, in practical financial terms.

8.2.3. Capitalistic Tendencies and Conflicts with the Maqasid

A major debt mode of financing under Islamic finance, referred to as 'commodity murabaha' has become acceptable in the Islamic finance industry. In practical terms, if an Islamic financial institution wants to provide debt to another Islamic financial institution, the fund provider would buy a commodity from e.g. the London Metal Exchange on the instruction of the obligor and then sell the commodity at a mark-up to the obligor or buyer. The buyer gets value in terms of cash and engages in other sale or lease contracts with such funds. The commodity murabaha transaction is certainly Shariah-compliant, since there is an underlying asset which, in this case, would be gold. There is no interest payment, since one part buys and sells to another. There is no uncertainly or extreme speculation, since the goods are tangible and there is information on the price yield curve. This transaction does not involve any sort of financial gambling. Dealing in hard commodities like gold or silver makes the transaction free from unethical concerns.

This model allows funds to move from the Middle East to London and to Nigeria. It provides assurance to Shariah scholars. Where there is a moratorium, a low mark-up rate and repayment flexibility, the funds entering the receiving bank in Nigeria may be used for impact investments. Alternatively, it may be used for any viable transaction which would usually be a debt-based one. The first leg of the commodity murabaha transaction, with London Metal Exchange, may, however, have little or no real impact on any community.

There is a difference with the Malaysian model. Herein, perceptible agro-commodities are traded in lieu of a stationary metal exchange. So, for struggling economies to enjoy a real communal impact, through such commodity murabaha transactions, actual commodity trading must take place. This helps to provide employment opportunities to poor communities while reducing communal poverty. When this trade is consistent, the value-chain of activities increasing the impact to society, through real value, is created.

Advanced Western economies are able to survive without transporting agricultural goods everywhere. They enjoy company tax savings and adopt a more welfare economic arrangement for their populations, while offering Shariah-compliant financial services. But, for more struggling economies, commodity murabaha, which seeks to satisfy Shariah rules, make an acceptable rate of profit and achieves human well-being and communal prosperity, and provides a good alternative, in all senses. This operates within the spirit of the Maqasid, which is the intent of the Shariah. As such, Islamic finance actors should seek to embed models that have a positive multiplier effect on the economy. But, at the moment, Islamic finance is caught between traces of capitalism and the actualisation of the Maqasid al-Shariah.

Consequently, current expectations hinge on Islamic finance requiring struggling economies to identify a handful of viable commodities either, as import substitution, or as an export promotion strategy. An Islamic bank may, then, seek to distort market forces for those specific commodities, as outlined in the enlarged strategy of the government, while learning quickly from the development-state's agenda, propelled by far Eastern economies. This strategy must, then, quickly graduate from agricultural production to light and heavy manufacturing, thereby increasing the variety of goods for sale on local and international markets. This push towards impact development is what naturally improves and lubricates the service industry.

More advanced Western economies, practising Islamic finance, are enjoying the benefits of industrialisation and effective institutions, where the service industry has matured. In fact, a large part of Islamic finance dealing benefits high-street law firms, public notaries, trustees and accounting firms, all of whom structured the Shariah-compliant transaction in the first place. Having such structures keeps the tax-man interested, but also allows excessive financial engineering in the Islamic finance industry. This means that Islamic finance becomes characterised by variations in equity, debt and service structures. This leads to implementing even more advanced forms of commodity murabaha, which further complicates the matter for struggling economies, since they are always behind the curve of Western cases, which have been endorsed by famous Shariah scholars.

To further achieve communal impact, struggling economies that are adopting Islamic finance should have established real and actual commodity exchanges, for priority commodities, such as oil and gas, real metal trading, to complement agro-commodities with process ones. It becomes important to further develop propositions around other manufactured or finished goods whilst seeking digital approaches to the trade. This bulk of activities, over time, should eliminate the lack of short-term liquidity instruments in the Islamic finance industry. This flow and real cycle of trade lubricates a weak and dying economy, so that it can be brought back to life. This has been the aim of the Malaysian economic trajectory, only activated a few decades ago, which becomes an interesting path to follow. This can be enhanced with learning from others of the Asian Tigers. What discoveries can we, then, take from Western-type management of the Islamic finance space?

8.2.4. Respect for Western-type Management

Without a bias towards the Islamic finance industry, Western Europe was quick to accept the Islamic finance proposition and vie with the Middle East to be the Islamic financial hub. While Islamic scholars, in many struggling economies, were arguing over debt modes of finance, or the acceptance of interest, where there is no established interest-free banking model, the West started to implement and learn from the process very quickly.

Aside from trying to define interest and money from a Shariah perspective, since the late 60s and early 70s, one may argue that the Muslim world was rather slow in the implementation of practical Islamic finance. Furthermore, Africa only woke up to this reality less than a decade ago. Many Western economies, especially in Western Europe, had already started to adjust their tax laws to accommodate this growing financial model. Research and Development started to spring up in the UK and France. The West quickly supported Malaysia in the *sukuk* industry, while the big banks created Islamic finance windows. These institutions, then, moved to the Middle East to support the Islamic finance agenda, which was helpful in mobilising funds needing Shariah-compliant destinations.

Models, structures and concepts around the new Islamic financial agenda began to refresh balance sheets. Experts from Europe moved swiftly to the Middle East to buttress this new financial agenda. While the United States tried to put Islamic finance in context, despite ideological resistance, Canada started to build institutions in this new arena, as anti-Islamic sentiment was less evident north of the 49th Parallel. The West leveraged its sound institutions and good governance base to build Islamic finance quite easily, ensuring they received the endorsement of Shariah scholars. Religious bias was relatively low and the focus was clear. Naturally, ethical concerns, the green agenda, environmental protection and other human development programme, in Western guise, were not, typically, blended with finance (see earlier chapters). But, what Islamic finance sought was to avoid gross financial speculation and the sale of debt structures.

Noticeably, the West introduced sound corporate governance which is a requirement for effective regulatory policies, rule of law, control of corruption and overall governance. Inevitably, the drive for neoliberalism, competition, profitability, and to minimise challenges became the driving force for these new financial and economic achievements. Equally, the public liability company structure accommodated and protected stakeholders, reducing nepotism and patrimonial behaviour. Consumer protection laws shielded depositors from aggressive capitalism, while the Basel Committee requirements on loan-book holdings enhanced banking supervision and oversight. Thus, the Islamic finance industry enjoyed yet more financial shelter.

The Profit Equalization Reserve (PER) and the Investment Risk Reserve (IRR) were, also, there to foster customer confidence in the Islamic finance world. Unlike Egypt's Mit Ghamr Savings Bank experience between 1963–1967, Islamic banks are now designed for long-term sustainability, where proper corporate governance is established. Even so, the cost of such structures may be too expensive for start-up companies, except where investors consciously capitalise to a sufficient extent. But, the ever-present 'ghost at the feast' is the motive of shareholders to ensure good returns on equity whilst remaining Shariah-compliant. These have been some of the main features of Islamic finance entering the sphere of Western financial institutions.

But, the question remains: how to align this with our primary purpose, for an integral approach that takes nature and the communal, culture, spirit and impact seriously, supplementing the economic motives of investors, whilst embedding the best ethical practices? How can such an impact be GENE-rated within a full debt-prioritised establishment? For example, Silicon Valley start-ups in the US, as well as German and Japanese industrialisation, were heavily based on equity options which allowed patient and convenient capital to be consistently lodged in production, thereby leading to rapid technological advancements within a relatively short period.

Yet, today, the Islamic finance industry substantially mimics interest-based financial products, through its debt-based contracts, thus slowing down innovation on the equity side. While learning from the South and East, North and West can be rich and relevant, the path toward creating that true integral financial institution is still a mirage, found in the writings of a few but hardly evident in any practice.

8.2.5. Setting up a Truly Integral Financial Institution

Many have argued that Islamic finance, at least in Western guise, is not any different from conventional banking, where interest is simply changed to profit. The Grameen Bank model shows that there can be impact investment aimed at reducing poverty, without making it Shariah-compliant, though it does not explicitly draw on an Islamic moral economic core, in the way that Akhuwat does (see Chapter 6). Why, then, expend time and energy building Shariah-compliant impact investments when any investment proposition can simply be tailored to societal impact?

In Chapter 6, we saw that one powerful imperative lay in the Akhuwat model, driven by solidarity bonds, through benevolent loans targeted at the bottom segment of the population, in Pakistan. Akhuwat is 'a self-sufficient regenerative model' of 'reciprocal endowments' (*mawakhat*) coming from its borrower's pool of reciprocity' (5), thereby creating a renewed trading community, where spirituality and economics are aligned. More so, readings around ethical finance also ensure that ethical standards, based on natural law, are met.

The interest here, however, is to leverage ethical foundations for Islamic finance offering, which draw together the deeper semiotic meanings of ethical finance with the spirituality of the Islamic tradition. To do so would be to re-GEN*E*-rate broad financial foundations, as truly integral financial institutions, based on positively touching human life, enriching faith, inspiring posterity, stimulating the intellect and multiplying wealth in a holistic manner. This could cumulatively create an individual, family, community, society, nation marked by happiness and well-being (see Chapter 2).

So what does it take to set up a financial institution that is truly integral? This means that the shareholders of such an institution must seek benefit beyond financial gain. They must, also, be able to measure such impact gains and, therefore, need other forms of bottom line performance of the balance sheet (see Chapter 4). They must seek a broad spectrum of measurable social benefits, which span the constituents of the Maqasid or anything that enhances or seeks to achieve human happiness. Measurability, or calibration—both qualitative and quantitative—firstly needs organisational ownership of such, on the one hand. On the other hand, indicators need to be identified, as with Mark Anielski's well-being economics (Chapter 2, or through the GIIN-IRIS network). These may, however, vary from formal jurisdictions to the meeting of real needs.

With respect to ownership, the Chief Impact Officer must have his/her own business case clearly spelt out. The content of any impact proposition, in London or Morocco, will certainly be different from the one in Poland or Bangladesh. The Islamic financial institution, as the pilot agency to drive impact investment, must understand the macro-economic variables at play in the country and, then, draw out tailored solutions in line with the Maqasid. Just like the Sekem initative in Egypt (Chapter 4) or the Ewu Community impact in Nigeria (Chapter 5), Islamic financial institutions need to channel their impact programmes to defined communities. By so doing, from one community to another, the fruits of organised impact investment will be felt.

Again, like the Silicon Valley arrangement, impact equity investments into specific trades, production or services can be enlarged and appropriately institutionalised. It really does not matter whether equity or a debt-mode of finance is used. What really matters is that the impact destination is clear, and the deliverables must be specifically aimed at impacting people and communities towards sustainable prosperity. In other words, the impact investment officer's business case or action research statement will seek to highlight impact-measurable indicators for selected communities.

The need in the West for affordable homes for specific income groups, will focus the impact officers' action-research to a totally different set of parameters, compared to considering the needs for sustainable sources of income in sub-Saharan Africa. This does not in any way affect the ability of such an impact institution to make money or declare profit. The impact proposition may, however, have different asset classes, each with varying returns. Other social returns, as integrally depicted in Chapters 3 and 4, can be explored further. Even so, regardless of the financial models that the West adopts, profitability remains ubiquitous, if sustainability is to be ensured.

Conventional or Islamic finance fund arrangers will not even listen if the funding proposition does not show a competitive return on equity. The business case must, also, show how to effectively mitigate repayments or credit risk, foreign exchange risks and even key-man risk. Thus, impact investment in the West will only supplement profitability except, perhaps, where such funds are from development institutions. What unique value proposition does one, then, expect from development agencies in the West or from Sovereign-wealth family funds from the Middle East? In other words, how do we start to dilute core capitalist investment funds with developmental funds, to reduce the cost of funds and the pressure on immediate profitability, allowing finance to become more patient?

8.2.6. The Drive for Profitability and Shareholders' Expectations

Investable funds coming from rich families in the United States, Saudi Arabia or an investment bank from Hong Kong would still require a competitive return on their investment. The price escalates when the fund is to be used in a struggling economy. Country risk matters are almost eliminated when the funds go to Western economies or the newly industrialised far Eastern economies, including the GCC. UAE is such a comfortable destination for funds across the Mediterranean. Pricing of debt and equity funds will be in low single digit figures. This is because of sound institutions, good governance, enforcement of contracts and availability of tradable items.

The big commercial and investment banks will accept these funds and may, then, pass on a retail proportion to smaller institutions, while increasing the price. The motivation for the big financial institutions or fund arrangers is to get a much greater return on capital, thereby increasing profitability. The same rule applies in the Islamic finance industry. A consortium of Islamic commercial or investment banks would ordinarily structure a 'syndicated murabaha' (syndicated mark-up sale product) for projects, companies and Islamic banks in struggling economies. Other banks in the West and Middle East will create a short-term or revolving treasury murabaha (mark-up sale) line with LIBOR as the benchmark profit base.

Once again, the primary agenda is to maximise profit. This financing term-sheet comes with all sort of fees to further increase the profit margin of fund owners and their consultants. In the Middle East, fund arrangers would, also, request that an investment committee's costs are borne by the obligor institution, regardless of whether they are funding a start-up or a company close to collapse and needing to keep its head above water. At the same time, all service providers want their fees paid upfront. As we have repeatedly noted, in such circumstances, the question of societal impact takes a back seat.

Of course, struggling economies in need of liquidity may accept or reject these terms. In extreme cases they may accept them, seeking soft loans to meet capitalist conditions. Then, every time local currency is converted to USD and sent overseas, it further underdevelops the country of the obligor. Even if funds were designed for impact, the obligor institution is forced to transfer these costs to the final recipient, so that the social impact envisaged may be misplaced, or completely lost. As indicated above, the capitalist tendency of the West swiftly penetrates the struggling Islamic financial institutions and their drive for social and environmental impact can, swiftly, vanish.

There are, however, some cases where funding institutions from the West are willing to take out the fee, as the time value or facility amount hits the account of the obligor bank. This way, an overwhelmed business, within the developing economy, is able to gain a quick financial balance while ensuring profitability is achieved. Subsequently, emerging and struggling countries quickly follow the practice of Western banks when local obligors seek financial intermediation or debt/equity financing. The multiplier effect of this practice is that economic development patterns in struggling economies are slowed down even further. More so, the appetite for impact investment becomes diluted. In this light, it becomes important to address issues around impact investment risk, as congealed in other financial risk.

8.2.7. The Inherent Risk in Impact Investments

Every transaction has its own unique type of risk. Taking equity investment or business risk is associated with huge moral hazard, so that fund owners may lose their entire investment. This is the same situation in *mudarabah* (partnership) and *musharakah* (joint venture) contracts, under Islamic finance. Mitigating such risk is beyond the financing partner being on the board of the expert partner or even appointing the Chief Financial Officer. Very close monitoring is expected in order to mitigate unexpected spending or withdrawal. This means that specific experts for the particular industry that funds are directed towards need to be contracted.

Practically, we might envisage an integral financial institution, using Islamic finance principles, to ensure impact, that embarks on a hospital project. Such a project will have three major activities: construction, purchasing of medical equipment and medical consumables. The initial set of funds will go into construction, to certain specification and would require that a construction company, which specialises in such, is brought in to complete the project. The financing partner must, also, appoint an independent project manager on its own cost, to manage milestone disbursements and performance.

In a conventional financial institution, the financier will simply give funds to the obligor and expect interest payments. Performance risk mitigation will come in the form of having performance bonds or bank guarantees from another financial institution, with an Advance Payment Guarantee accepted in certain circumstances. To further reduce performance risk, or the risk that the expert partner will simply walk away from the deal, it will be expected that the expert partner will, equally, provide the land, or, at least, have verified joint-venture arrangements with the land owner.

The same close monitoring is expected for the purchase of medical equipment. An effective control system must be in place to verify the cost of equipment, while ensuring that Letters of Credit (LC) are opened. Consumables will, also, need their own form of supervision, which will include getting an agent to ensure the right price deals are secured. Overall, funds need to be disbursed in a well-defined manner to mitigate waste and unscrupulous spending. In the same way that this approach would work for a retail transaction, it should also be applied to more corporate ones, in order to avoid the Abraaj Group experience (which we comment on below). Funders with impact intent must set forth a close review mechanism including use of project, operating and investable funds, which should be embedded in their investment business case. Analysis of risk exposures and mitigating strategies must be sound and coherent. Both inherent and residual risk must be factored in to the impact proposition.

Regardless of whether the investment is Shariah-compliant or impact bias, actual realities coupled with strong corporate governance are imperative. Thus, it is not enough to have a well-written business case for societal or communal impact, with attractive projections and sound profiles of the founders. It is vital to manage costs effectively, perfectly match funds with projects, avoid debts to meet costs—except, perhaps 'interest-free loan' or *Qard-al-Hasan*—and pay attention to the character of obligors. The fall of the Abraaj Group, as a typical impact private equity company, provides a salutory lesson. They aligned with the Western-type of financial structure, to create impact, but failed after 16 years. They attracted funds from Islamic banks and reputable development organisations who trusted their management style, up until 2018.

8.2.8. The Case of Abraaj Group

With over USD 3M of capital and USD 60M of assets under management, Arif Naqvi, a Pakistan expatriate, living in Dubai, founded the Abraaj Group in 2002. His primary aim was to embark on impact investments through a conventional private equity arrangement. Abraaj Group sought to use a pure Western-based model to touch lives in struggling economies. The company secured USD 3BN funding in 2015 alone, to impact communities in Africa and mobilised another USD 526M for investment in Turkey.

The Abraaj Group understood the challenge of poor health facilities in sub-Saharan Africa and South Asian communities, and thus launched its USD Abraaj Growth Market Health Fund (AGHF). Abraaj managed over USD 14BN and had 25 offices worldwide. Funds rolled in from the Kuwaiti Public Institution for Social Security (PIFSS), the Bill and Melinda Gates Foundation, the World Bank, Proparco, the Centre for Disease Control and Prevention (CDC) and several UAE and Kuwaiti establishments. Abraaj's impact investing agenda covered healthcare and healthcare technologies, clean energy, real estate and education, aside from supporting sustainable initiatives and foundations, while developing financial institutions.

Abraaj had a USD 1BN portfolio for healthcare-related projects alone and invested another USD 1BN in the Karachi power company, K-Electric. Their attempt to exit from the power deal through Shanghai Electric from China was stunted by regulation and elections in Pakistan. The company went into a partnership with ENGIE to foster a wind power platform in India and took a majority stake in Jhimpir Power aimed at constructing a 50 MW wind project in south-east Pakistan. In 2017 the company sealed a partnership with the International Federation of Red Cross and Red Crescent Societies in Kenya. This arrangement concentrated on education and primary healthcare matters.

Abraaj invested in Indorama Fertilizers based in Nigeria and natural gas projects in Chihuahua, Mexico. In Nigeria, land was acquired for impact projects while building regulation problems started to emerge in Pakistan and political issues affected investments in Kenya.

Abraaj may have been mismatching its investment funds with very long-term projects, including equity stakes which, thus, exposed them to huge impact investment risk, in addition to widespread equity specific risk. They were quick to finance operations with loans which were not publicly listed, which is quite unusual with a private equity firm. By 2017, they also held a lot of the health funds in treasury units with the World Bank, the Gates Foundation, the Centre for Disease Control and Prevention (CDC) and Proparco, which was frowned upon as an inappropriate use of funds, leading these investors to call in their investments in the impact initiatives led by Abraaj, in 2018.

As an unsecured lender, the Kuwaiti Public Institution for Social Security (PIFSS) had invested over USD 731M. They identified repayment and fiduciary risk and demanded liquidation proceedings. Abraaj may have also been exposed to market risk, country risk and ineffective managerial competencies. Overall funds mismatch was present and heightened their trials and tribulations. Survival imperatives led the company to pursue fee income and short-term profit from treasury investments, which did not align with the impact-drive of funders. In the same vein, the company's main revenue never covered its operating costs for years while law firms and audit firms continued to earn their fees, even while liquidation processes proceeded apace.

All of these crises reached their peak in 2018 and a company valued at USD 2BN, which supported impact investments in 200 companies, especially in struggling economies, filed for provisional liquidation in the Cayman Islands. Debt to unsecured and secured creditors stood at USD 501M and USD 572.4M, respectively, totalling USD 1.1BN. Investors lost funds and impact drive, impact projects were stopped and communities were hit with further poverty.

8.2.9. Emerging Laboratories – Struggle Between Cost, Profit and Impact Investments

Over the decades, global Islamic finance has grown to become worth more than USD 2.4TN, as at end of 2017. The sukuk market, Islamic commercial banking and fund management have been exceptional, while the *takaful* or insurance market is showing huge growth. The Islamic private equity market is also growing quickly. The industry has adopted Western styles of growth in terms of balance sheet growth or funds undermanagement. The impact on communities and countries has, however, been very limited. The industry is yet to evolve as a 'socio-economic laboratory' that is truly and sincerely integral, with such an ecological and social, cultural as well as economic orientation.

The Maqasid al-Shariah or purpose of Shariah, as the original foundation of the industry, is either misplaced or ignored. Countries and communities with majority Muslim populations harbour the poorest people on the earth. The growth has indeed not translated into a good life. Such offerings have been Shariah-compliant and have recorded competitive returns.

Even so, Sterling Bank's Islamic finance window in Nigeria, led by myself, with a background in development economics and Islamic finance, as well as being an alumnus of both Trans4m (France) and Da Vinci Institute (South Africa) showed returns on real equity of 45% in 2017–18, which constitutes a decent return on investment. The bank has, also, given priority to transactions in sectors such as health, education, agriculture, renewable energy and transportation, in the HEART sector.

Sterling Bank promotes impact, by engaging in both equity and debt structures for these selected sectors, with additional interest in affordable housing for the people at the middle and middle-bottom part of the income pyramid. The overall strategy for Sterling's Islamic banking window is to closely monitor investments in these sectors, with reputable agents, while mitigating overall risk on the one hand. At the same time, prudent cost control and avoidance of wastage is prioritised. The bank is also particular with the character of its customers. This has helped to keep non-performing assets (NPA) at 0.5 percent. The company also goes an extra mile by helping obligors or expert partners with free technical consultancy, alongside building competences in the HEART sector.

A new kind of socio-economic laboratory for the Islamic finance industry would be based upon an integral private equity firm that would build expertise in selected impact sectors, attract equity funding or a low-cost senior debt like *wakala* or agency-based contract for its operations. Each funding type would be specifically tailored to a particular project, so that fund mismatch issues should not arise. While matching these funds, the timing for cash-flow or profit would be fixed to the particular proposition and funders would have adequate information on this arrangement. The laboratory would have a sound corporate governance regime with key-man risk insurance for its top management.

The impact focus of funders and management, moreover, must be perfectly aligned. The impact laboratory must also identify only jurisdictions where there is a good understanding of the socio-political environment. From the beginning, impact segments should be limited to only a handful of key sectors that benefit the host communities most. Evaluation of impact, qualitatively, as well as quantitatively, should be validated by the host community and society. Profitability must also be achieved, within appropriate budgetary timelines, while return should also be qualitatively based on the indicators arrived at by the Impact Investment Officer. In the same light, the Islamic finance contracts covering equity, debt and services should be focused on unique combinations of corporate, commercial and retail transactions that are people-oriented. That, indeed, is the envisaged impact laboratory for the 21st century and a more purposeful Shariah-compliant institution.

8.3. Conclusion

The future of Islamic finance is rooted in its ability to positively impact life as a whole. A socio-economic laboratory, accordingly, within and around a financial institution, would seek to achieve Shariah-compliance, ensure defined profitability and achieve targeted communal impact. The position of a Chief Impact Officer would be given priority and such office will take the responsibility of building a business case that matches impact investment funds with projects. There is much more inherent and residual risk in impact investment using mudarabah (partnership) and musharakah (joint-venture) contracts, which must be identified and adequately analysed in order to achieve set impact goals. Country risk and communal needs are, also, of utmost importance in deciding the use of impact funds, while a Western-type profit drive must be supplemented by a people-oriented approach. When this happens, the true Islamic finance value proposition is achieved. More so, Western financial systems relying on laissez-faire economic liberalism are failing, whilst integral finance bent towards achieving communal impact through ethical considerations will be, at least, one way forward to true prosperity.

The West has introduced prudential guidelines to assist banks stabilise while protecting customers' funds. The primary sources of the Shariah have simply prohibited interest and would certainly not frown at any derivations from the text, even if they were leveraged on the basis of Western thinking. Islamic finance, on the other hand, avoids uncertainty or extreme risk in business ventures, gambling of all categories and anything unethical. This places restrictions on Western-type financial betting, trading in receivables and other debt sales, but promotes business involvements and partnerships. Profitability is the common factor between Islamic banking and Western-type motives. And so, to date, sadly, Islamic finance has misplaced its primary aim of community activation and happiness in favour of the balance sheet bottom line. As indicated, we propose a different way forward.

Seek after the **'Positive Facts'**
Separate Facts and **Values**
Collect Data and Build Inductive Theories
Control through **'Closed Systems'**

Table 8.1. Empirical Accounting

It is this incongruity, then, that sets the stage for practical integral financial institution learning from the appearance of AmeenArthur global venture designed to impact selected communities in the South and the West, to which we will turn in Chapter 10. But, before we do, we examine the Semiotic Economics methodology applied to a range of faith-based economic systems.

8.4. Bibliography

1 **Lessem**, R and **Schieffer** A (2010) *Integral Research and Innovation: Transforming Enterprise and Society.* Farnham. Gower Publishing

2 **Oshodi**, B A (2014) *An Integral Approach to Development Economics – Islamic Finance in an African Context.* Farnham. Gower Publishing Company

3 **Todaro** M P and **Smith** S C (2009) *Economic Development.* Upper Saddle River, NJ. Pearson Education.

4. **Lessem** R, **Adodo** A and **Bradley** T (2019) *The Idea of The Communiversity.* Manchester. Beacon Academic

5 **Saqib** A. and **Malik**, A. (2018) *Integral Finance: Akhuwat – A Case Study of Solidarity Economy.* Abingdon. Routledge

PART FOUR

*Semiotic Economics and
Islamic Finance in Prospect*

CHAPTER 9

The Semiotic Economics of Faith-based Finance

Tony Bradley, Lecturer in Social Economy,
Liverpool Hope Business School, UK

9.1. Introduction

9.1.2. Re-introducing the Model of Semiotic Economics

> I suggest that [neoclassical economics] is a religion because its basic precepts are not subject to verification; and so, like a religion the tenets must simply be taken on faith. This wouldn't be so serious were it not for the fact that neoclassical economics as a system of thinking dominates policymaking and academic thought across the globe.
>
> Kurt Cobb, *Environmental and Natural Resources News*

> The only function of economic forecasting is to make astrology look respectable.
>
> John Kenneth Galbraith

As we draw towards the final sections of this volume, on *Islamic to Integral Finance: A Semiotic Approach*, the purpose of this chapter is to indicate how the Semiotic Economics methodology connects, directly, to many of the themes explored in preceding chapters. Thence, in the final substantive Chapter 10, Dr. Basheer Oshodi will indicate a current practical case of Islamic finance; that is, adopting the principles that have been outlined here and which, as he examined in Chapter 8, are lacking in so much Islamic finance practice, that has become enmeshed in the meaning-systems of neoliberalism.

Using the preceding chapter as the contextual backdrop, following from Chapter 7, I wish to show how the new sub-discipline of Semiotic Economics helps to situate each faith-based economic model within the sphere of an evolved integral economics. This has emerged from research conducted at Liverpool Hope Business School. As we saw in Chapter 7, Semiotic Economics analyses the meaning-systems underpinning economic models that seek to challenge the dominance of neoliberalism, within contemporary economies. In particular, here, the focus turns to using the methodology of Semiotic Economics in respect of models that emerge from Christian, Islamic and Impact Investing finance communities, each of which can claim a legacy in either religious or secular faith traditions.

Yet, as the opening quote indicates, from Kurt Cobb, the idea of mixing conventional economics with faith sounds like anathema, ironically. We might agree with him that the principles of neoclassicism do have a certain 'evangelical zeal' about them. But, where we disagree is in seeing genuine faith as somehow detached from the signs of economics, albeit models that are divergent to neoclassical or neoliberal approaches. Instead, in this chapter, we suggest that the semiotics of faith-based traditions, when applied to economics, yield important outcomes. Because the faiths are not 'blind', as so many secular commentators, such as Cobb, would have us believe, as articles of their faithing. Nor are they akin to astrology, as in the mocking quote about economic forecasters, from J.K. Galbraith. Rather, the People of the Book and their scriptures are important signifying sources for economics, as we will show.

In Chapter 7 I indicated that there is a missing 'meaning giving' fourth, even in an economics that challenges the dis-embeddedness of capitalism, from Polanyi. This is homologous to the missing fourth in all but the most recent semiotics, thereby giving *meaning* to finance and economics. Following the work of Carl Jung, in seeking understanding of the unconscious depths of the human psyche, I have labelled these as 'archetypes of signification'. Emerging and uncovering these represents a second step in the method of Semiotic Economics.

These lie within the pre-conceptual sub-structures of spirituality and culture, that are hardly articulated and, certainly, not within conventional economics. As such, in Table 9.1. I outline, in synoptic form, the GEN*E*alogy for a semiotic economics method: **g**rounding economic objects, **e**merging archetypes of signification, **n**avigating signs of economic significance and **e**ffecting interpretants, reminding readers of how this methodology connects with the themes introduced in previous chapters. These are shown for eight economic systems, contrasted against that of conventional economic neoliberalism.

Specifically, I indicate eight economic systems, as examples, in order to show two that pertain to each of the four Integral Realms. These cycle from Southern, based in community activation, through Eastern, emerging from models of cultural consciousness, Northern pointing to models based in particular systemic techniques, around to Western, effecting systems based in financial models, that are alternative to those that dominate the horizon of the contemporary world. Inevitably, space doesn't permit a full articulation of the Semiotic Economics methodology for all eight systems, alongside that of the neoliberal.

As such, given the overall focus of this chapter, I concentrate on three systems, one drawn from the East and two from the West. Firstly, I indicate how the meaning-system of 'Kingdom Economics' derives from what can be termed the *Biblical Quaternity Archetype* (1). This helps to show how deep structures of indigenous meaning ground the emergence of spiritual economics. Second, I consider the semiotic processual development of the Akhuwat model of Islamic finance, particularly derived from the Eastern, Sufi, tradition, to connect the case from Chapter 6 to the methodology of Semiotic Economics.

Then, having established the deep connections to indigenous meaning-systems and ways in which the 'missing fourth' signify economic challenges to neoliberalism, I take the first of the two economic models that connect, directly, to the world of Western finance. This indicates the methodology applied to contemporary economic models. Inevitably, I leave the reader to connect the interpretations of the others. But, I hope to have developed the basis for Semiotic Economics sufficiently to enable this process to be more fully articulated elsewhere.

Table 9.1. Semiotic GENEalogies contrasted with neoliberalism

FOURFOLD SEMIOTICS METHOD (See Chapter 7)	An economic object (G) Peircean 'object'	Economic pre-signifier (archetype of signification) (E) De Morentin's 'pre-Conceptual sub-structures'	Sign of economic significance (N) Peircean 'representamum'	Effective interpretation (E) e.g. specific innovations Peircean 'interpretant'
NEOLIBERAL ECONOMICS (See critiques in Chapters 2, 3 and 7)	Money Values	Individualistic 'homo economicus' (money) Power/ Hubris (personal & corporate) How do we acquire more?	Gross Domestic Product/ Money Wealth (rich list)	Corporate share-ownership e.g. the FANGS (Facebook, Amazon, Netflix, Google, Starbucks)
ECOLOGICAL ECONOMICS (S)	Nature/ Natural capital	The Commons How do we create sustainability?	Circular economy	Blue Economy e.g. WRAP (Waste & Resources Action Programme) and Provenance
NHAKANOMICS (SHONA) (S) (See Chapter 5)	Inheritance	Traditions and legacy How do we develop our heritage?	Community holding	Communal land, property and resource holdings e.g. Zimbabwean Tribal Trust Lands, Mexican Ejidos
SOULIDARITY (SUFI ISLAM) (E) (See Chapters 6 and 8)	Mawakhat Sharing abundance in 'brotherhood'	Ihsan How do we attain perfection/ excellence through advocacy for oppressed/ vulnerable?	Infaaq – process of creating a chain of solidarity, through dispersal and pleasing God, without expecting any return.	E.g. Akhuwat in Pakistan and the diaspora community in the UK, using Qard-al-Hasan, benevolent, interest-free loans.

ASSOCIATIVE ECONOMICS (E)	Stakeholder Associations	Rights How do we co-operate?	Three-folding	Biodynamic agriculture e.g. L'Aubier and Sekem
CORE ECONOMICS (N)	Unpaid non-marketised work	Human bonds How do we care for one another?	Household Satellite Accounts (HHSAs)	Domestic life (e.g. millions of functioning and dysfunctional households)
WELL-BEING ECONOMICS (N) (See Chapter 2)	Social health (real prosperity)	Love How do we create true wealth?	Social value	UN Human Development Index e.g. closing life-wide gender gap in Rwanda
IMPACT ACCOUNTING (W) (See Chapters 1 and 4)	Impact Investments	Value How do we make a difference?	QBLA (quadruple bottom line accounting)	Various accounting protocols e.g. IRIS
KINGDOM ECONOMICS (JUDAEO-CHRISTIAN) (W)	Charisms (Lukan dynamic/ Grounding)	Grace How do we give away? (Markan dynamic/ Emergence)	Sacrificial (for) giving (Johannine dynamic/ Navigation)	Debt annulment (personal and national) e.g. HIPC debt relief in Zambia (post Jubilee 2000) (Matthean dynamic/ Effecting)

9.2. The Methodology for Uncovering Economic Semiosis

In Chapter 7 I introduced the four basic steps of the Semiotic Economics methodology, which are to:

- Identify the economics object e.g. for impact accounting: impact investments.
- Uncover the cultural/spiritual/integral/*archetypes of signification* e.g. the (initial pre-conscious) emergent desire to effect change and make a beneficial difference in the world, as the practical financial objects become clear.
- Specify the sign/symbolic question (*signifier/representamum*) to be addressed e.g. how do we develop quadruple bottom line accounting?
- Effect the co-creation of local material interpretations (*interpretants*) e.g. of impact investing, such as various accounting protocols.

In the following sections I apply this methodology for uncovering economic semiosis, within three of the examples from Table 9.1: Kingdom Economics, Islamic finance and Impact Investing, with which I am directly involved.

9.2.1. The Biblical Quaternity Archetype – Uncovering the Deep Structure of 'Kingdom Economics'

The Christian Church has embraced a variety of understandings of alternative economic systems, over the centuries, that emerge from its traditional communities, history, theological hermeneutics and contemporary culture. We may use the portmanteau term 'kingdom (of God) economics' to bracket together a wide range of different, 'upside-down' (2) economic systems that have emerged within the Church, since the 'primitive commun(al)ism' of the Acts of the Apostles (2:44–45, 4:32–35). These include the social humanism of John Calvin's Geneva, the American Puritans, Dutch Mennonites, English Methodists and the medieval Italian Catholic 'economia civile' (3, 4, 5, inter alia).

The common denominator for each of these expressions of radical economics is their basis in the biblical tradition and what I refer to as the Biblical Quaternity Archetype (BQA), as the predominate archetype of signification for Christian economics. It is possible to point to specific biblical injunctions, such as the Levitical laws on support for the poor (*tzedakah* e.g. Lev 19:9–11, 25:35–55), the three Jewish tithes system (Num 18:21, Deut 14:28–29, Deut 12:17–18), warnings against economic oppression (e.g. 1 Kings 21, Ezekiel 34, Nehemiah 5), a divine 'bias towards the poor' (e.g. Exodus 12:49, 22:21ff, Proverbs 10:4), Jesus' emphasis on sacrificial giving, from the heart (e.g. Mark Chapters 10–12), his commandment to mutualism in agape love (e.g. John

15:1–11) and the kingdom of God, as one where the Lord is recognised in the face of the most marginalised and destitute (e.g. Matthew 25:31–46). Even so, we only begin to identify the depth structure of these stresses when we recognise the overall quaternity shape of the scriptures.

If we examine the structure of the Judaeo-Christian Scriptures we see that the quaternity archetype provides the organising principle for the entire biblical worldview. This is reflected in the main sections of both the Old and New Testaments and in many details of the Bible's structure, but is most exemplified in the four canonical New Testament Gospels, which present four interlocking perspectives. These have significance in respect of integral economics, alongside many other aspects of social and spiritual life.

The four perspectives fit together, in that the Gospel of Luke (together with his second volume, The Acts/Praxeis) reflects a Southern mode, grounded in the integration of community. Mark has a far more Eastern orientation, in his emphasis on the immediacy of the encounters that Jesus has, together with his power to bring the supernatural into the everyday. The Gospel of John is, equally, more mystical, more conceptual and more readily earthed. In these respects it is navigational, in a Northern sense, with an economics that uses signs of transformation as pointers to a deeper reality within the ordinary. Fourthly, when we come to the Gospel of Matthew, we enter very directly into the Western world of economics and finance.

As such, we can place Kingdom Economics in the Western realm, so that, whilst it is informed by each of the four Gospel perspectives, it is most readily expressed through the Gospel of Matthew. Matthew was a tax-gatherer (9:9) and familiar with the details of financial transactions. It is worth noting the significant amount of Matthew's Gospel that is devoted to questions of money, possessions, poverty, wealth and economics.

With reference to money, for example, amongst the Synoptics, there are 6 passages in Mark, 22 in Luke and 44 in Matthew. More significantly, certain aspects of Jesus' teaching in Matthew display a remarkable level of understanding of economic principles, as well as how Jesus turned these upside-down. For example, the *Parable of the Workers in the Vineyard* (20:1–16) speaks of the amazing generosity of God's grace in the face of human economising. The day-workers hired for only one hour receive the same as those who have worked all day, because God is generous, even to those who arrive last in the kingdom.

Grounding in the Economic Object of Gift-Graces: Charism

Nevertheless, when we come to considering the semiotic economics process—aligned with the integral GEN*E*alogical dynamic—it is possible to identify sequential features deriving, in turn, from the worldviews of each Gospel redactor (See Table 9.1.). Kingdom Economics has a meaning-system that is grounded in the economic object of 'charism', which substantially reflects a Lukan perspective. Charisms are the gift-graces of the Holy Spirit. They are the gifts that are given, by the love of God, through the Spirit of God, in the name of Jesus Christ, to the community of the Church. They *ground* God's life and work in the people of God.

Whilst the pneumatological charisms are not exclusively narrated in Luke-Acts, more than 50% of NT (New Testament) references to the charismatic work of the Holy Spirit are recorded by Luke, within writings that represent 25% of the NT material. As such, they are doubly 'over-represented' in Luke. Furthermore, although this is not a conventional treatment—which is usually reserved for 'spiritual' lessons—at least nineteen of the charisms listed in the NT, have a clear economic and managerial dimension. These include helping (1 Cor 12:28), administration (Acts 6:2–3), service (2 Tim 1:16–18), teaching (Eph 4:11–14), encouragement (Heb 10:24–25), giving (Acts 4:32–35), leadership (Acts 13:12), mercy (Luke 5:12–13), guidance (Eph 4:11), hospitality (1 Pet 4:9), and grace (Eph 3:7).

Emergence Through the Archetype of Signification: Grace

When brought together these present a profound basis for a Kingdom Economics, which upends mainstream neoliberal rationality. The *emergent* 'archetype of signification' for this economic meaning-system is represented in the final charism listed, which is, equally, their core feature, namely, grace (χαρις). This is, often, indicated to mean an abstract divine quality (God's graciousness). But, as Professor Jimmy Dunn (6) puts it:

> In Paul... χαρις is never merely an attitude or disposition of God (God's character as gracious); consistently it denotes something much more dynamic—the wholly generous *act* of God. Like 'Spirit,' with which it overlaps in meaning (cf., e.g., [Rom] 6:14 and Gal 5:18), it denotes effective divine power in the experience of men.

'Grace' has a clear, archetypal and semiotic economic dimension. It is, often, colloquially, defined as 'God's free, undeserved, favour'. The idea of reception that is free, unmerited and given, simply (sic) out of love, challenges notions of markets, labour and rights-in-exchange. Another conventional mnemonic for grace is 'God's riches at Christ's expense'. Again, this is to use the economic language of wealth, expenditure and exchange.

Although 'grace' language—of the *emergence* of God's love—is not explicit in Mark's Gospel, it is the archetypal underpinning for it. We see this in the miracles of the raising of Jairus' daughter (5:25–43), the healing of a deaf man (7:31–37), Jesus' wrestling with the call to crucifixion, in Gethsemane (14:33ff) and his 'cry of dereliction' from the cross (15:34). In each of these

and many other Markan passages, we are presented with a pattern of signific
cation which indicates a vocation to self-giving, sacrifice and service of others.

The Representamum of Sacrificial Giving – Economic Navigation

Sacrificial, self-giving is the sign of economic significance, the 'representamum' in Peircean terms. This is displayed in an immensely complex way in
John's Gospel, as a compass-bearing, that *navigates*, via an inter-connected series of icons, pointing to how to follow the way of Christ. The first twelve
chapters of John are often referred to as 'the book of seven signs'—indicating,
remarkably, that the semiotic methodology, which is a Northern abstraction,
was, already, embedded in the Gospel pattern—with Chapters 13–21 being
'the book of suffering'. Although these signs are not, usually, seen in economic
terms, they have that precise and practical association. For example, the very
first sign in John is of Jesus turning water into wine at a wedding feast (2:1–
12). The resources had run dry, by implication, because either the wedding
planners had over-economised or the guests had over-indulged. But, the grace
charism is reflected, economically, in over-flowing love, literally presented as
twelve (number of the tribes of Israel, reflected in Jesus' disciples) large stone
jars of 'new wine'.

Furthermore, the final sign of the seven is *the* sign, namely the raising of
Lazarus (11:1–46), pointing, as it does, to the implications of Christ's resurrection, as *navigating* humanity heavenwards. This may seem antithetic to
economic analysis. Rather, it is a pointer to the possibility that kingdom (of
heaven) activity can begin in the everyday, which can, equally, mean to transform economics. The dead can come to life. Even financial accounting practice
can become enlivened, which is one of the abiding themes of this volume.

Debt-forgiveness – An Exemplary Interpretant Effect

The sign that this sign has, in fact, taken on signification, will be in the
self-giving and forgiving work of the Christian community. That acts—the
Praxeis is the book of the early Church, immediately following the quaternity
of the Gospels—as the pointer to the effect of this representamum (signs) in
the interpretants that flow from it. One of the most powerful of these has been
in the movement towards 'debt forgiveness', by the IMF and World Bank, of
loans to many heavily-indebted nations.

I, vividly, remember standing in a human chain, surrounding the great
cathedral of Koln (Cologne), Germany, in the year 2000, as part of the *Drop
the Debt* campaign. This had been orchestrated by Jubilee 2000 and the Christian economist Ann Pettifor, with support from such luminaries as the singer
Bono and the, then, UK Chancellor of the Exchequer, Gordon Brown. My old
colleague Archbishop Justin Welby has recently described it (7) as:

> ... perhaps the churches' finest hour in dethroning Mammon... Sustained support from Christians and others across the world led to the cancellation of more than $100 billion of debt owed by 35 of the poorest countries.

This would have been heartily approved by St. Matthew, as an *effective* interpretation of Kingdom Economics principles. The Matthean version of The Lord's Prayer (6:9–13) contains the phrase 'forgive us our debts' (ὀφειλήματα) whereas, in the Lukan version, it is most closely translated 'forgive us our sins' (ἁμαρτίας). Both continue, 'as we forgive our debtors'. But, Matthew's language is much more directed towards the economics of financial exchanges, whereas, as we would expect, Luke's language is more rooted in the home, community and *grounding* in human relationships. In this way, it is possible to cycle around the GEN*E*, using the BQA as a guide.

Overall, as this brief survey indicates, we can see, within the pattern of the four canonical NT Gospels, a broader Biblical Quaternity Archetype, holographically reflected in the GEN*E*alogy of the Four Worlds model. This archetype of signification provides the basis for a meaning-system which has significance far beyond economics. Even so, it does, equally, hold signification within the economic realm. In this respect, we can see how, as one of many alternative systems—such as the eight listed in Table 9.1. above—it is possible to present a semiotic economics which provides in-depth contestation of economic neoliberalism. In the following section I turn from a Christian perspective back to Akhuwat, as an Islamic source of meaning, to reconnect to the case presented in Chapter 6, at this point through the direct lens of Semiotic Economics.

9.3. Mawakhat to Akhuwat – A Semiotic Economics Example of Islamic Finance

As we have seen, there is no single approach to Islamic finance. Indeed, just as the Christian Church has many branches and, historical divisions, so the Islamic community and family of national cultures and diverse traditions—particularly between Sunni, Shia, Ahmadiyya, Sufi and Wahhabi communities—offers diverse theological interpretations of Islamic principles. Even so, it is possible to identify certain over-arching aspects which indicate the direction of flow for a semiotic economics analysis of Islamic finance, in this case from a specifically Eastern perspective. In this case I have drawn on the work of Amjad Saqib and Aneeqa Malik, concerning microfinance in Pakistan for insights into the tradition that underpins the microfinance institution of Akhuwat, which operates in Pakistan and amongst the Pakistani community diaspora.

9.3.1. Grounding the Economic Object in Mawakhat

Following the Semiotic Economics methodological process, we first identify the economic object. As we saw in Chapter 6, this rests on the foundational principle of *mawakhat*, or 'brotherhood' (a more gender-neutral term might be 'kindred'). But, the original meaning does proceed from the male-line fraternal history of the Prophet (blessed be he). As in the mythic depiction of Adam (the man) and Eve (the help-mate), in the biblical account of Genesis 1–3, the Holy Qur'an points to humanity having its origins in a single male-female pair-bond:

> O, mankind! Surely we have created you of a male and female and make you tribes and families that you know each other, surely the noblest among you unto Allah is one who fears him. Lo! Allah is the All-Knowing.

> Holy Qur'an, al-Hujurat, 49:13, English translation

The significance of this *ayah* (verse) is to *ground* the commonality of all human beings. If all people are members of the same family, then, we are all equal in the sight of God (Allah). Such equality is to be worked out in every aspect of human society, including that of the economic. The richest and most powerful ('the noblest') are to fear God and, thus, respect the poorest and least economically dominant.

Furthermore, this verse indicates the practical implication of being a single family. The (Islamic) community is to 'know each other'. The theological principle is to be worked out in direct, societal and cultural relationships, so that where people are known to be part of the community, under Allah, they are to practise equality. This establishes a foundational economic object, namely, institutionalising equality-before-God, as kin, or 'mawakhat', in financial and economic dealings.

As we have reflected on several occasions, in the preceding chapters, the historical origin of this principle derives from the flight (*hijrah*) of the Prophet and his followers from Makkah (Mecca) to Yathrib (Medina), in 622 CE. On arrival, Muhammad recognised various tribes of Jews and Arabs living in the latter city. Reputedly, he identified that many of the Jewish merchants practised usury, or the charging of excessive interest-rates on money or property loans, which he sought to outlaw. Equally, he differentiated the refugees from Mecca, which he named *Muhajireen* (people of the pilgrimage, or *Hajj*), from the Muslim settled population of Mecca, designated as *Ansar* (native brethren).

As might be expected the Ansar were, initially, wealthier than their Muhajireen brothers. Even so, given that many of the refugees had been prosperous merchants in Mecca, some swiftly established new businesses and restored their wealth, whilst others chose to continue a more ascetic lifestyle of preferred poverty. Additionally, many of the Jews recognised Muhammad's authority in

211

Medina and associated themselves with the brotherhood, whilst retaining their distinctive Jewish faith.

On this basis, Muhammad instituted the Charter of Medina, which institutionalised equality between the Jews and Arabs and, also, between the Ansar and Muhajireen, in Medina. Part of the Charter was to issue an article which paired together 'brothers' from the two Muslim groupings. This reflected a remarkable act of generosity from the resident Muslims, who took their refugee brethren into their homes, sharing their family wealth and seeking to integrate them into the economic prosperity of the city. The act of the Ansar towards the Muhajireen became a model of mawakhat, in respect of economic equalising. Unfortunately, this situation was short-lived, as a year later (623 CE) Medina was over-run and the system of wealth-sharing was eradicated. Nevertheless, it had become an object of economic equality, upon which much of Islamic teaching concerning financial relationships—within the brotherhood—was founded.

Fascinatingly, in terms of the integral economics GEN*E*alogical fourfold, during the second year following the hijrah, Muhammad changed the orientation of prayer, for his followers from Jerusalem, to the North, to Mecca, in the South, reputedly because he had lost confidence in the possibility of converting the Jews to Islam. As such, the foundation of the economic object, in mawakhat, was grounded in a Southern orientation. This indicates the relative metaphorical and literal aspect of the geographical poles in the Four Worlds model, given that for biblical Judaism the South was represented by Jerusalem, in Judah, when viewed from the Northern Kingdom of Israel. Equally, it reflects the mysterious, near universal, homology of the four realms, wherein the South is associated with community, human nature, brotherhood and the grounding of economic objects.

In practical terms, several organisations across the Islamic world, such as Akhuwat and the Alkhidmat Foundation, both in Pakistan, practise the principle of mawakhat. They offer interest-free microfinance, as acts of 'solidarity' (8). Akhuwat seeks to harness the spiritual principle of brotherhood giving and sharing, by inviting those at the top of the income distribution to donate towards relieving poverty at the bottom, whilst redistributing from the upper-middle to the lower-middle, through the use of small-scale financial loans. Following our earlier discussion of Polanyi's economic taxonomy, these Islamic models integrate together Southern (reciprocity-based relief, based in mawakhat), Northern (redistributive microfinance) and Western (within a market-based capitalist economy) aspects of the GEN*E*alogy. The question is: to what extent do they emerge a sub-structural archetype of signification, to complete the integral cycle?

9.3.2. The Emergent Archetype of Signification – Ihsan

The starting impulse for the Akhuwat model rests in the East, with spiritual faith. In terms of the spiritual life there are three 'levels' of faith defined within the Sufi tradition: *islam, iman* and *ihsan*, each representing a 'higher state' of 'closeness to God'. These appear to correspond, within the contemplative Christian tradition, to prayer, meditation and contemplation. To these higher states, of iman and ihsan, have been added the practices of *ikhlas* (sincerity) and *makhuwat* (solidarity), to generate a fourfold process of integral development.

But, in this Sufi Islamic model, the impulse for the GEN*E* appears to begin in the Eastern Pilgrimium (9, in the language of the Communiversity), with the spirituality of iman, after which the Akhuwat model turns North into the Academy of Sincerity, as the place for understanding Truth. Thence, the GEN*E*, turns West, into the Laboratory of Excellence, as the place of drawing close to God through actualising faith. The final turn is towards the South, into the makhuwat (Islamic community) of solidarity (or, Soul-i-darity, as Aneeqa Malik puts it), as the place of effecting a connection between the people of faith, established in the institutions of Akhuwat.

There is no need to be too deterministic about this. The point is that the grounding and emergence of Islamic finance are inextricably connected together, wherein the community (Southern) is defined according to spiritual and cultural (Eastern) faith and belief aspects. In terms of the current elaboration of this model, as a case of semiotic economics, it is important to identify that the practice of Islamic finance, within this approach, emerges the archetype of signification as 'ihsan' or the ascent towards perfection and excellence.

It makes sense to refer to ihsan as the Islamic archetype of signification, or the hidden sub-structural, unconscious place-holder for faith. In every spiritual tradition there is a 'ladder of prayer' (cf. Jacob's Ladder, Genesis 28:10–19). Equally, most faiths point to the futility of attempting the ascent, as a hope of reaching to God. As we observed in respect of Kingdom Economics, the archetype is that 'grace', which cannot be earned, or reached. Rather, it is a gift.

Even so, it is possible to perceive ihsan as several steps beyond islam (religious obligation), or iman (spiritual reason). Within the Sufi understanding of ihsan there is the sense of having uncovered a divine intention or inner compulsion to the highest form of worship (also referred to as *ibadah*). That means to serve God for no other reason than as love towards Allah. It has a rough correspondence with the Christian understanding of contemplation (10).

The emergence or uncovering of this archetype of economic signification can only occur through deep personal faith, commitment, prayer and reflection on how to put faith into practice, as righteous acts. Once again, we see that the meaning-system underpinning the economic form of Islamic finance, when truly practised, emerges from a trans-rational place, within the sub-conscious or, frequently, unconscious self. Contrary to neoliberal principles, this economic rationality doesn't emerge from values of acquisitiveness and maximising surpluses, but from a commitment to the vulnerable, economically weak, poor and oppressed.

Indeed, ihsan is usually connected to the 'hadith-Jibreel' or the word of the Angel Gabriel to the Prophet, which contains the verse:

> Then he further asked, 'What is Ihsan (perfection)?' Allah's Messenger replied, 'To worship Allah as if you see Him, and if you cannot achieve this state of devotion then you must consider that He is looking at you.'

> Holy Qur'an, Hadith-Jibreel, English translation, al-Bukhari version

This reflects the principle of each of the monotheistic faiths (*Ahl al-Kitab*), that, whilst God is unseen, 'He' is all-seeing, so that whatever is done in secret is not unknown to God/Allah. The archetype of signification is that out of a secret place God's word will become flesh. In the Christian biblical tradition this is the word of Gabriel to Mary, that she had found favour with God and would give birth to a Son, Jesus, through the activity of the Holy Spirit. Within the Islamic tradition this secret activity of Allah is demonstrated in the lives of those who are aware of the fact that their every action is seen by God, not least in the sphere of the economic.

9.3.3. Navigating through a Chain of Soulidarity – Infaaq; Pointing to Akhuwat

There is little need to specify the third and fourth steps of the GEN*E* here, as these are elaborated at length in Chapter 6. But, whilst the archetype of signification, in terms of the prayerful practice of ihsan is largely hidden, the technological expression of *infaaq*, as a chain of soulidarity, needs to be clearly represented. This is the sign/representamum of this model of Islamic finance, pointing to such practical programmes (interpretants) as Akhuwat and Alkhidmat, each operating from Lahore and Karachi, in Pakistan (see Chapters 5, 6 and 8 for full depictions of the chain of 'soulidarity' in Akhuwat and other navigational forms of Islamic finance).

It is, however, important to make some comment on the representamum (sign) aspect of infaaq. This is very directly consequent on the hidden nature—archetype of signification—of ihsan. Because, whilst infaaq (derived from *nafaq*, which can mean to spend profitably) is, clearly visible, as a form of dispersement of moneys, funds or capital, it is performed on the basis of not expecting any return. Once again, this parallels teaching that is biblical, in both Jewish (Deuteronomy 15:8) and Christian (Luke 6:33–35) scriptures.

In this respect infaaq is a sign that points from the hidden spiritual economic principle of God seeing 'the heart', or spirit, behind transactions, to its expression in particular examples (interpretants), which require giving, as both free gifts and non-interest-based loans.

The purpose of this section has been to indicate, in synoptic form, the way in which the methodology of Semiotic Economics can be applied to Islamic finance, through the familiar, in these chapters, case of Akhuwat. It begins through an identification of the economic object. As such, we, finally, need to ask the question: what does economics mean in this context?

Herein the answer lies in an understanding of mawakhat or equality based on 'kinship', that all believers belong to a single family. In that respect Islam can be seen as extending far beyond the boundaries of those who call themselves Muslims. Its archetype of signification emerges from the trans-rational conscience of the believer, who acts on the basis of an inner awareness of the all-knowing sight of Allah. The sign that this ihsan is truly represented is demonstrated in the navigational form of the infaaq, or unexpectant loan-as-gift.

But, of course, in addition to the faith-based models of Kingdom Economics and Islamic finance, we can, also, specify the working of other 'alternative' economic meaning-systems, such as current practices in terms of 'impact investing'. As such, finally, I turn to a methodology for uncovering economic semiosis in contemporary models of capital investment, for a purpose other than purely maximising a monetary ROI. Although this doesn't proceed from a spiritual and religious faith, it does reflect values of what might be understood as a secular, humanitarian faith to organise economics and finance on the basis of making an impact in addressing human need. In this respect, we return to the territory that Ronnie Lessem critically addressed in Chapters 3 and 4.

9.4. The Semiotic Methodology Applied to Impact Investing

The development of impact investing, currently being further evolved by one of the Trans4m Fellows in the UK, Robert Dellner (see Chapter 1), is little more than two decades old and has very significantly increased in the years since the Crash. It recognises the desire—within conventional capitalist economics—for investors to intentionally generate social and environmental impacts, alongside financial returns, from their investments. One of the leading arenas, for investors and financiers, to navigate their way through the plethora of virtuous schemes, by which to construct their portfolio, is the Global

Impact Investing Network (GIIN). Once again, we can deploy the Semiotic Economics methodology, as an evolution of the integral economics GEN*E*.

9.4.1. The Economic Object (G)

The key grounding object for the economics of impact investing is the investment itself. But, drill down deeper into this object and a spectrum emerges from more conventional 'market-rate' investments to others, termed 'below-market' (or concessionary) investments, which might, in other contexts, be considered as charitable donations.

As such, this demonstrates one of the complexities of Semiotic Economics, which is the specification of an economic object itself. Some reasons why concessionary investments may not be considered as traditional charity are that they may represent aspects of 'virtue signalling'. By engaging such investments an institution may enable the release of other asset classes, for leveraging enhanced standard financial returns, for example, by an ROI of political or other forms of social capital, such as trust-building amongst clients. Even so, we may regard the investment as the basic economic object.

9.4.2. The Archetypes of Signification (E)

The stated purpose of impact investing is to enable investors to intentionally provide capital to challenge some of the world's most pressing social and environmental needs and concerns. The emphasis is placed on the emergence of *intentionality*. This indicates an understanding that, hitherto, investors may have unintentionally invested in enterprises and projects that either provided social and/or environmental benefits, or, alternatively, acted to undermine social development or degrade the environment. The GIIN exists to offer a wide range of methodologies (through IRIS) and exemplar opportunities for impact investors.

But, as will have become immediately obvious, the focus on intentionality masks the purposes behind investment in social and environmental concerns. Indeed, until relatively recently, much debate about accounting practices, in this sphere, had been predicated on the idea of triple bottom line accounting, which takes people and planet into account, alongside profit. But, more recently, a fourth 'p' of purpose has been added, in quadruple bottom line accounting (QBLA), which gets to the heart of the question surrounding archetypes of signification.

It will be a matter of empirical investigation to uncover the precise origins of these archetypes. But, as indicated in Table 9.2. we suggest that the deep spiritual/cultural impulse behind much genuine impact investing is a search for *value*. Of course, this is an ancient economic question that was at the heart of much early political economy, particularly in respect of the work of David

Ricardo and Karl Marx. They, each, solved the question of value-in-production by applying it to the inherent 'cost' (Ricardo) or 'congealed exploitation' (Marx) of labour.

Later, neo-classical economists established value as a function of exchange, eliding value with price, in marginalist theory. By the mid-20th century post-Keynesians, such as Sraffa, had returned to a productive use-value understanding. Correspondingly, 21st century impact investors are identifying value with conscious impulses to develop society and conserve ecological capital. There is, however, in the notion of purpose a deeper cultural and spiritual impulse that can be associated with fundamental meaning. Discovering the emergence of such meaning-systems—on the basis of innate releasing mechanisms—in particular enterprises, state actions and investment decisions is one of the tasks of Semiotic Economics.

9.4.3. The Signifier ('Representamum', N)

As suggested above, the sign-relation of impact investing is QBLA, with its emphasis placed on the 'purpose' underpinning an investment and the accounting procedures used to measure this meaning-system and its outputs. Beginning to fully investigate this sign-relation, within Peircean semiotic terms, it will be necessary to construct a table such as 7.1, with purpose as its example. Table 9.2. represents an initial attempt at this.

What becomes, immediately, apparent in such an articulation is that it is far more complex than even seeking to establish the sign-relations of the object 'elephant' (see Chapter 7). Economic objects are multi-faceted phenomena in themselves. But, whilst this makes the task of Semiotic Economics intensely challenging, it is, also, vitally important to reveal the pre-judgments on which different economic meaning-systems are based. Most importantly, from the perspective established here, is the need to both comment on specific local cases of each economic system, such as that involving impact investment and, equally, to signify the development of innovations which can more fully embody these meaning-systems, having articulated the signification archetypes of the missing fourth.

	Sign quality (grounding)	Sign-reaction/ resistance (pointing/ navigation)	Sign-mediation/ further representation (effect)
Sign-relation type (base)	**Qual-sign** Object: Purpose-aligned enterprise	**Sin-sign** QBLA	**Legi-sign** Indicators for the measurement of 'purposive impact' e.g. New Zealand government's measures of cultural continuity amongst indigenous 'Maori' peoples.
Sign-object relation (primary relation)	**Icon** Picture of: Quaternity model	**Index** Applications of QBLA in e.g. customer, employee and supply-chain relations	**Symbol** e.g. Fairtrade sourcing and the use of the Fairtrade Labelling Organisation (FLO) symbol, which combines images of a person waving, ying-yang, a river flowing, an embryo and an Aztec depiction of an eagle's head, all in a circular motif (cf. individuation)
Sign-interpretant relation (secondary relation)	**Rheme** The quest for meaning	**Dici-sign** Situated enterprises e.g. seeing work as alienating and lacking in sustaining communities	**Argument** e.g. in Buddhist economics there is a fundamental concern for inter-dependence between people, communities, Nature and an enlightened understanding of prosperity.

Table 9.2. Peircean Classification of Sign-Relations for Purposive Impact Investing

9.4.4. Effective Interpretation ('Interpretant', E)

This fourth, completing, aspect of the GEN*E*alogical cycle—in respect of the methodology of Semiotic Economics analysis—requires the co-creation of particular local cases in which the specific signification is being effected. In a short chapter such as this it isn't possible to provide detailed case examples of enterprise operations where impact investing is making a meaningful difference. But, even to look at those listed on the GIIN Case Studies pages, there are several dozen, together with many more that are the subject of research profiles.

Equally, GIIN is, essentially, focused on the impact investing movement in the USA. Consequently, it only reflects a tiny proportion of those enterprises, corporations and individuals who are exploring purpose-driven investment opportunities, using QBLA and associated signifiers, recognising the trenchant critiques of such, as raised by Ronnie Lessem, in Chapter 4. Equally, in the UK, ethical banks such as Triodos, more conventional financial institutions, such as Barclays, independent foundations, such as the Inclusive Economy Unit and arms of government, such as the Advisory Group on Growing a Culture of Social Impact Investing in the UK, each contribute to explicating the meanings that investors place on impact and purpose-driven finance.

9.5. Meaningful Conclusion

The objective of this chapter has been to, briefly, introduce and apply Semiotic Economics to the themes introduced in the previous chapters, by looking into three meaning-giving instances: Christian, Islamic and humanitarian. As I have sought to demonstrate, there is a clear and pressing need for deeper understanding of so-called alternative and, for us, *meaningful,* economic systems as such. Of course, these are only alternative if we take our compass-bearings from neoliberalism, which we indeed consider to be 'meaningless' because it lacks specific context.

The economic consensus, surrounding this previously dominant model of economics, is increasingly, breaking down. As such, we are seeing the emergence of a broad range of collaborative (rather than competing) economic meaning-systems, that have assumed the mantle of presenting, to use Schumacher's famous dictum, as the sub-heading to 'small is beautiful', 'economics as if people mattered'. Semiotic Economics should aim to uncover the archetypes of signification which awaken consciousness and release communities to co-create new enterprise innovations.

These will be signalled by sense-making that rejects neoliberal and marginalist economics as the sole nature of the discipline. There are many more economic worlds to understand, interpret, analyse and build practical enterprise structures onto. That task is underway. It will emerge over time, through the pages of this publisher, in our series on *Insights in Semiotic Economics*. But, for the moment, that mission of developing further economic signification must await another day. Meanwhile, in conclusion, we turn to Basheer Oshodi's presentation of AmeenArthur, as a model of Islamic finance that is taking principles underpinning the chapters of this volume seriously, prior to Ronnie Lessem concluding the volume with a plea to bring finance and accounting back to its humanistic home.

9.6. Bibliography

1 **Bradley**, T (2019) Innovating Arts, within the Cultural-Economy nexus of the Liverpool City-Region: Towards a Communiversity, using the Biblical Quaternity Archetype model. *Unpublished doctoral thesis, Da Vinci Institute*. Johannesburg. Da Vinci Institute

2 **Kraybill**, D B (2011, updated) *The Upside-down Kingdom*. Harrisonburg, Va. Herald Press

3 **Redekop**, C, **Ainlay**, S A and **Siemens**, R (1995) *Mennonite Entrepreneurs*. Baltimore. John Hopkins University Press

4 **Bruni**, L and **Zamagni**, S (2006) *Civil Economy – efficiency, equity and public happiness*. Bern. Peter Lang

5 **Wilentz**, S (2016) *The Politicians and the Egalitarians – the hidden history of American politics*. New York. W.W. Norton & Co

6 **Dunn**, J D G (1988) *Romans 1–8: Word Biblical Commentary 38a*. Dallas, Tx.. Word Books

7 **Welby**, J (2016) *Dethroning Mammom: making money serve grace*. London. Bloomsbury

8 **Saqib**, M A and **Malik**, A (2019) *Integral Finance: Akhuwat – a case study of the solidarity economy*. Abingdon. Routledge

9 **Lessem**, R, **Adodo**, A, and **Bradley**, T (2019) *The Idea of the Communiversity: releasing the Natural, Cultural, Technological and Economic GENE-ius of Societies*. Manchester. Beacon Academic

10 **Carrigan**, H L (2002) *The Ascent of Mount Carmel* (modern version of St John of the Cross). Brewster, Ma. Paraclete Press

CHAPTER 10

AmeenArthur Venture: An Integral Islamic Case

Basheer Oshodi, Head of Islamic Banking at Sterling Bank in Nigeria and Founder of CISER

10.1. Introduction

As we saw in Chapter 8, as things currently stand, the Islamic finance industry has grown on the backs of neoliberalism. As such, and crucial for our purposes in this book, there is not yet a clear proposition targeted at socio-ontology, related to specific communities, whether in the South or East, North or West. Many Islamic financial institutions simply copied the Western model and ensured products got the *Shariah*-compliance stamp.

There has been very little thought given to fine-tuning Islamic finance products and propositions to merge the local (communal) with the global (international). The salutary Abraaj case (see Chapter 8), showed an example of good intent towards localised impact, but lost its way as a result of this gap in communal knowledge and particular focus. It is in this vein that a new impact investment proposition propelled by Islamic finance principles is being launched. This unfolding proposition, as articulated here, moulds Islamic finance in integral guise with blends and ingredients from a handful of jurisdictions, in Europe and Africa, with extra focus on areas of comparative and competitive advantage.

An organic growth is, indeed, being explored. Islamic finance, as a dynamic proposition, is being applied to investment banking, structured trade and real estate, as top priorities and, initially, limited to seven countries in Africa, Europe and the Middle East. This is reflected in the name, AmeenArthur, which demonstrates a mashing of three vibrant worlds of Africa, of Europe and of the Middle East.

10.2. Achieving Integral Finance Through a Global Private Equity Company

Changing the face of Islamic finance towards more societal impact is the clear agenda for AmeenArthur. AmeenArthur has its roots in Lagos, Nigeria, spurred on, initially, through a research project undertaken at the University of Lagos, in their Faculty of Environmental Services, Department of Estate Management (1). Such action research, then, led to the development of the integral finance business case in 2018. The particular value proposition—as articulated in this concluding chapter—is the further outcome of the seminar which initiated this volume (see Preface). It provides a culmination for this book, setting out 'propositional knowing' (2) as in John Heron's *Co-operative Inquiry*.

The next practical step is to evolve a vehicle and entities that will pass through the rough lands of Africa and experience the cool climate of a European banking location, resting its arm in the Middle East, and its Islamic financial wealth funds. Through experience gained in the Islamic finance field it is able to use its understanding of cultural elements, gained from listening to 'the beats of the communal drums and paying attention to the colourful beads around the waist of the village girl'. Thus, a major strength in this emerging venture is the way in which it involves an understanding of the needs of the communal South, the African communities.

The proposed UK-based European arm serves as an investment and advisory vehicle, with a sound corporate governance structure, to attract funds from around the globe while maintaining its registration, close to the source of financial funds in the Middle East. As such, in this chapter we present something of the business case for AmeenArthur, as an Islamic finance fund, operating in integral terms, where the company's high-level strategies are exposed and where the constituents that make up the value proposition are revealed. The core of the value proposition is to achieve one hundred percent Shariah-compliance, exceptional profitability and, also, most distinctively in the context of this book, societal impact, on an integral basis. AmeenArthur will apply learning from Africa, Europe and the Middle East.

Generally, modern business dealings, especially in financial services, require legitimate licences to operate in several jurisdictions. As fintechs, telcos and technology companies increasingly compete with financial institutions in providing financial services, the need for banks to quickly measure up to the challenge cannot be overstated. It is very important for each business to include the ability to acquire customers, pursue innovation, utilise and transform data and protect itself from competition (3). Two main additions are then required for this local-global entity to capture the rudiments of what Lessem and Schieffer (4), have called the moral economic core. One is to have the requisite Islamic finance licence. The other is to adopt the emerging norms (5) of integral banking aimed at overall social impact, whereby nature and community, culture and spirituality, in and of a particular society, take pride of place alongside technology and enterprise.

The structure of corporate governance and engagement of stakeholders are of vital significance. The motives behind any company are closely linked with the expectations and desires of such stakeholders. Thus, many stakeholders will expect a financial services house, such as AmeenArthur, to have an all-round societal impact, that will involve making investments in specific human, natural, cultural and social, as well as financial capital (see Mark Anielski's 5 Capitals model, in Chapter 2).

So, beyond profitability, shareholders—under an integral finance model—will want *integral* impact investments; to reach out to communities; to see happiness on the faces and in the homes of their clients; and they want to see sustainability of such impact, in a particular society. For this to happen, the emerging integral private equity firm will have a global Chief Impact Officer (CIO), who will ensure that all ventures being financed impact society directly. The measurement or scorecard for performance will go beyond Return on Investment (ROI) and Return on Equity (ROE) to Impact on Communities (ROC) and Impact of Value-based Investments (IVI) (see Robert Dellner's discussion of Integral Impact Return (IIR) and Return on Impact Investment (RII), in Chapter 1).

Practically, this integral private equity company will be similar to a holding company and will be involved in two main types of equity: equity in companies and equity in business transactions. Equally, it will have a dedicated Research Academy, geared towards safeguarding, and continually evolving, its integral impact within a particular society, serving to secure a 5 Capitals return. Such *integral* equity positions will be located in other financial institutions, real estate companies, technology firms, fintechs, telcos, agriculture, commodity trading companies and manufacturing companies. It may, also, be engaged in long-term equity investment in business ventures, while maintaining executive or non-executive management position in these firms. It may then sell its shares at much higher value in the future. With priority in real estate, the integral PE fund could take considerable equity in real estate companies, real estate related projects, while seeking for an Islamic home finance institution licence.

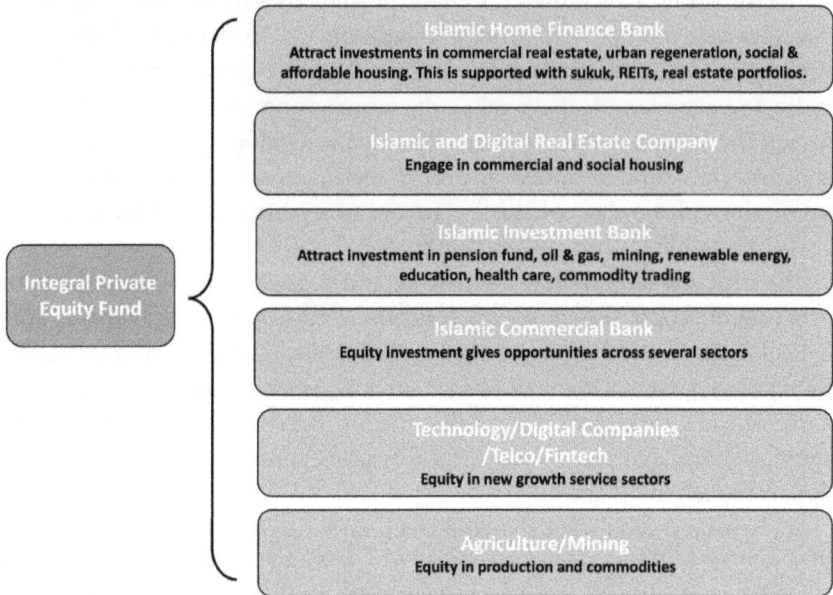

Figure 10.1. The integral private equity fund

10.3. Initiating Integral Real Estate Opportunities

There are few financial institutions offering distinctive Islamic home finance services in Africa. We started close to Lagos, Nigeria, with the aim of reducing the housing deficit of twenty million homes. A quick response to this challenge was to evolve a housing finance laboratory or financial institution aimed at providing affordable housing to various income segments. This was coupled with a unique programme for social housing, while embedding children's orphanages within regular housing estates, thereby enhancing social and human capital.

Vulnerable widows were allowed to live and take care of orphans in residential units, participating in schools attended by children from other families within the same estate. There was, also, a real estate endowment or *waqf*, where a certain percentage of profit from the home finance institution was set aside to acquire homes for the weak, while others would attract rental income to further support the social agenda. This Islamic home finance institution created a range of housing classes, from commercial properties to affordable ones, and from urban regeneration to social housing. There is an almost infinite volume of opportunities for investing in urban renewal in emerging economies where the housing deficit is huge, as in sub-Saharan Africa. This included zero-coupon *sukuk*, for social or affordable housing where the unemployed in such neighbourhoods were the builders, labourers and suppliers.

This new institution, then, took termed and perpetual equity in other building companies and building projects; patiently takes part in the construction of estates for all segments; supports with sales efforts; and shares profit when the units are sold. Such convenient funds are what the integral finance model seeks as the supply side of housing delivery. Other more interesting housing delivery funding instruments includes sukuk, real estate investment trust (REITs) and real estate portfolios. The instruments are used to mobilise more funds for housing, with some preference for social and affordable housing.

AmeenArthur relies on several types of funding for real estate development projects. Firstly, the capital of the home finance bank is expected to be far above the regulatory minimum, while this allows the institution to provide higher risk assets. Secondly, local and foreign liabilities, tied to specific real estate projects, are mobilised. These deposits are, mainly, based on partnership (*mudarabah*) contracts or agency (*wakala*) contracts. Thirdly, there are several off-balance sheet structures, in the form of real estate sukuk. AmeenArthur ordinarily acts as the obligor, while top-rated local and foreign partner financial institutions provide guarantees and underwrite the sukuk. Fourthly, where AmeenArthur has a huge portfolio of income-generating assets, a Real Estate Investment Trust (REITs) option is invoked, such that more funds for other real estate projects can be generated from the equities market. The fifth supply-side strategy is to attract other top-rated foreign real estate companies that will come and build affordable houses, where AmeenArthur provides land, off-takers and home finance facilities to buyers.

On the demand side, home finance facilities are created using debt-based Islamic finance instruments, such as lease or forward lease contracts, and mark-up sale contracts, where the term is much shorter, with diminishing partnership for other home finance arrangement. Preference is, however, given to the diminishing partnership mode, since it gives the obligor more rights when rental repayment challenges occur. In this instance, the property can be sold at its present value or as force sale value, thereby giving the obligor back his or her equity stake in the asset.

So, what is integral about this model? Essentially, it rests in the ability of the bank to relax the overall terms of the facility, such as the percentage of security deposit and equity contribution, the ease with which such deposit is contributed, and the relatively low pricing on the facility amount. In some other instances, AmeenArthur wishes to refinance its home finance facilities through other mortgage refinancing banks and private equity investors. Furthermore, the demand side would be digitised, such that the entire home finance or 'mortgage' process takes place on mobile devices, including equity contribution or security deposit and home facility repayment. The repayment schedule and other information on the facility is, then, provided as a platform through an app. This is coupled with equity investment in property fintech companies or platforms. In order to consistently raise the housing demand side sukuk or 'mortgage'-backed sukuk, it was necessary for the AmeenArthur private equity fund to take equity in an Islamic investment bank.

10.4. The Essence of Investment Banking

Apart from household poverty, struggling economies are exposed to huge infrastructural poverty which, then, affects their ability to develop their social, as well as physical, capital effectively and efficiently. These economies do not have adequate tradable assets and are characterised by coordination gaps, in relation to people, value, states, and markets (6). Their stock market is characterised by unstable foreign direct investment, which evaporates at the slightest shock. Opportunities in structured trade finance and structured corporate finance are also enormous. Consequently, the AmeenArthur fund prioritises 5 Capitals value-based investments, that impact communities and countries, helping the *maqasid* principles and create communal well-being.

The Chief Impact Officer (CIO) from AmeenArthur private equity monitors the activities of the CIOs of partner companies and franchise other jurisdictions while drawing on integral indicators (see Chapter 4), and an overall accounting approach that supports social ontology. This approach to integral accounting becomes a major bedrock in the integral finance storyline due to its ability to engage in such rounded business and social ventures, the latter also drawing on Muhammad Yunus' (7) recent insights into eliminating poverty, unemployment and environmental degradation through his so-called 'social business'. We are prioritising such investments in Nigeria, South Africa and Kenya while the UK, Finland and the UAE will focus on delivering a percentage of acquired profitability into the global charity fund. Even so, Bahrain, in the Middle East maintains its ceremonial leadership role, while the UK plays the advisory instrumental role.

In the same light, the integral investment bank creates its own assets and investment portfolios alongside investments in other liquidity instruments. It nourishes these enterprises, places shares in them and supports their growth process. It picks community projects that are beneficial to a particular society, helping them to grow, giving ownership status to its workers and the surrounding communities, sustaining and enhancing the natural environment, as well as helping to identify markets. This continuous and circular process is expected to bring genuine happiness and prosperity to the hearts of households and communities. When such impact is felt, it means that finance, integrates with human needs culminating in (wo)man's happiness (see Mark Anielski, Chapter 2).

Whilst each community has a different set of needs, the overall, integral, human and more-than-human needs are prioritised. These include the creation of employment opportunities or entrepreneurship opportunities within the overall context of what we term 'communipreneurship'; the creation of health-related needs and health infrastructures; the establishment and upgrading of educational institutions and other support needs; and the provision of clean energy for communal and industrial needs. This is the integral value proposition of AmeenArthur, aimed at improving human well-being.

But, will such envisaged happiness reach the bottom segment? How quickly can convenient funds get to them? What role will an integral investment bank want to play here? Can digitisation strategies be a useful approach? This brings us to the role of technology, which is critical, integrally, set alongside the other capitals.

10.5. Making an Impact Through Digitised Business Strategies

From the start of the new millennium, digital platforms created disruption to all business sectors. The village child in Central Africa or the forest dweller in Columbia finds the tablet a thing of amusement and can operate it with relatively limited education. Even despite the late 90s dot-com bubble, companies engaged in technology and digitisation are being valued much more highly than huge manufacturing car companies, financial institutions, telecommunication companies and even countries with natural endowments. The entrepreneurial world now quickly searches through their Google site looking for new domains. They go in search of 'the wizard that has taken their lunch away'. It is little wonder that Rogers (8) identified the five domains of digital transformation—customers, competition, data, innovation and value—to which we add natural, cultural, human and social value. As such, we are partnering with Finnish fintech companies, recognising the opportunities that they provide.

It is the task of AmeenArthur to identify those core needs that will create impact and innovation through daily lifestyle data collection and monitoring the value system. Little will be achieved where the integral financial institution is unable to transform society digitally, thus reaching out to multitudes, valued customers and partners via their mobile phones. As an example, Nigeria's Sterling Bank was quick to introduce trading platforms alongside its products, as part of its Islamic banking window, to address aspects of competition. Lifestyle goods are sold to corporate communities in minutes and real trade grows almost unconsciously. Thus, AmeenArthur's response to overall competition is to get financial services to communities in good time, with some emphasis on rural communities and the vulnerable. International organisations, aid organisations and other non-government organisations always want to go physically to displaced communities and war zones, when, in fact, the emerging integral Islamic bank and indeed AmeenArthur, uses community members as agents to deliver these services. These communities and communipreneurs (9) are, then, with mobile phones for logistics, selling and buying of agro-commodities, and to aid their academic learning.

The emerging AmeenArthur private equity fund and its partners rely heavily on insights, concepts and information from the integral research academy (see above), aligned with our integral bank. Such is based on the integral transformative rhythm (10) where the conditions of the four layers would be met: origination, foundation, emancipation and transformation. This integral model assists us in understanding the pattern of communal behaviour, communal needs, and overall societal challenge and need for social innovation (11). The research academy, thus, needs to be aligned with the bank-as-laboratory, lodged in an overall communiversity (12).

In essence, the integral private equity company and its partners, subsidiaries and obligors need to expand the scope of the research academy, so that its integral orientation, both transculturally and transformationally, is specifically aligned with the worlds of finance and accounting with which we are engaged, and as this book has revealed. Such research academy, technologically (as well as naturally, culturally, economically) must, then, take up the new challenge of using artificial intelligence algorithms to gather and analyse information that will translate to overall impact. Thus, impact-oriented decision-making must be data-led, leading to innovation.

But, innovation in the home finance bank, the investment bank, the microfinance bank and other partners should not be about new banking style. These financial institutions should start to see themselves as digital social platforms, with a banking licence. Islamic home finance institutions will not require branches and other channels when both the supply and demand side of real estate transactions can be concluded on platforms and mobile phones, thereby heralding a veritable socio-economic transformation.

This value-based communal and societal impact, learning from an authentic fusion of Southern and Western horizons, and, occupied in the Eastern, through specific Islamic finance on the one hand, and overall moral economics on the other, is the strength infused in this new way of banking. As a digital platform, AmeenArthur is, then, beyond a bank and exposed to various types of competition. Competition, again, becomes the most dynamic of the five domains since co-laboratories will not have control of the external environment. Symmetric competitions are within the same industry and a combination of prescriptive and emergent strategies are being applied over time.

Asymmetric competition-and-cooperation for the integral financial institution means that fintechs, telcos, technology platforms and companies will provide the same services as the integral bank, whilst reaching out to more communities and being more integral in their approach. Can one imagine if a 'Westernised' Apple or Facebook launches a private equity fund to expand the technology business horizon? How quickly can the overtly integral ecological-cultural-socio/technical-economic bank respond to such a single-minded economic challenge? Equally, what if Uber starts to produce computer software and phones? What if Airbnb seeks to create industrial hubs for manufacturers to fabricate their goods for a fee? The strategic response for the integral financial institution, thereby evolving Islamic finance in most specifically Southern guise (see Chapter 5) is to align nature and culture, technology and enterprise, as a true integral financial institution. This will, however, be within the realm of people, value, intellectual and social impact thereby further supporting those at the bottom of the pyramid, through a newly integral brand of microfinance, indeed drawing now Eastern lessons (13) from Pakistan's Akhuwat (see Chapter 6).

10.6. The Dynamics of the Microfinance Institution

The bottom segment of the population is largely neglected in both advanced and struggling economies. The case of Grameen Bank in Bangladesh and the Akhuwat model in Pakistan are practical examples, then, of a co-laboratory, in our communiversity (14) terms, that can reach the expected segment. Rather than reinvent the wheel, the option before the world may just be to purposefully evolve these models, since they contain key elements of the integral. As such, our Center for Integral Social and Economic Research (CISER) has set up an integral microfinance institution, at least aligning the economic with the social, running as a platform rather than physically going into every community.

From microfinance, there is a need to migrate to micromanufacturing industries, where the Islamic integral bank takes a long equity position in the venture. Considering that 98% of companies in sub-Saharan Africa are micro and small, it means the opportunity to touch lives is there in abundance. Practically, it becomes inevitable for AmeenArthur to directly or indirectly establish such platforms or institutions in Nigeria, Kenya and South Africa in the immediate term. The alternative is to enhance or strengthen communal or social co-operatives with grants from the global charity funds, since most of such co-operatives' members are hardly able to repay such facilities. The Ewu Village, near Benin City in Edo State, Nigeria, for example, became a typical pilot case for impact—socially, physically and psychologically. Such communities are found in virtually every sub-Saharan African country.

Most struggling economies do not have enough funds for priority sectors; they are unable to convert their endowments to communal good-life; their production activities, bearing in mind also the narrowly conceived notion of 'production'—see also (15)—are insufficient to meet the population explosion, causing colossal unemployment which then exposes such economies to conflict. As future conflicts and insecurity brew, the need to extend a helping hand to the growing population becomes integral to the Islamic private equity laboratory. Microfinance institutions and co-operatives, arguably (see below), play a key role here, while financial inclusion is a response to the poverty trends.

Practically, microfinance banks in Nigeria happily give loans to high-street corporate workers with the confidence that the funds and profit would come back. But, the woman selling dried fish by the roadside gets nothing, while the fashion designer with an MBA qualification cannot get USD 500 to buy a fairly used sewing machine. This calls for an urgent financial intervention, whereby the owner of funds consciously directs such towards the bottom segments by selecting pilot communities. Thus, AmeenArthur as an integral financial institution is embarking on such, via collaboration with co-operatives, microfinance institutions and banks to serve communities.

In Islamic finance practice terms, such integrality is based on three main Shariah-compliant business models. One is the Akhuwat model, where communities enjoy interest-free loans (*Qard-al-Hasan*), while compulsory alms (*zakat*), voluntary alms (*sadaqa*) and donations/contribution (*tabarru*) are channeled towards the emancipation of communal poverty. This incorporates a social as well as an economic mission, while building on Islamic culture, albeit to this point bypassing physical, as well as human, nature. The cost of funds under the Akhuwat model is close to zero except for minimal operational cost. The repayment risk is hinged on the peer-group collateral or community-induced collateral. AmeenArthur, through communal leadership, will be involved in monitoring performance and repayment. Grants will also be acceptable under the Akhuwat model.

The second Shariah-compliant model is another debt structure using sale, lease or agency contract which attracts mark-up or profit. A further aspect of AmeenArthur's model is to provide credit guarantee through another related party. This guarantee arrangement need not be one hundred percent, while

AmeenArthur and other relevant institutions would contribute to this guarantee scheme.

The third Shariah-compliant mode of financing micro-businesses, including micro-manufacturing for AmeenArthur, is the use of equity modes. It isn't very different from venture capital investments in start-ups and existing businesses. In order to mitigate moral hazard and equity risk, such investments go directly into communal business ventures, while AmeenArthur, as fund provider, would enhance the business case, offer financial expertise and be directly involved in the day-to-day running of the venture, using communal partners. This proposition seeks to impact lives, satisfy the conditions of ethical finance and Shariah-compliance, while ensuring that the maqasid is also upheld, starting from an educational-related agenda.

10.7. Education as a Priority

The bedrock of any society is formed by people who are equipped with the knowledge and skills required to transform it. These are evolved out of natural and cultural attributes that are indigenous to them, albeit ripe for further indigenous-exogenous evolution. The enrichment and safeguarding of intellect (in our case 'intellect' that is innate to that particular community) is, also one of the major desires of the maqasid, touching communal and human lives positively. Education is the key to societal success, but the kind of education that is sensitive to, and indeed born out of, a particular physical and human nature, preferably bearing in mind, in a Southern context, traditional age-sets.

These 're-sources' are much more potent than those of the extractive industries. Knowledge of the world, both locally and globally, and of science and technology, indigenously and exogenously, is more valuable than material (mineral) endowments. Integral banking is fully committed to raising skills, towards economic emancipation. The ability of an economy to have inclusive economic growth and development is inextricably linked to having a population that is productive, naturally, culturally, technologically and economically. The case of Finland, which rose from one of the least developed countries in Europe to, possibly, the highest educated in less than a century, is inspiring, showing the possibilities for organising productive capacity.

The experience of many struggling economies is that only a small proportion of the population are productive, beyond subsistence levels. At the same time, we should not equate economic development with market-based production, as we have repeatedly seen throughout these chapters. Nevertheless, more 'advanced' economies have, at some point, addressed a crisis in skills, knowledge-creation and educational attainment. This is highlighted, in terms of connecting tradition and modernity, by the Nigerian psychologist and artist

Akomolafe (16), through his extraordinary insights in *These Worlds Beyond our Fences,* on humanity's search for home. The wealth of Taiwan, South Korea, Japan, Hong Kong, China and Finland, to name but a few countries which have rapidly transformed, is its people. Investment in people is an integral business proposition for AmeenArthur. Such an investment agenda is wrapped around producing innovative and technology-driven propositions, that will help weak economies to catch up quickly with more advanced economies.

In today's digital age, struggling economies are still mapping out strategies in the agricultural sector to reduce import bills, inflation and hunger in the community. They invest in the knowledge base around effective food production, efficient storage systems and commodity exports. These efforts will certainly reduce poverty when successful, but would certainly not take these economies to the next stage of industrialisation, let alone digitisation, and would certainly not necessarily draw on the nature and culture of a particular place. The focus of education needs to be rechanneled towards the trajectory of re-GEN*E*-ration, drawing on local, natural and communal **G**rounding with a view to transformative economic and enterprise *E*ffect, not so much on the exploitation of natural resources. Over the last 50 years, countries with huge natural resources have generally performed worse than those without, with rare exceptions, such as Botswana and, more recently, Rwanda in Africa. These latter are, increasingly, drawing on their Grounding, politically, if not, also, economically.

Venezuela, the Democratic Republic of Congo and Nigeria have had calamitous experiences. To catch up with, say, Malaysia, knowledge-creation, both indigenous and exogenous, needs to become paramount as the path of socio-technological advancement. It is in this vein that AmeenArthur is building a generic proposition to support a learning-for-life agenda and specifically pursue knowledge that will help enhance development, foreign exchange inflows and communal cash flows. So, while building hostels for universities, giving scholarships to deserving students and buying educational tablets for village primary schools, AmeenArthur is purposefully engaged in social research and innovation at every educational level, most especially in relation to co-evolving newly integral financial and economic systems. The resultant effect, in terms of people improvement, communal wealth-creation and societal impact is, then, periodically assessed, qualitatively as well as quantitatively (see Chapter 4) by AmeenArthur's impact officers, particularly in the housing and health sectors.

10.8. The Creation of Wealth around Health

Many struggling economies suffer from deaths caused by preventable diseases. Malaria alone killed over 445,000 people in 2016 while cases of cholera, typhoid fever, hypertension and accidents kill multitudes. Out of the death of 440,000 people in 2018 due to global malaria, 400,000 were recorded in Africa, out of which Nigeria alone recorded 300,000, let alone another 215,000 deaths from HIV/AIDS. Equally, cancer and HIV cases are also growing rapidly, whilst millions of people feel that they have nowhere to turn to, but to cry out to their Creator. But, this can breed a form of folk mythology that is disconnected from indigenous knowledge-creation. For example, recent accounts have surfaced of sickle-cell anaemia deaths in Africa being attributed to repetition of the gods when this is a preventable health condition.

Rates of premature infant mortality remain high because hospitals do not have incubators, while heart disease and stroke in Africa accounted for 15.2 million of the 56.9 million worldwide deaths in 2016 (all statistics, 17). AmeenArthur's focus on the health sector will be centred around financing diagnostics centres, medical equipment and programmes towards reducing diseases and stroke, mainly in public hospitals to further impact those at the base of the income pyramid. Moreover, and through our association with Paxherbals in Nigeria (see Chapter 5), we are aligning conventional and complementary approaches to such, combining Southern and Western approaches.

AmeenArthur is partnering with public and private hospitals to set up diagnostic centres for communal benefits, again, here, aligned with our integral partners Medlabs (18) in Jordan. Equally, AmeenArthur is engaged in more Islamic finance partnership models, using Islamic finance instruments in hospital projects or asset purchases, which are more integral than offering debt contracts through short payback loans. Where a debt mode is used, the cost of funds will be lower than the market, whilst AmeenArthur will be more directly involved with financial advice and overall monitoring. Funds from AmeenArthur's global charity pool will, also, be given to provide common malaria drugs, alongside the treatment of other preventable diseases. Collaboration with the Bill and Melinda Gates Foundation and WHO will be explored in the area of research on vaccines for preventable diseases. Addressing these healthcare issues, together with the provision of stable power supplies for hospitals are urgent issues for AmeenArthur to address.

10.9. The Conflict between Fossil Fuel and Clean Energy

In the UK, at the time of writing (May 2019), the government is poised to declare a state of climate emergency, with more than 100 British local councils having already done so. In a world of over 7.7 billion people, 1 billion are without electricity while another 3 billion use polluting fuel, as observed by the World Bank. Struggling economies in the tropical south are particularly vulnerable to storms, as witnessed by the impact of hurricanes in Zimbabwe and Mozambique in 2019. Equally, many sub-Saharan African countries have some of the worst records in terms of per capita use of dirty fuels. People simply want power from whatever source they can get, to keep one or two bulbs on and charge their mobile phones. Open market settings, which are common in developing countries, do not have different needs from the residential communities. Equally, the ravages of nepotism and predation have impaired governments' abilities to provide 6 hours of power daily. As such, the people call for a complete deregulation of the power sector, so that more competent investors can move into the space. At the same time, our colleague, Father Anselm Adodo (19), has proclaimed the virtues of *Nature Power*, and duly acted upon it via Paxherbals (see Chapter 5).

However, such weak states still argue in favour of providing power through the national grid, since it is an opportunity to award white elephant projects, when, in fact, entrepreneurs can conveniently provide power to their communities and cities if backed by favourable regulation. So, communities simply seek power from whatever source they can, whether fossil fuels or clean energy. Again, regulation has a role to play, where clean energy entrepreneurs are further incentivised. Communipreneurs are, then, caught in between policies around licence for communal power, incentives for the clean energy option and the huge demand for 'power'. With limited power generation, very poor transmission and fair distribution, communipreneurs are required to meet household and industrial needs.

Fortunately, the use of solar energy is increasing exponentially. But this becomes yet another import-based industry, while the weaker industrialised economies use their hard-earned foreign exchange to, excitingly, buy the panels rather than produce them for their own needs. This creates a two-tier power supply system, with middle-income households able to use their own inverter and solar panels, whilst much industry and low-income households remain dependent on large plants, powered by fossil fuels. Consequently, AmeenArthur is partnering with a range of Finnish suppliers to fund the indigenous production and installation of solar panels throughout sub-Saharan Africa. There is an opportunity for AmeenArthur to concentrate on providing clean energy for industry, through the use of Islamic finance equity or debt contracts. But, there is, equally, the need for such intermediation in the agricultural sector, which is pre-eminent.

10.10. Beyond Agricultural Production

Agriculture engages, either in employment or community mobilisation and subsistence, about 50% of all labour in these regions. As such, multilateral agencies, central banks, commercial banks and special funds are being allocated to improve investment in agricultural production. But, effective and refrigerated storage remains a major brake on products reaching any market. Furthermore, 'pig-cycle' type gluts and famines, with major price fluctuations continue to hamper agriculture. Incredibly, many governments fail to seriously scrutinise the volume of their local needs and export capabilities. At the same time, they are unconscious about how to channel their comparative and competitive advantage. There are no serious quantitative and qualitative strategic plans, considering import substitution or export promotion of the agricultural value chain.

AmeenArthur is assisting local economies to learn lessons from other global regions. By contrast, in post-war South Korea, the state directed development towards strategic goods and services that would attract volumes of foreign exchange, as early as the 1950s. But in West Africa, there is little, if any, coordination of the minimum volume of cocoa to be produced that will earn the economy a defined income. Links in the value chain are hardly connected, although some Fairtrade distributors, such as Divine, have sought to rectify this situation, channeling greater income proportions to primary cocoa producers. The strategic response for AmeenArthur is to invest in a commodity exchange while digitising the entire process in order to absorb global funds and indeed, digital money. The exchange will have all forms of commodities—hard, liquid and gaseous—included in the money exchange. It will, also, support the value-chain that allows at least minimal processing of commodities so they can attract higher prices in the international market. The bank will further support the processing of a handful of commodities and precious metals that will earn the targeted economies a decent income.

Globally, Islamic financial institutions have challenges around short-term liquidity instruments. The commodity exchange becomes a viable investment platform which will lead to further growth of the Islamic finance industry. More funds will be invested from corporate and retail clients, while commercial banking, investment banking and the overall capital market structure will be enlarged. With regards to societal impact, sleeping communities will suddenly be exposed to rising opportunities.

10.11. Impacting Communities Through Society Building

The rather tired and conventional terminology of CSR (Corporate Social Responsibility) is ill-suited to integral, if not Islamic, finance, whereby equity and efficiency, morality and economy, nature and culture, technology and enterprise are, together, aligned. In such an environment, CSR becomes a misnomer. Even in the most viable economies and business destinations of New York, Chicago and London, one will find the weak, the feeble, the poor. This is all too normal an experience in India, Nigeria, Pakistan, Bangladesh, South Africa and so on. In the absence of a welfare system (see Chapter 2), diminishing communism and callous capitalism (see Chapters 1–4) one needs to set forth the spirit of the maqasid (see Chapters 5 and 6), which is the primary purpose or intent of the Shariah.

In struggling economies, corporates spend so much money sponsoring trivialities, social events where the rich are invited to dine with the rich, purposeless talk shows called conferences, and activities that are fun but baseless. In fact, CSRs have often become an opportunity to waste funds, because they have already been budgeted for anyway. The problem is that few question what private companies do with their funds after they have paid their taxes. Of course, in many instances, large globalised corporations also have the capacity to avoid, if not evade, paying tax. Instead, they support sports, entertainment, culture, and other social events. They pay celebrity artists and footballers huge sums to display their face on a programme. Meanwhile, research is ignored and no one bothers to buy extra beds for the community health centre or general hospital. Struggling economies display much more income inequality than advanced ones, yet the political and entrepreneurial actors only remember to organise weddings in UAE, Turkey and on cruise boats sailing the Mediterranean. It is in that light, and in relation to our notion of an integral enterprise (20) that we, at Trans4m, have come up with the notion of *society building* as opposed to CSR.

AmeenArthur's society building initiatives will be channeled towards three areas: action research, primary healthcare and primary and secondary education. African students study in the West and become outstanding, contributing meaningfully to their new host countries, whose institutions are effective. In their home countries, institutions tend to rise and fall with the movements of leadership teams. As such, research academies are weak; they never get grants from alumni or corporates. AmeenArthur is occupying that space by supporting the expansion of useful knowledge aimed at improving self, others and society. Such intellectual enhancement is at the integral heart of the maqasid.

In Nigeria and connected to AmeenArthur, we have created the CISER integral research academy, geared towards the evolution of Islamic into integral finance, using the communiversity model (21): with a co-laboratory, a learning community, a regenerative sanctuary, alongside the research academy. In Nigeria, 12 million children were still out of school as at the date these words were being written (May 2019). AmeenArthur wants to get them back to their classes, aligned to traditional age-sets, albeit in new communiversity guise.

Our vision is to stop deaths from preventable illness in a decade, across Nigeria. It is a shocking indictment of global inequality that vulnerable citizens only need USD 10–30 to remain alive, but they aren't able to earn or receive it. They struggle to have one fair meal a day and rely on gifts to survive. This is why AmeenArthur is setting aside, as a minimum, 5 percent of its gross profit to facilitate this much-needed, real societal impact.

10.12. The Starting Point

As we saw in Chapter 8, the Abraaj Private Equity company wanted to be everywhere at the same time and failed, despite initial good intentions. That's why our proposition is limited to six countries for the first five years. Our priority countries are Nigeria, South Africa, Kenya, the United Kingdom, Finland and the UAE, while retaining Bahrain as the administrative arm. The UK will write the financial advisory script, alongside support its housing needs, while the UAE will serve other financial intermediation roles.

Moreover, returning to Trans4m's original work (22) on *Managing in Four Worlds*, in psychological and cultural terms, if not also economic ones, the North needs the South, as much as an abstract 'mind' is bereft without a concrete 'soul', not to mention the fact, also, that Africa (in the South) is the original cradle of humanity (including the North). Pragmatically speaking, AmeenArthur has been set up with like-minded investors, who are conscious of the Maqasid al-Shariah, committed to societal impact, and willing to accept balanced social and financial returns. Our principles rest in the wisdom of humanism, feminism, ethical radicalism and communipreneurship, all yoked to deep Islamic faith, within an integral worldview.

10.13. Conclusion

The integrity of any business venture lies in the values, worldview and commitments of its leaders. That's why we insist that the stakeholders of AmeenArthur seek to align natural and cultural, technological and economic expectations. But, we always, in a financial world, need to ask the question: what integral bottom line are they looking for? Is it a financial Return on Equity (ROE) of 25–50%? Is it a return on and for nature, on and for culture, on and for technology and economy? Is it Shariah governance or the maqasid intention of the Shariah? Whichever, it shapes the direction of the communiprise leading to communipreneurship and communitalism. For the redoubtable Islamic scholar, Ziauddin Sardar (23):

> The freezing of interpretation, the closure of the 'gates of ijitihad',
> has had a devastating effect on Muslim thought and action. In reality,

Shariah is nothing but a set of principles, a framework of values, that provide Muslim societies with guidance. But these sets of principles and values are not a static given but are dynamically derived within changing contexts. As such the Shariah is a problem solving methodology rather than a law. It requires the believers to exert themselves and constantly reinterpret the Qur'an and look at the life of Muhammad with ever changing fresh eyes. The only thing that remains constant in Islam is the text of the Qur'an itself—its concepts providing the anchor for ever changing interpretations.

It is relatively easy to get investors to put funds into a private equity company, just like any other greenfield and brownfield project. What is distinctive about the investment fund and projects outlined here is their ability to approach the purpose of investment with an integral mindset. Such integrality involves anything that impacts nature and culture, as well as technology and economy, altogether positively.

But, intention is insufficient, in itself. The integral impact must be carefully assessed, both qualitatively and quantitatively, to weigh whether or not communities and nations are deriving genuine social, as well as technological, innovation. The purpose of a Research Academy in Integral Finance, aligned with AmeenArthur as a pilot laboratory, is to change the destiny of communities. It is to provide them with their heart's desires, take them out of housing and infrastructural poverty, create employment and groundbreaking opportunities, reduce national inequality and strive to become a cohesive integral state.

In this final chapter we have addressed the question, at the very heart of this volume: how can the power of the integral permeate into Islamic finance, so that the impact of local economic development is felt communally? We have sought to set forth the parameters for genuine impact investment, contextually evolved across different jurisdictions. Nigeria is as different from the UK as Igboland is different from Yorubaland, within Nigeria, and Scotland from England, within the UK. The nature of money, in each case, will certainly be altered and bent towards an integral guise. It is this reconstruction of money and finance, imbued with nature and culture, as well as technology and enterprise, that reflects the integral light.

10.14. Bibliography

1 **Centre for Housing Studies** (2018) *Funding Housing Delivery in Nigeria through Three Real Estate Investment Portfolios – REITs, Asset-backed Bond/Sukuk and Restricted Real Estate Portfolios.* Lagos. University of Lagos
2 **Heron** J (1994) *Co-operative Inquiry.* London. Sage
3 **Rogers**, D L (2016) *The Digital Transformation Playbook – Rethink your Business for the Digital Age.* New York. Columbia University Press

4 **Lessem** R and **Schieffer** A (2010) *Integral Economics: Releasing the Economic Genius of your Society.* Abingdon. Routledge

5 **Lessem** R and **Schieffer** A (2009) *Transformation Management: Toward the Integral Enterprise.* Abingdon. Routledge

6 **Oshodi** B (2014) *An Integral Approach to Development Economics: Islamic Finance in an African Context.* Abingdon. Routledge

7 **Yunus** M (2016) *A World of Three Zeroes.* London. Scribe Publications

8 **Rogers**, D (2016) *op cit*

9 **Oshod**i B and **Adeojo** J (2018), in Lessem, R and Bradley, T, *Evolving Work: Employing Self and Community.* Abingdon. Routledge

10 **Lessem** R and **Schieffer** A (2010) *Integral Research: Transforming Enterprise and Society.* Abingdon. Routledge

11 **Lessem** R, **Mawere** M and **Taranhike** D (2019) *Nhakanomics.* Mazvingo. Africa Talent Publishers

12 **Lessem** R, **Adodo** A and **Bradley** T (2019) *The Idea of the Communiversity.* Manchester. Beacon Academic

13 **Saqib** M and **Malik** A (2018) *Integral Finance, Akhuwat: A Case Study of a Solidarity Economy.* Abingdon. Routledge

14 **Lessem** R, **Adodo** A and **Bradley** T (2019) *op cit*

15 **Lessem** R, **Mawere** M, **Matupire** P and **Zongololo** S (2019) *Integral Kumusha: Aligning Policonomy, Nature, Culture, Technology and Enterprise.* Mazvingo. Africa Talent Publishers

16 **Akomolafe** B (2017) *These Worlds Beyond our Fences: Letters to My Daughter on Humanity's Search for Home.* Berkeley. California, North Atlantic Books

17 **World Health Organisation** (2019) https://www.who.int/ne/news-room/fact-sheets/detail/the-top-10-cases-of-death (Accessed 1 May, 2019)

18 **Al Nimer** M (2017) Organizational Learning and Development at Medlabs, in **Lessem** R, *Embodying Integral Development.* Abingdon. Routledge Focus

19 **Adodo** A (2012) *Nature Power: A Christian Approach to Herbal Medicine. New Edition.* Edo State. Benedictine Publications

20 **Lessem** R and **Schieffer** A (2009) *op cit*

21 **Lessem** R, **Adodo** A and **Bradley** T (2019) *op cit*

22 **Lessem** R (2001) Managing in Four Worlds: Culture, Strategy and Transformation. *Long Range Planning*, 34, 9–32

23 **Inayatullah** S and **Boxwell** G (2003) *Islam, Postmodernism and Other Futures: A Ziauddin Reader.* London. Pluto Press

Humanity's Search For Home

Ronnie Lessem and Tony Bradley, Series Editors

Only if we are capable of dwelling, only then can we build.

Tim Ingold, *The Perception of the Environment*

According to Big Others' architects these walls must come down. There can be no refuge. The universe takes up residence in our walls. Now they are simply the coordinates for 'smart' thermostats, security cameras, speakers, and light switches that extract and render our experience to actuate our behaviour. That our walls are dense and deep is of no significance because boundaries that define the very experience of our home are erased.

Shoshana Zuboff, *The Age of Surveillance Capitalism*

Introduction

Contemporary Transnationalism

According to Peter Mandaville (1), introduced in Chapter 3, having been brought up in the Gulf and, thereby, exposed to the Islamic world, trans-nationalism creates forms of political identity which do not fit the taxonomies of political modernity. Hybridity and cultural melange often feature heavily in these spaces, and such syncretism often gives rise to new post-national forms, as well as to reformulated understandings of what and where the nation can be. The *trans-local*, is a space in which new forms of (post) ethnic and (post) national identity are constituted, rather than a space in which prior identities assert themselves. This has been the positioning of our *integral* and *semiotic* approach to Islamic finance.

Trans-locality, then, can be theorised as a mode for how people move *through* places. It is a form of travel. It involves studying the flows that ripple through localities, rather more than what is in them. The political implications of such hybrid spaces become evident as we look at Muslim trans-locality today. The same forces which have brought about trans-local spaces have also given rise to phenomenal increases in the extent to which people communicate and encounter each other across boundaries of cultures, ethnicities, nations and communities. In the few minutes I've been writing this I have communicated with colleagues in the US, London, Nairobi, Harare and Lagos. Nor is this a strange experience. It is the patina of the 21st century world.

In cosmopolitan, trans-local spaces like London, the myriad range of cultures, ideas and people that flow through these spaces produce rich sites of hybridised intellectual activity. The syncretism and inter-mingling which constitute these cities also constitute the cutting edge of critical Islam. As Malaysia's Anwar Ibrahim (2) argues:

> Recapturing the meaning of the umma would necessitate that Muslims engage with other people, nations, worldviews, religions and ideologies to work for a set of moral objectives that we can and must define together. But it takes us much further. It requires that we accept the umma of other people... the history of the umma as shown exemplary, almost unique models of multiracial, multicultural, multireligious, pluralist societies. If ever we had the need of recovering such an imperative it is now.

It is in this trans-local, trans-cultural light that we have reconsidered *integral* Islamic finance, and economics, across our South and East, North and West. Yet, there appears to be something of a contradiction, or, at the very least, a discontinuity in our approach. Here we are, discussing the future role of finance in a world of trans-local places, and, at the same time, we have returned, repeatedly, to spiritual principles and religious texts that have their situatedness in very specific locations in the Middle East, over the past 3,000 years.

But, that is the 'GEN*E*-ius' of the integral in each specific societal context. Every culture both absorbs and interprets its traditions and changing worldview in the light of its multi-faceted and, often, contradictory experience of social relations, not least in the sphere of the economic. For this reason, we have referred to this collection of essays as a *semiotic* approach, being the first volume in a series on *Insights in Semiotic Economics*. If nothing else, the shifting modalities of trans-localism remind us that there is no single definition of economics or understanding of what 'the economic' means. There may, in abstract theology, if not in concrete practice, be a single ummah, or Church, or Judaism or Humanity. Even so, in every cultural context—across the four worlds—the economic is reinterpreted, so that these alternative meanings may be exposed to the light of analysis and, thence, enabled to reshape integral economic societies. In this way the economic is grounded in their soil, emerges through their culture, navigates via their knowledge bases and effects innovative practices. That was the original intention of integral economics, now evolving in the light of semiotics.

Zen and the Art of Motorcycle Maintenance to the Worlds Beyond Our Fences

Meanwhile, when poised to write the Epilogue to our book, we happened to come across a remarkable recent work on *Humanity's Search For Home*, which represents a fitting conclusion. For, whereas Islam itself originated in the 'South-East', in Arabia, conventional approaches to Islamic finance have been overtaken by the economically predominant 'North-West' (see Chapter 8). What we have attempted to do in this book is to rediscover the 'middle ground' that was historically Islam's birthright, at least during its Golden Age in the 11th to 14th centuries, by repositioning integral Islamic finance and economics in the South, East and North, as well as the West.

For the itinerant Bayo Akomolafe (3)—as a clinical psychologist from south-western Nigeria, now living with his Afro-Indian wife in India—in seeking out *These Worlds Beyond the Fences*, he has been engaged in a search for humanity's new home. In doing so, he has articulated, today, for the South, what the social philosopher Robert Pirsig represented for the East. The 'counter-cultural' Westerner Pirsig (4), commented:

> You can find the godhead just as easily in the gears of a motorcycle transmission, or in an integrated circuit, as you can in the heavens above.

Now, for the 'Southerner' Akomolafe, also a trans-worlds traveller, the question is:

> Do we recognize our relatedness to all things, our real dependence on the land we supposedly transcend, and that to be human is not a magisterial decree of isolation but a chorus... a syncretic process of shared ecological participation?

Metaphysics of Quality to Humanity's Search for Home

Pirsig was writing, last century, on the *metaphysics of quality,* when the East was newly announcing itself in the West. In this second decade of the new millennium the time of the African South, the original cradle of humanity, has, seemingly, come. The very title of Akomolafe's book, *These Worlds Beyond our Fences,* and the subtitle *Letters to my Daughter on Humanity's Search for Home,* tells its own story. Indeed, this search for home today, as our opening quotes reveal, has become all-pervasive. This is, particularly, poignant, as we watch whole swathes of human cultures risking life-and-limb to escape Africa, believing in a false hopeful Europe that is, itself, on the edge of disintegration. In fact, and as the above opening quotes reveal, this theme of 'home' is one on our everyday lips. It also constitutes a backdrop, at least in Southern Africa, to our (5) *integral kumusha* (homestead), serving to newly align *policonomy* with nature, culture, technology and enterprise. Here, again, we find an utterly distinctive understanding of 'the economic', that would remain invisible without the vital work of uncovering it, semiotically and integrally.

In other words, and overall, we have been seeking to bring Islamic economics and finance 'home' to its original South-West to counterbalance, or at least complement, the 'North-West' with which it is more conventionally connected. For in many ways, Islam, as a whole, today, has acted as a counterweight to the West, albeit more often than not seen in negative guise, whereas what we have been seeking to high-*light* is the positive role that Islam, economically, can play, at least in its more integral modality.

Tears Do Not Fall in Space

According to Akomolafe, we live in a world governed under a kingdom of Light—as such the white West versus dark 'rest'—and this light implies a violent and forceful dichotomisation of the world. It needs everything neatly arranged and easily categorised. It cannot afford that things spill into each other. It needs binaries—inside and outside. The things that fall on the outside are thus thought to be evil, chaotic and corrupt. Modernity—from the fifteenth century onwards—set the stage for a massive repression and devaluation of the 'dark side' of a psychic life. Now is a time for a semiotic reappraisal, as much in the sphere of economics and finance as elsewhere, which this volume has attempted, in some small degree.

'Feminist materialists', like Californian physicist Karen Barad (6), sees her work as involving an attempt to crack open the sealed places, to dispute the ontological imprisonment of things in Cartesian categories. This is to show how the supposedly righteous and separate are already complicit in the 'crime' of entanglement. Consequently, we should pay attention to the interesting proposal that our psychic lives are richly embroidered with darkness. As such, 'a light at the end of the tunnel' relegates the dark to secondary status. In fact, in the shaman's tradition, firstly, the trickster is the black sheep of the pantheon, in archetypal terms, not because his/her jokes are bad, but because he/she embodies the primal generativity and diffractive ingenuity of things. In this dark lightness, interpreting the meanings of alternative financial models casts a shadow over the supposed ubiquity of neoliberalism, in all its forms.

Furthermore, *heading into the forest* to find the dark brings us into encounters with the nonhuman, thereby stressing some kind of intra-subjective ethos of trans-affectivity. Carl Jung took this even further, drawing entangling links between 'human minds' and base metals. Thoughts do not come from 'within', neither do they come from 'without'; they emerge 'between'. As such, healing in African indigenous systems is 'inter-actional'. There is no cure without the long dusty road travelled with others.

Asking Awkward Questions

It is often, moreover, taken for granted that the opposite of a question is an answer; there is a cosmic, platonic double-step logic about it. Black is to white as night is to day, and questions are to answers. What if questions, for Akomolafe, are like quests to return home—to be welcomed, spoken to affectionately, and put to bed. To slow down from the treachery of a swift resolution and the quest for a binding reconciliation of contradiction. To keep the world fresh. What if questions have colours, textures? Questions such as: what does this mean economically, when the object in question is the gift-of-grace that a mother has shown to a child, in the home?

When Akomolafe was younger, the world seemed a simpler place. Life was about 'making it', or 'following your passion'. To do this one needed to go to school, to speak one tongue, to develop entrepreneurial skills, identify problems. The purpose of human collectives was to use the natural resources God had given us to construct bridges, build factories, make rocket ships that went to the moon, and invent technologies that would save lives. Just as important, perhaps even more so, the meaning of life was to be holy and exclusively devoted to a single faith. All other faiths were stupid, ignorant or even wicked. But all of this started to change. First, in giving himself to one faith, he began noticing limitations. Many things did not add up: the notion of sin, the exclusivity of religious compliance in a world too culturally complex for single opinions, and narratives of destiny.

But, of course, and semiotically, there was some hidden dialectic in the concept of 'making it'—a 'me against the world', or 'me in competition with others'—which led him to begin to distrust that magical highway to the sun. And school? In most parts it represented the colonial heritage of a particular way of seeing the world. English. One tongue. Development. Yet another flight of Icarus to escape the sensuous and ethical extravagance of the material world. In short, he lost faith. The ego, he discovered, moreover, is not the problem; the problem is the paradigm that amputates it, treats it as diseased, cuts it off from the rest of the world, out of touch. The 'solution' is not to empty ourselves of it, therefore, but to notice the umbilical cords that still tether us to a festival of vitality.

So, what do we *do*? How do we respond to the fact that our 'normal'— this consistently grinding premise of social ascendancy, is built on the backs of generational occlusion? How do we 'rise' to meet a world that is well and truly skewed in favour of the rich? How do we interpret money, finance, the economy, once we have begun to achieve escape velocity from the uni-dimensionality of what we were taught to understand?

This raises yet more extremely awkward questions. In 2006, former US Vice President Al Gore (7) had an epiphany in these terms, which led to his stating that there was *An Inconvenient Truth*. How can we come to terms with the fact that due to rising sea temperatures, we will grow up in a world without the Great Barrier Reef? As Bayo thought about the world's problems and what to *do* about them, he learnt to offer different questions—more regenerative questions—hospitable and humbling questions: how are we *already* collectively responding, in response to our specific crises?

What these questions bring us to contemplate is the way we are already complicit in the production of certain realities at the cost of complementary others. They open up the possibility of redescribing our many activisms in terms of an ongoing *accounting* for the ways we are part of the universe touching itself… already a response to and being responded with. Or, to put it another way, we need to keep on questioning the semiotic meanings of things, not least in the ways we understand money and finance, its hold on us and multi-facetedness. As soon as we do this, we find that we need to grow up. The world is not as simple as the childish economics that we have learned.

As incredibly pressing as it may sound, the story of humans who are out to fix the world that they were destroying still feeds a politics of binaries. It tells a story of nature being the vassal of culture, of mind preceding matter, of 'thought' being an alien brooding over the deep, and of mankind rearranging the whole of language, meanings, semiosis. This isn't to deny what we feel in our bones to be urgent: the need to address poverty and inequality, to create governments that truly exist for people, or enact radically different political imaginaries that sidestep the biased distribution of suffering made possible in nation states.

'Saving the world', though, for Akomolafe, is sweet tongue for sidestepping, not only the troubling discernment that the world is more complex than language or thought (and therefore 'solutions'), but, the confounding realisation that the world is not a dormant palette for our most austere dreams or best intentions. In the language of the semiotic methodology introduced here and throughout this series, every economics sign fizzes with a fireworks display of interpretant effects. As soon as we have seen the incredible, complex and diverse meanings of accounting, finance, economics, in their myriad trans-local cultures, we may shrink back in awe and confusion. Atlas shrugs, and the world shrugs back.

From SDGs to carbon emissions trading and microfinance as a way of tackling poverty, our globalising crisis-response imaginary has at its core the sticky idea that we can—if we put our backs into it—rise above the fray and create the world *we* want. But, in this sense, how we are, already, responding to the crisis is *part of* the crisis. It is not a case of something *yet* to be done. Climate change is believed to be the single most threatening phenomenon facing humankind today. The elementary argument is that the planet is getting warmer, and this warming is causing adverse weather conditions that have multiplier effects on the ways we organise our lives and on the places we call home. It *is* an inconvenient truth and one that is predicated on a particular view of economics, accounting and finance.

Today's conversation about climate change insists that the only way to stop our certain demise, under towering pillars of water, is by adopting policies that modify the otherwise unregulated market production effects of the environment. Whilst we do need to invest in developing cheaper green technologies that remove dependence on extracted fossil fuels—the black oil that poisons skies in millions of internal combustion cars across the planet—the framing of the case easily slips into an abyss that makes matters far worse.

Like the hand of God on the wall announcing the end of the old era, this new myth inscribes new parameters of responsivity in the sky, infecting everything with its logic, and enfolding itself around the new enemy: carbon emissions. There is a reality to this. Carbon dioxide and methane are trapping ever-greater amounts of heat energy within the atmosphere. But, when we turn the science into financial dogma, about carbon trading, our accounting feeds the downward spiral. We find ways to account for our destructive activity and to persuade ourselves, economically, that we have a solution. Basically, carbon trading then assigns monetary value to the earth's shared atmosphere, forcing businesses to pay attributed fines proportionate to the damage done. Are these good practices? The prognosis, for Bayo, is not looking good.

Climate change politics is not so much the practice of depicting the truth about climate dynamics as it is the multi/agential co-production and maintenance of an abstraction—carbon metrics—with which a particular worldview sustains itself to the exhaustion of other complementary accounts to the ways climates matter. There are worlds of meaning involved in this and these really matter, if we are to prevent cataclysm. We need a new finance and economics. Or, rather, every trans-local culture needs to look into its own dark and light soul and discover its authentic economics that creates local solutions with global impact.

As we have seen, economic measures like GDP force us to privilege monetary transactions, income, and corporate/industrial activity by discounting the non-monetary practices of caring about what happens in small places. They cause us to neglect or forget the contributions of trees to weathering the planet and its well-being. Carbon metrics reduce climate change to the amount of carbon in the atmosphere and the ability of emissions markets to meet sustainability goals. As part of the climate imaginary that is produced by a neoliberal agenda of progress, linear time, anthropocentric control, separation form nature, and technological optimism, today's carbon discourse and activism obfuscate other ways of thinking about who we are in relation to the weather. And, that is an economic question. One that has a myriad of different answers.

Our conventional economics stems from the myth that human bodies are discrete in time and space, somehow outside of the natural milieu that sustains them and indeed transits through them. It denies the way bodies are already entangled with weather—in other words, weather is what 'we', collectively, are doing with each other. The whole apparatus, for Akomolafe, is in fact framed from a Newtonian perspective of human exceptionalism. The unit of climate change is, thus, not carbon emissions, measured by any neutral metric. *Carbon emissions* is an abstraction with universalising effects; it is too narrow, too linear, and too stunted to explain climate change. Moreover, it serves a single future. It is the colonising racetrack that imposes a teleology on the world, and tacks on the politics of sustain-*ability* to the furniture. It is lockstep, he says, with colonial time. What, then, if carbon reductionism was not the only way of understanding climate change? What if we weren't addicted to growth, progress, consumption, and independence? What would life look like?

Sustainable development is not our way of embracing our entanglement in the web of life; it has nothing to do with revitalising our inescapable tethering with 'nature' or recognising that we are normally constituted by agencies and actions outside our control. It is our way of sustaining the primacy of one understanding of economic advancement and cultural homogenisation. If you are in any doubt how skewed the paradigm of sustainable development really is, for Bayo, look at its indicators. They are all entirely economic, in one dimension. In other worlds, our alliance with nature is directly proportional to how estranged we are from her. Nature in this conception is the network of raw materials awaiting redemption in our Cartesian coordinates. Making 'nature' an 'Other' is the singular motif that keeps emerging in every approach to addressing our crises today. But, other meanings of 'the economic' are possible and, indeed, are amongst us, if we only open our semiotic eyes.

What indigenous cosmologies can teach us about the world is now making room for new kinds of polities, and economics, learning to take care with the non-human populations around us. Maybe a different home lies in another ethos that reframes the questions of survival. Maybe other places of 'power' open up when we relinquish our convenient narratives of human exceptionalism and triumphalism—those stories that centralise human agency and enthrone human interests as paramount in the multiverse. Do we recognise our relatedness to all things, our real dependence on the land we supposedly transcend, and that to be human is not a magisterial decree of isolation but a chorus... a syncretic process of shared ecological participation? If we do, a magnificent range of new economics opens up for us. If we don't, once again, Atlas shrugs.

Conclusion

The vital questions we might ask today, for Akomolafe, do not simply concern just the math of how we get from here to there, but questions about the thick politics of what we are co-becoming. Questions about the boundaries, and differences, and how we are imprinted with the lives of many others. The far is nearby.

In a sense, to entertain hope is not merely to give in to a linear unfolding of events; it is to allow oneself to be touched. It is to recognise that there are other possibilities—wild possibilities—and that these possibilities will not leave us intact. To meet hope open-faced is to surrender to a logic that is beyond our ken. We begin at the edges in the middle. Hope is an affair of material riddles.

What feelings we have not felt, what concepts we have not conceived, what possibilities we do not account for, what semiosis has not been interpreted, are tied to radical new places where we practise being middling agents of a home that is wilder than fences. And we leave the last words, thereby, to Peter Mandaville (8):

> Within the spaces of diasporic Islam there is emerging a new form of interstitial identity, a 'third space' in which the politics of the majority are not embraced but neither is that of the 'homeland', especially by the younger generation. Many therefore see in Islam the seeds of a new idiom of political community, as authentic as it is modern, one that perhaps even moved beyond modernity.

And, for us, the same goes for *integral* Islamic finance, as one starting point in a journey of *semiosis*.

Bibliography

1 **Mandaville** P (2000) *Transnational Muslim Politics: Reimagining the Umma.* London. Routledge Research in Transnationalism
2 **Ibrahim** A (1996) *Asian Renaissance.* New York. Times International Books
3 **Akomolafe** B (2017) *These Worlds Beyond our Fences: Letters to My Daughter on Humanity's Search for Home.* Berkeley. California, North Atlantic Books
4 **Pirsig** R (1991) *Zen and the Art of Motorcycle Maintenance: An Inquiry Into Values.* New York. Vintage Classics

5 **Lessem** R, **Mawere** M, **Matupire** P and **Zongololo** P (2019) *Integral Kumusha: Aligning Policonomy with Nature, Culture, Technology and Enterprise.* Mazvingo. Africa Talent Publishers.
6 **Barad** K (2007) *Meeting the Universe Halfway: Quantum Physics and the Entanglement of Matter and Meaning.* Durham. North Carolina. Duke University Press
7 **Gore** A (2006) *An Inconvenient Truth: the planetary emergency of global warming and what we can do about it.* London. Bloomsbury Press
8 **Mandaville** P (2000) *op cit*

Index

A

B

C

D

E

G

www.ingramcontent.com/pod-product-compliance
Lightning Source LLC
Chambersburg PA
CBHW021553210326
41599CB00010B/430